Better Governance for Development in the Middle East and North Africa

Better Governance for Development in the Middle East and North Africa

Enhancing Inclusiveness and Accountability

THE WORLD BANK
Washington, D.C.

ISBN 0-8213-5635-6

Cover photos from Getty Images and World Bank Photo Library.

Library of Congress Cataloging-in-Publication Data *has been applied for.*

Contents

Foreword   xiii

Acknowledgments   xv

Glossary of Terms   xvii

Abbreviations and Acronyms   xxi

Overview   1

Enhancing Governance in MENA   1
Governance Is Typically Weaker in MENA than in
  the Rest of the World—Qualitatively …   3
… And in the Measure of Good Governance   5
Weak Governance Has Contributed to Weak Growth
  in MENA …   8
… Because Poor Governance Has Shackled the Business
  Environment   10
Weak Governance Has Also Limited the Quality of Public
  Goods and Services   12
Bridging the Region's Governance Gap Is Both a Challenge
  and an Opportunity   14
Any Program to Enhance Governance Requires Attention
  to the Twin Values of Inclusiveness and Accountability, …   17
… Starting with an Open Commitment by Countries …   17
… To Formulate and Act on a Program to Enhance
  Governance …   18
… With Five Pathways to Good Governance: …   18
… To Enhance Inclusiveness, …   20
… To Strengthen External Accountability Through
  National Actions, …   20
… To Strengthen External Accountability Through
  Local Actions, …   21

... To Improve Internal Accountability Through National
    Checks and Balances, ...   21
... And to Improve Internal Accountability Through
    Administrative Reforms   22
In Sum: Follow Commitment with Action   23
Notes   23

**Analytical Framework for Good Governance in the
Middle East and North Africa**   **25**

The Good Governance Relationship   25
    Inclusiveness   27
    Accountability   27
Making Governance "Good"   31

1. The Governance Gap in MENA   **35**

Introducing Governance in MENA   35
Describing Governance in MENA   39
    Inclusiveness in MENA   39
    Accountability in MENA   42
    Measuring Governance—How Does MENA Compare?   56
    Overall Governance Quality   58
    Quality of Administration   58
    Public Accountability   62
Why Governance Has Not Been Improving in MENA   65
    Geopolitics   66
    Conflict—or Its Threat   68
    Oil Wealth   68
Notes   73

2. Better Governance for Economic Development   **75**

The Governance Gap and Development   76
Governance Deficiencies Are at the Root of Slow Growth
    in MENA   78
    The Link Between Good Governance and Growth   80
    Growth in MENA: Sluggish, with Low Private
        Investment and Productivity   81
    The Governance Gap Slowed Growth in MENA   83
Better Governance Improves the Environment for
    Productive Investment   87
    Better Governance Reduces the Scope for Arbitrary
        Government Policies   87
    Better Governance Reduces Uncertainty and Costs of
        Doing Business   92

Better Governance Ensures Effective Public Services for
    Businesses   98
  Notes   101

3. Better Governance for Social Development   105

  Service Delivery in MENA: Commitment and Achievements   108
    Overall Outcomes Show Improvement over Time …   108
    … Because of a Strong Commitment by Governments   110
    A Mixed Record in Public Services Delivery   114
  Governance Matters for Public Service Delivery   119
    An Accountability Framework for Governance and Public
      Service Delivery   120
    The Link Between the Politicians or Policymakers and
      the Service Agencies   123
    The Link Between Service Agencies and Client–Citizens   133
    The Link Between Citizens and Politicians   141
  Challenges for the Future   148
  Notes   149

4. Pathways to Better Governance   151

  The Urgency for Action—Development and
    Governance Gaps   151
  Overcoming the Governance Gap   152
    Enhancing Inclusiveness   156
    Gaining Stronger Accountability   157
    Improving External Accountability—National Actions   158
    Improving External Accountability—Local Actions   162
    Improving Internal Accountability—National Checks
      and Balances   166
    Improving Internal Accountability—Administrative
      Measures   168
  Moving the Governance Agenda Forward   172
    A Commitment for Action …   175
    … And Formulation of a Program to Enhance Governance   177

Appendixes

  A. Construction of Governance Indexes   179
  B. Governance and Income Correlations   187
  C. Estimating the Effect of Governance on Growth   193
  D. Literature Review: Examining Factors that Help Explain
      the Governance Gap in MENA   199
  E. Governance and Growth: Reviewing the Evidence   207
  F. Country Tables   211

References   245

Index   271

Boxes

1.1   No Documents—No Identity   36
1.2   An Analytical Framework for Good Governance   38
1.3   The Strong Executive in Egypt   45
1.4   Parliamentary Independence in MENA   46
1.5   Judicial Independence in MENA   48
1.6   Judicial Independence in Tunisia Is Lacking   49
1.7   Clientelism in the Bureaucracy Weakens Governance
       in the Syrian Arab Republic   50
1.8   Improving the Relationship Between Public
       Organizations and Citizens in Tunisia   51
1.9   Informal Mechanisms of Participation in MENA   56
1.10   Measuring the Quality of Governance in MENA—
       Not an Easy Job   57
1.11   Constructing Indexes of Governance for MENA   59
1.12   The Debilitating Impact of Administrative Regulations
       and Behavior—Examples from the Arab Republic of
       Egypt and Lebanon   64
1.13   Military Spending in MENA Is High   69
1.14   Botswana's Good Governance Helps Overcome
       the Resource Curse   72
2.1   Governance, Policies, and Growth—a Complex Link   88
2.2   Better Processes for Public Procurement Counter
       State Capture   90
2.3   Reducing Red Tape in Lebanon   94
2.4   Improved Regulatory Framework for Investment
       in Morocco   95
2.5   Corruption—Not a Synonym but a Symptom of
       Bad Governance   99
3.1   Deciding When Government Action Is Needed   107
3.2   Community Schools in Upper Egypt—Bringing
       Education to Girls   114
3.3   Regulating Telecommunications in MENA   120
3.4   Quantifying the Effectiveness of Institutional
       Arrangements in the Budget Process   125
3.5   The Move to Performance Budgeting   129
3.6   Greater Accountability in Procurement   131
3.7   Public Administration Reform   132
3.8   Citizen Surveys in Bangalore   136
3.9   Public Expenditure Tracking Surveys   137

3.10   Promoting VOICE in India—Online Delivery of
        Municipal Services   138
3.11   Colombia's Targeted Voucher Program for
        Secondary Education   139
3.12   China and SARS—the Need for External
        Accountability for Complex Public Services   142
3.13   Community Management of Schools—the EDUCO
        Program in El Salvador   143
3.14   Participatory Budgeting in Pôrto Alegre, Brazil   144
3.15   Tribal Governance in Jordan—Then and Now   147
4.1   The Move to E-government in MENA Countries   159
4.2   Expanding Consultative Organisms—Algeria's
        National Social and Economic Council   161
4.3   Service Delivery Surveys in the West Bank and Gaza   164
4.4   Decentralizing Political Power—Local Economic
        Development in Aden   165
4.5   Cooperating with Civil Society   166
4.6   Toward External Accountability in Algeria:
        The National Ombudsman   169
4.7   Good Governance Can Improve Economic Policies—
        Lessons from the Europe and Central Asia
        Transition   173
4.8   Political Pluralism and Economic Recovery in Mexico   174
4.9   Toward Governance Reforms in Morocco   176

Figures

O.1   Inclusiveness and Accountability Are the Values
        Underpinning Good Governance   3
O.2   Compared with Other Regions, MENA Shows a
        Clear Governance Gap   6
O.3   For the Quality of Administration, MENA's Governance
        Gap Is Narrower and Incomes Matter   7
O.4   For Public Accountability, MENA's Governance Gap Is
        Wider, Irrespective of Incomes   8
O.5   For MENA's Oil-Dependent Countries, the Public
        Accountability Gap Is Even Wider   9
O.6   A Program to Enhance Governance   19
AF.1   Public Governance Is the Authority Relationship
        Between the *Government* and the *People*   26
AF.2   Inclusiveness Implies Equal Rights, Including
        Equal Opportunities to Participate   28
AF.3   Accountability Can Be Internal (by Checks and Balances
        within the Government) or External (by the People)   29
AF.4   Multiple Channels of Accountability   30

AF.5   Inclusiveness and Accountability Are the Values
       Underpinning Good Governance   33
1.1   Inclusiveness Implies Equal Rights, Including Equal
       Opportunities to Participate   40
1.2   Female Representation in MENA Parliaments Is Low   41
1.3   Accountability Can Be Internal (by Checks and Balances
       within the Government) or External (by the People)   43
1.4   MENA's Governance Gap Compared with the Rest
       of the World   60
1.5   For the Quality of Administration, MENA's Governance
       Gap Is Narrower and Incomes Matter   61
1.6   Within MENA, There Is Wide Variation in the
       Quality of Administration   62
1.7   Regulatory Quality Varies across MENA Countries   63
1.8   For Public Accountability, MENA's Governance Gap Is
       Wider, Irrespective of Incomes   65
1.9   All MENA Countries Have a Gap in Public
       Accountability with the Rest of the World   66
1.10   Compared with Other Regions, MENA Shows a
       Clear Governance Gap   67
1.11   For MENA's Oil-Dependent Countries, the Public
       Accountability Gap Is Even Wider   71
2.1   Governance Improves Growth by Improving the
       Business Environment   77
2.2   MENA versus East Asia Shows Divergent
       Per Capita Growth   79
2.3   A 20-Year Growth Slowdown … and a Record
       of Volatility   80
2.4   High but Declining Investment Rates   82
2.5   The Share of Private Investment Is Low   82
2.6   Incomes Are Positively Correlated with Governance
       Quality in the World and MENA   84
2.7   Better Governance Brings Added Growth   85
2.8   Better Administration Speeds Economic Recovery
       in East Asia and in MENA   86
2.9   Some Court Systems in MENA Are Especially Slow   93
2.10   Challenges for Business in MENA Shown by Lengthy
       and Costly Registration and Contract Enforcement   96
2.11   Large Variation in Corruption Exists in MENA   98
2.12   Poor Public Infrastructure Forces Businesses to
       Spend on Private Alternatives   100
3.1   Years of Schooling Are Up Significantly   109
3.2   Youth Illiteracy Is Down by 20 Points   110
3.3   Infant Mortality Is Down by Almost Two-Thirds   111
3.4   Immunizations Are Expanding Rapidly   112

3.5   Health Spending Is on Par with Other Middle-Income
       Countries   115
3.6   Education Spending Is Even Higher than in Some
       Leading Middle-Income Countries   116
3.7   In Health Spending, Most MENA Countries
       Are Efficient ...   117
3.8   ... But in Education, MENA Countries Are Either
       Inefficient or Underachievers   118
3.9   Multiple Channels of Accountability   121
3.10   Good Governance Matters for Health ...   126
3.11   ... And for Education and Infrastructure Services   127
3.12   Performance Orientation and Internal Accountability
       Are Low   128
4.1   Multiple Channels of Accountability   155
4.2   A Program to Enhance Governance   178
B.1   Governance and Per Capita Incomes: Estimating
       the Average MENA Effect   189
B.2   MENA's Governance Gap Compared with the
       Rest of the World   190

Tables

3.1   Constitutional and Legal Provisions for Education
       in MENA   113
3.2   Food Subsidies, 1995   114
4.1   Modern Governance Institutions Took a Long Time
       to Develop   172
B.1   Governance and Per Capita Incomes: Estimated
       Coefficients and *t* Values   188
B.2   MENA's Governance Gap: Estimated Coefficients
       and *t* Values   190
C.1   Estimating Growth   198

Foreword

Improving public sector performance and governance is a key pillar in the World Bank's engagement strategy for the Middle East and North Africa (MENA). To guide and support this strategic priority over the coming years, we at the World Bank have worked with a network of leading scholars and opinion leaders who are from the region and work in the field of governance. Their ideas, their papers, and their consultations have been instrumental in shaping our effort to translate this strategic orientation into vision and action.

The ambition of this regional book is not to offer answers to the complex challenge of improving governance. Those matters are for people in the region to decide. More modestly, the book seeks to enhance the dialogue in MENA on governance. To accomplish this goal, the book proposes an analytical framework for discussing and measuring governance. It also marshals evidence showing that good governance matters for development—globally and in MENA. Our hope is to work more closely with those in government and in civil society—and they are many—who are passionate about improving governance.

Globalization and demographic pressures put a premium on faster economic growth, yet growth in the region remains below potential. The same pressures are raising people's aspirations—for public services that work for everyone, for wider participation in governance, and for better social and human development. But as the book shows, weak governance translates into slower growth, less-than-effective public services, and missed opportunities because of the limited participation of citizens in shaping their future.

That an economic institution such as the World Bank would venture into the delicate societal issues surrounding governance reflects the growing recognition that development is more than an economic challenge. The business environment for growth led by the private sector—plus the quality of public services essential for economic efficiency and social equity—depends everywhere in the world as much on governance arrangements as on technical design.

The book documents several encouraging experiments and positive trends in the region—even if measuring governance is made difficult by the region's legacy of limited public disclosure and debate. On the quality of administration, including the rule of law, countries in the region compare well with others at the same income level. Still, the progress in governance varies widely by country. Along other key indicators of governance, especially those that measure public accountability, the countries in the MENA region consistently lag behind the countries with which they have to compete in the global economy. The rest of the world has much to offer in terms of innovative governance mechanisms, and the region is beginning to draw on such experience. We hope this book will help in that process.

If improving governance were easy, it would have improved already. But improvement is a long, uncharted, and risky process. The challenge may be relatively easy to diagnose, but it is not easy to surmount.

A first step could be defining a program to enhance governance. The book proposes two universal criteria that have resonated in our consultations in the region: inclusiveness and accountability. On the premise that people are the source of public authority, inclusiveness means that everyone is treated equally by governments and can participate equally in governance. Accountability means that those who act on behalf of the people are answerable for what they do. Accountability also requires transparency (allowing everyone to be fully informed of relevant information), as well as contestability (enabling everyone to participate in the choice of leaders, policies, and service providers).

The next steps are in the hands of the countries in the MENA region—to commit to improve the quality of governance and to bring quality up to par with the best in the world, and to do so in a participatory process of formulating their own programs to enhance governance.

Measures to improve governance are a key ingredient in the success of other reforms, including in the areas of trade, investment, employment, job creation, and gender equity—all of them critical for improving the lives of people in MENA. These concerns are taken up in companion volumes to this book. Together, our books aim to review the challenges and opportunities that the region faces as it fashions a new development strategy to meet the evolving needs of its people in coming decades.

Jean-Louis Sarbib
Vice President
Middle East and North Africa Region
The World Bank

Acknowledgments

The MENA Development Reports are coordinated by the Office of the Chief Economist for the Middle East and North Africa Region of the World Bank, led by Mustapha Kamel Nabli.

Under the supervision of Mustapha Kamel Nabli, chief economist of the MENA Region at the World Bank, this book was written by a core team of Charles Humphreys, Arup Banerji, J. Edgardo Campos, Paloma Anos Casero, Edouard Aldahdah, Laila Al-Hamad, and Marianne El-Khoury.

The team benefited from the guidance and contributions of an advisory network of scholars and opinion leaders from the MENA region, including Aziz al-Azmeh, Mohammed Charfi, Farideh Farhi, Abdou Filali-Ansari, Burhan Ghalioun, Salah Hejailan, Isam Khafaji, Rami Khouri, Ahmed Mahiou, Chibli Mallat, Salim Nasr, Abdel Monem Saeed Ali, Paul Salem, Mustapha Kamel al-Sayyid, and Mohamed Tozy. Advisers in this network prepared country and regional background papers (to be published separately), participated in several discussions and consultations, reviewed the book in draft, and provided continuing feedback to the team. Special thanks go to the Lebanese Center for Policy Studies (under Salim Nasr, with Lina Ghoussoub), which organized and chaired a major workshop in Beirut. The work of this network is supported in part by a grant from the Governance Knowledge Sharing Program, which was funded by the Netherlands.

Within the Bank, the work was formally reviewed by Shantayanan Devarajan, Cheryl Gray, Joel Helmann, Dani Kaufman, Philip Keefer, Sanjay Pradhan, and Nemat Shafik.

The book has benefited from numerous inputs and comments from others, including Theodore Ahlers, Petros Aklilu, Pedro Alba, Zoubida Allaoua, Regina Bendokat, Subash Bhatnagar, Nabil Chaherli, Nadereh Chamlou, Monali Chowdhurie-Aziz, Francoise Clottes, Dipak Dasgupta, Chantal Dejou, Sebastien Dessus, Hadi Esfahani, Ahmed R. Eweida, El Mansour Feten, Habib Fetini, Emmanuel Forestier, Faris

Hadad-Zervos, Heidi Heinrich-Hansen, Robert Hindle, Farrukh Iqbal, Steve Karam, Omer Karasapan, Amine Khene, Jamal al-Kibbi, Aart Kraay, Nicholas Krafft, Catherine Laurent, Jenny Litvack, Mohammed al-Maitami, Caralee McLiesh, Nadir Mohammed, Ranjana Mukherjee, Mohamed Mustapha, Carmen Niethammer, Setareh Razmara, Omar Razzaz, Ritva Reinikka, Keith Rennie, Mohammed al-Sabbry, Shaha Riza, Nigel Roberts, Joseph Saba, David Sewell, John Speakman, Helen Sutch, Giulio de Tomasso, Hasan Tuluy, Victor Vergara, Najat Yamouri, Tarik Yousef, Paolo Zacchia, and Leila Zlaoui.

Giles Hopkins provided special networking support to the team. Alexandra Sperling, with Brigitte Wiss, formatted and processed multiple versions. Gerry Quinn prepared the special charts on governance concepts. Bruce Ross Larson and his associates at Communications Development Incorporated, along with Publications Professionals LLC, edited the text. The cover was designed by Naylor Design, Inc., with Arabic calligraphy by Mamoun Sakkal (www.Sakkal.com). The World Bank's Office of the Publisher managed book design and production.

The team warmly thanks all those who contributed to this book, including any people inadvertently not mentioned, but it bears full responsibility for the final version.

Glossary of Terms

Accountability. A multifaceted principle underpinning good governance across the spectrum of government activities.

Public accountability is the requirement that anyone acting with the authority of the state (whether elected or otherwise) should fully disclose and explain his or her actions to the people (often labeled transparency, answerability), and should abide by electoral, legal, or administrative sanctions if the actions are judged not to be in the public interest (often labeled contestability, competition, or enforcement).

External accountability means that citizens hold public officials to account—say, through voting or public advocacy campaigns or through direct oversight of a public agency.

Internal accountability means that one public agency holds another accountable, as when courts rule on the constitutionality of laws, when parliament votes against the executive, or when the audit agency investigates procurement by a ministry.

Contestability. A keystone of accountability. Fundamentally, contestability means that citizens should have choices among government leaders, policies, and agencies—and that processes should exist to allow citizens either to choose among existing alternatives (for example, among candidates or among alternative service agencies), or to lobby for different alternatives (for example, through public debate), or to have recourse and remedy if the citizens judge a policy to be a violation of their rights.

Contestability means that those who act with the authority of the state should be required to compete for that privilege—whether as political leaders or as public service agencies. It is through such contestable, or competitive, processes that citizens have the opportunity to exercise effectively their right to hold government officials and agencies accountable for acting in the public interest.

Contestability can sometimes be economic—the availability of alternative service providers, for example, acts as a discipline for public providers to improve services or to face a drop in demand. It can also be political, such as when recurrent elections encourage elected officials to be more responsive to their constituencies. Or it can be administrative, such as when merit-based recruitment and promotion encourage civil servants to pay more attention to service delivery.

Governance. The rules and process governing the exercise of authority in the name of a constituency, including the selection and replacement of those who exercise that authority. In public governance, this process takes place between two actors, broadly characterized as the people (citizens) and the government.

Public governance is good when this process is inclusive of everyone and when the people can hold accountable those who make and implement the rules.

Government. Includes all branches of government—parliament and judiciary, not simply the executive. It also includes all administrative agencies that operate with the authority of the state, at all levels: national, regional, and municipal.

Inclusiveness. Means that all citizens have equal rights before the law (such as protection of property) and have equal opportunities to exercise those rights. For good governance, a key right is to participate in the governance process. Thus, inclusiveness means that all those who have a stake in a governance process and who want to participate in it can do so on an equal basis—and that no class of citizens is systematically excluded or treated differently. In short, there is equal participation.

Inclusiveness also means nondiscrimination in access to services that a government is mandated to provide through social consensus, such as public health or education services and public goods (for example, justice and the rule of law). In short, there is equal treatment.

Index of governance quality (IGQ). Assesses the overall quality of governance processes. It aggregates, for all countries, governance indicators available for MENA. The IGQ is separated into the broad categories of IPA and IQA (see next).

Index of public accountability (IPA). Assesses how well the citizens can access government information and hold their leaders and public officials accountable. Among other things, the IPA assesses the process of selecting and replacing those in authority.

Index of quality of administration (IQA). Assesses the strength of the rule of law and protection of property rights, the efficiency of the bureaucracy, the quality of regulations, and the control of corruption. The IQA assesses both the capability of the public administration to formulate and implement sound policies and the respect for the institutions that govern interactions between citizens and government.

Institutions. Encompasses the rules, including behavioral norms and codes of conduct, that govern the interaction among participants in the governance process. The organizations, themselves, through which this interaction takes place are often included in the definition of institutions.

Parliament. Used in the general sense of legislature, irrespective of whether the form of government is a parliamentary, a presidential, or a hybrid system. It consists of an elected body, an appointed body, or a combination of the two, which represents the people, thereby, in principle, providing a counterweight on executive power.

Participation. Defined broadly—to include all the mechanisms for citizens to take part in the governance process. Simply put, participation consists of the range of activities through which citizens seek to influence government actions, either directly by affecting the formulation and implementation of public policy, or indirectly by affecting the selection of public officials. Citizens can exercise their participation in governance by voting, by joining civil-society organizations that lobby government, by playing a greater role in the management of public services, or by taking part in the public debate on governance issues—whether as a protagonist or simply as an informed observer. This definition is distinct from others that define participation in terms of economic activity, such as participation in the labor force.

Transparency. Encapsulates citizens' right to know. It requires the regular disclosure of information on what government officials and agencies are supposed to be doing, what they are actually doing, and who is responsible. It also involves clear and publicly accessible information on the rights of citizens; services for which citizens are eligible; ways to access such services (such as what fees must be paid, how to pay them, and what avenues of recourse are available in case of a dispute); and regulations that citizens are expected to comply with (including the agencies responsible, sanctions, and recourse mechanisms).

Abbreviations and Acronyms

CID	Center for International Development
CIDCM	Center for International Development and Conflict Management
CPIA	Country Policy and Institutional Assessment
DPT	Diphtheria, pertussis, and tetanus
EDUCO	Community-Managed School Program ("Educación con Participación de la Comunidad")
EU	European Union
FDI	Foreign direct investment
FLN	National Liberation Front (*Front de Libération Nationale*)
FRH	Freedom House
FSC	Federal Supreme Council (of the United Arab Emirates)
GCC	Gulf Cooperation Council
GDP	Gross domestic product
GNP	Gross national product
GNI	Gross national income
HWJ	Heritage Foundation/*Wall Street Journal*
IGQ	Index of governance quality
IPA	Index of public accountability
IQA	Index of quality of administration
IV	Instrumental variable
LIC	Lower-income countries
LMIC	Lower-middle-income countries
MENA	Middle East and North Africa
MIC	Middle-income countries
NBER	National Bureau of Economic Research (U.S.)
NGO	Nongovernmental organization
OECD	Organisation for Economic Co-operation and Development
OLS	Ordinary least squares

PPBS	Planning, Programming, and Budgeting System
PPP	Purchasing power parity
PRI	Institutional Revolutionary Party (*Partido Revolucionario Institucional*)
PRS	Political Risk Service
SARS	Severe acute respiratory syndrome
TOT	Terms of trade
UAE	United Arab Emirates
UGTT	*Union Générale Tunisienne du Travail* (Tunisian labor union)
UMIC	Upper-middle-income countries
UN	United Nations
UNDP	United Nations Development Programme
VOICE	Vijaywada Online Information Centers
WHO	World Health Organization

Overview

Enhancing Governance in MENA

Most governments and people share the aspiration of national development, with its many interpretations. Development is often defined in terms of its economic aspects, as increased material well-being through ensured employment and income for all who want it. But as knows anyone whose children go to schools of poor quality, have no clean water to drink, or face the threat of violence, development is also about having access to adequate social services. And development is ultimately about human development—the quality of material living, with wider choices and opportunities for people to realize their potential, plus the guarantee of those intangible qualities that characterize all more-developed societies: equality of treatment, freedom to choose, greater voice, and opportunities to participate in the process by which they are governed. Virtually all constitutions in the Middle East and North Africa (MENA) region enshrine those values of development, and public governance is one of the mechanisms through which the values are secured for the people.

From getting a driver's license in Casablanca to voting in municipal elections in Beirut, public governance relationships in the MENA region, as elsewhere, manifest themselves in almost every situation in which individuals and groups interact with the government. The challenge for governments and people throughout the region is to expand the interactions that are smooth and productive and to minimize the ones that are frustrating and wasteful—in a move toward "good" governance. If public governance is the exercise of authority in the name of the people, good governance is exercising that authority in ways that respect the integrity, rights, and needs of everyone within the state.

Good governance relationships can be analyzed in a framework that is based on two universal values that are particularly relevant to MENA: *inclusiveness* and *accountability*. The first draws on the notion of equality, which is enshrined in virtually every constitution in the region. Equality,

1

when translated into governance, means that all those who have a stake in governance processes and who want to participate in them can do so on a basis equal to all others. In short, governance is inclusive, not exclusive. Inclusive governance maintains mechanisms to define and to protect the basic rights of everyone, and it provides remedies and recourse guaranteed by a rule of law. Rights include fairness and tolerance among the people themselves, and good governance means those rights are protected. Rights also include how governments treat the people, and good governance means that governments treat everyone with equal rights before the law and without discrimination and ensure equal opportunities to access the services provided by governments.

The second value draws on the notion of representation, a notion as ancient as the first caliphs. Representation, when translated into governance, means that those selected to act in the name of the people are answerable to the people for their failures and credited for their successes. In short, they are accountable to the people. That accountability rests on knowledge and information—and thus on transparency in governance mechanisms. It also rests on incentives that encourage those who act in the name of the people (government officials) to do so faithfully, efficiently, and honestly. Such incentives come both from contestability in the selection of public officials and policies and from fostering an ethic of public service so officials act in the public interest.

Accountability can be both external and internal. *External accountability* is when people themselves hold the government accountable, as when the residents in a village select their councilman. But it also includes instances where the recipients of public services (such as parents of students) hold the service provider (teacher or school administrator) directly accountable. *Internal accountability* is when the government, to protect the public interest, institutes various systems and incentives to govern the behavior of different agencies within the government, such as separating powers and setting up independent checks and balances. Together, inclusiveness and accountability are the flowering of good governance (figure O.1).

A particular, and common, manifestation of poor governance is corruption—manifested in favoritism, nepotism, or bribery. By denying the right of equal treatment, corruption denies inclusiveness; it results from a lack of accountability, internal or external. Thus, it is a symptom of poor governance, even if eliminating corruption will not by itself guarantee good governance.

The thesis of this book is that development in MENA—economic, social, and human—is being handicapped by weaknesses in the quality of public governance, in which the region lags behind the rest of the world. A prominent group of Arab scholars writing in the United Nations De-

FIGURE O.1

Inclusiveness and Accountability Are the Values Underpinning Good Governance

Inclusiveness means that all those who have a stake in a governance process and want to participate in it—men and women, rich and poor, rural and urban—are able to do so on an equal basis, whether by voting, by contributing to consultations, or by overseeing local public service agencies.

Inclusiveness also means that governments treat everyone equally, that they protect the rights of everyone with equal vigor, that exclusion and discrimination are absent in the provision of public services by governments, and that everyone has equal rights to recourse and remedy if there is discrimination by public officials.

Accountability is based on the idea that people have the right to hold their governments answerable for how they use the authority of the state and the resources of the people.

Accountability needs transparency or full access to information— the people need to know about the functioning of the government, to hold it answerable, and governments need to provide access to such information.

Accountability also needs contestability—being able to choose among alternative political and economic entities on the basis of how well they perform. It also means recourse and remedy when government actions contravene basic rights—especially those of inclusiveness—or violate the rule of law.

velopment Programme's (UNDP) *2002 Arab Human Development Report* decry the region's "freedom deficit [that] undermines human development and is one of the most painful manifestations of lagging political development" (UNDP 2002a, p. 2).

Governance Is Typically Weaker in MENA than in the Rest of the World—Qualitatively …

Governments in MENA have typically sought to provide a broad range of public goods to everyone, with some astounding increases in coverage. (Lebanon increased the rate of childhood immunizations from virtually none to more than 90 percent in about a decade. Tunisia increased the number of phone lines 20-fold, also in about a decade.) And even with some of the driest countries on earth, the region has some of the best access to water for its people.

But beneath those gains are weaknesses in inclusiveness. Pressures from rising populations, increasing urbanization, and the growing complexity of modern public services strain the coverage of many public services. Although the spotlight of weak inclusiveness often falls on gender inequalities in the region, other groups suffer as well. Inclusion is weak wherever rural dwellers have fewer public services, thus leaving in its wake some of the highest levels of illiteracy among middle-income countries. Inclusion is also weak when the government effectively controls the conduct of elections, as in virtually all national elections. And it is weak when nepotism, tribal affinity, patronage, or money determines who gets public services and who does not—as well as who gets access to lucrative business opportunities and who does not.

Thus, there exists a wide and persistent social gap between countries in the region and those with which they have to compete. Infant mortality in the Arab Republic of Egypt was still 69 per 1,000 live births in 1999, much higher than the 42 per 1,000 in Indonesia, a country with half of Egypt's per capita income. Only the United Arab Emirates, one of the richest countries in the region, matches Hungary and Malaysia, with a rate of 8 per 1,000. Almost two in five adult males in Morocco are illiterate, and well over three in five adult females—on par with much poorer countries, such as Mozambique or Pakistan. Ensuring equitable treatment is a challenge worldwide, but the challenge is greater when there are few avenues for accountability, recourse, and remedies.

And what about accountability—and the transparency and contestability that it depends on? There are glimmers of greater transparency in some countries. The Islamic Republic of Iran fully publishes its national budget and televises its parliamentary debates, as do some other countries in the region. The media are contributing to the public debate on government accountability in countries like the Islamic Republic of Iran and Algeria and are especially vocal in Lebanon. Satellite television channels allow information to travel across previously impenetrable borders.

But in general, countries across the MENA region exhibit a pattern of limited and reluctant transparency, which is reflected in the fact that it is the region with the least empirical data on the quality of governance. No country guarantees citizens the right to government information; some countries actively repress that right. In Egypt, the detailed government budget is not fully published and discussed outside parliament. The freedom of the press is carefully monitored and circumscribed in most countries and is periodically assaulted in some countries by the harassment or arrest of journalists, thereby damping public debate. Many countries have laws restricting press freedom, subjecting them to controls, and imposing penalties. The war on terrorism, more intense after September 11, 2001, has provided excuses for tightening controls in many countries.

Accountability requires—as much as transparency—contestability: debate, questioning, choice, and competition among alternative representatives and policies. Parliaments can enhance internal accountability; Morocco and Bahrain, for example, have recently created parliaments. Local elections can enhance external accountability; in Lebanon and the Islamic Republic of Iran (where the 1999 elections brought 200,000 locally elected representatives into the political sphere), local elections have improved local governance and created a proving ground for future national political leaders. Within administrations, easing the rigid civil service policies and pressures—which put the unemployed on the public payroll and that award jobs on the basis of personal connections—will improve accountability through competition for bureaucratic appointment and advancement.

In most MENA countries, internal accountability mechanisms within the government administration are generally comparable with those of other countries at similar incomes. But internal checks and balances across the branches of government are uniformly weak. Why? Because of the excessive concentration of power in the executive—not only in the seven monarchies, but also in the more notionally "pluralistic" governments, such as Algeria, the Arab Republic of Egypt, and Tunisia. Regarding external accountability, contestability for public officials—in the form of regular, fair, competitive processes of renewing mandates and of placing no one above the law—has been rare in the region, especially for national leaders. MENA governments remain the most centralized of all developing countries.

... And in the Measure of Good Governance

A complex, multifaceted concept, governance is difficult to collapse into a few empirical measures that can be compared across countries. Various efforts to do so have sought to identify critical dimensions of good governance, ranging from the rule of law, to controlling corruption, to public sector efficiency, to citizen voice, to "democracy." Many of the measures are based on observer perceptions and opinions, making the measures subjective. And the lack of data on the quality of governance in this region compounds the difficulty of measuring governance empirically. Even so, the analysis in this book supplements the qualitative assessment and allows comparisons among countries worldwide by drawing on past work and by aggregating the available empirical data into broad indexes of governance.

The quantitative picture reveals a gradation in the quality of governance in MENA, thus reflecting the region's diversity, which makes generalizations difficult. But on close examination, some robust regional patterns emerge.

For the most part, the quality of governance in the region increases with incomes—a worldwide pattern that has been found in every study on governance. In terms of the overall index of governance quality used in this book (based on 22 indicators with comparable data for most countries), upper-middle-income countries around the world, as well as in MENA, have average governance quality about twice that of lower-income countries. So any study of governance needs to take account of variations in income.

When compared with countries that have similar incomes and characteristics—the main competitors in the global marketplace—the MENA region ranks at the bottom on the index of overall governance quality (figure O.2).

That overall governance gap has two components: an index of the quality of administration in the public sector and an index of public accountability. The first measures the efficiency of the bureaucracy, the rule of law, the protection of property rights, the level of corruption, the quality of regulations, and the mechanisms of internal accountability. On this index, MENA countries largely track their counterparts worldwide, typically running only slightly lower. With few exceptions, they have individually and on average lower levels of the quality of administration in the public sector than would be expected for their incomes (that is, they are below the income-adjusted world average in figure O.3), with the gap tending to be worse for countries that have higher incomes that rely on oil resources.

FIGURE O.2

Compared with Other Regions, MENA Shows a Clear Governance Gap

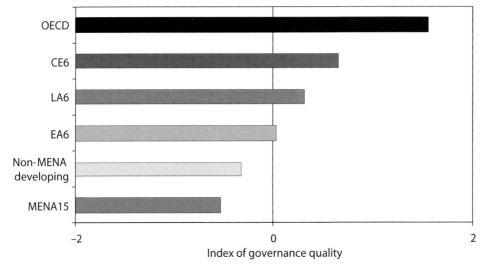

Notes: OECD includes Australia, Austria, Belgium, Canada, Denmark, Finland, France, Germany, Greece, Iceland, Ireland, Italy, Japan, Luxembourg, the Netherlands, New Zealand, Norway, Portugal, Spain, Sweden, Switzerland, the United Kingdom, and the United States. Central European countries (CE6) include Bulgaria, the Czech Republic, Hungary, Poland, Romania, and the Slovak Republic. Latin American countries (LA6) include Argentina, Brazil, Chile, Mexico, República Bolivariana de Venezuela, and Uruguay. East Asian countries (EA6) include Indonesia, Malaysia, the Philippines, Singapore, Thailand, and Vietnam. MENA15 includes Algeria, the Arab Republic of Egypt, Bahrain, the Islamic Republic of Iran, Jordan, Kuwait, Lebanon, Morocco, Oman, Qatar, the Republic of Yemen, Saudi Arabia, the Syrian Arab Republic, Tunisia, and the United Arab Emirates.
Source: Authors' calculations, which are based on the index of governance quality, covering 173 countries worldwide.

FIGURE O.3

For the Quality of Administration, MENA's Governance Gap Is Narrower and Incomes Matter

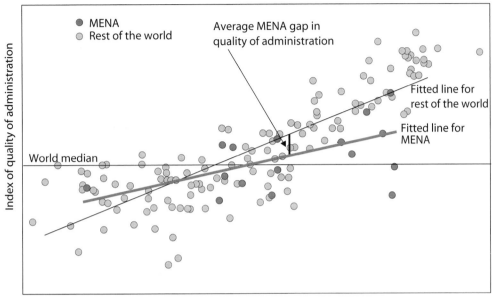

Notes: Refer to appendix B for the measurement of the governance gap. Data are insufficient to include Djibouti, Iraq, Libya, and the West Bank and Gaza.
Source: Authors' calculations, which are based on the index of the quality of administration, covering 173 countries worldwide.

The index of public accountability measures the openness of political institutions and participation, respect of civil liberties, transparency of government, and freedom of the press. Here, the MENA region falls far short. In the rest of the world, the quality of public accountability increases as incomes increase, but not in MENA (as shown by the flat line for MENA in figure O.4). For some of the richer MENA countries, the gap is particularly wide when compared with similar countries worldwide. Moreover, not a single country in MENA appears above the world median for the quality of public accountability, whether adjusted for income or not. Individually and collectively, the region lags on measures of public accountability, and the richer the country, the worse the gap.

Within MENA, there is a stark difference in the quality of public accountability between the countries that have very little or no oil or gas (the Arab Republic of Egypt, Jordan, Lebanon, Morocco, and Tunisia) and those that do (figure O.5). This is because the high incomes of the latter depend less on a good environment for business activity (as, say, is

FIGURE O.4

For Public Accountability, MENA's Governance Gap Is Wider, Irrespective of Incomes

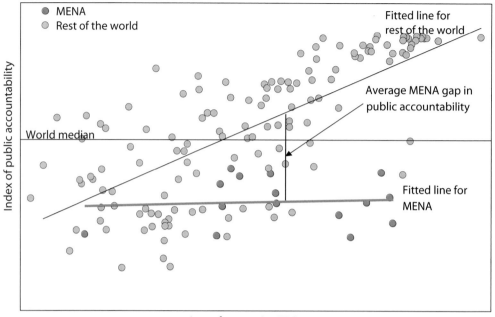

Notes: Refer to appendix B for the measurement of the governance gap. Data are insufficient to include Djibouti, Iraq, Libya, and the West Bank and Gaza.
Source: Authors' calculations, which are based on the index of public accountability, covering 173 countries worldwide.

the case for some of the richer East Asian countries such as the Republic of Korea and Singapore) than on the exploitation of oil and gas resources.

Weak Governance Has Contributed to Weak Growth in MENA ...

Since 1980, the average annual per capita economic growth of the MENA region as a whole has been 0.9 percent, even less than that of Sub-Saharan Africa.[1] Productivity has been on the decline for three decades. Even more troubling is the volatility of growth. Increases in incomes have been difficult to sustain, and declines in income have not been quickly reversed—for both oil exporters and the non–oil-dependent countries. Contrast that with East Asian countries, which grew faster at sustained rates, except for the regional crisis in 1997–98.

At the root of MENA's growth gap is its governance gap. Indeed, simulations find that if MENA had matched the average quality of adminis-

FIGURE O.5

For MENA's Oil-Dependent Countries, the Public Accountability Gap Is Even Wider

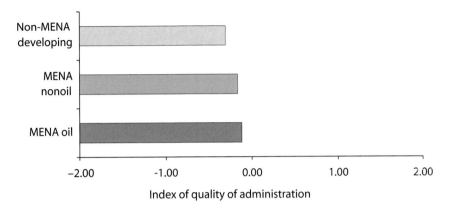

Index of quality of administration

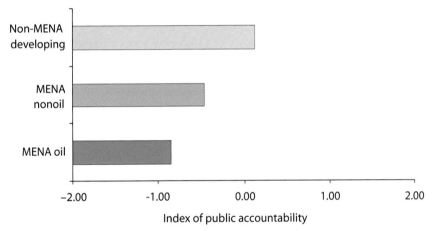

Index of public accountability

Notes: MENA oil includes Algeria, Bahrain, the Islamic Republic of Iran, Kuwait, Oman, Qatar, the Republic of Yemen, Saudi Arabia, the Syrian Arab Republic, and the United Arab Emirates. MENA nonoil includes the Arab Republic of Egypt, Jordan, Lebanon, Morocco, and Tunisia. Data are insufficient to include Djibouti, Iraq, Libya, and the West Bank and Gaza.
Source: Authors' calculations, which are based on the indexes of quality of administration and public accountability, covering 173 countries worldwide.

tration in the public sector for a group of good-performing Southeast Asian countries (Indonesia, Malaysia, the Philippines, Singapore, and Thailand), its growth rates would have been higher by about one percentage point a year.[2] The development gap is reflected in this growth gap: if the region had grown as fast as Hungary, Malaysia, and other top performers over the past decade and a half, average incomes would be twice what they are today—twice! The shortfall may be even higher, because the calculations do not include the full effects of public accountability, which is much less well developed in MENA countries than in those good-performing comparators.

... Because Poor Governance Has Shackled the Business Environment

Many factors contribute to the region's disappointing economic performance, with weak governance at the origin of many. Governance helps determine policy formulation and implementation that, in turn, determine whether or not there is a sound, attractive business environment for investment and production.

Businesses react to incentives, costs, and constraints, which are often summarized as the "business environment" or, more narrowly, as the "investment climate." Influencing the environment for business and investment are the actions of the government in shaping and implementing policies. Needed are good policies—and good administration of policies. One without the other would be ineffective.

For most MENA countries, the bureaucratic environment for doing business still lags far behind that of their comparators elsewhere in the world. In Morocco, about half the firms in a recent survey said that they had to hire intermediaries or maintain full-time workers to deal with the bureaucracy (World Bank 2000a). In Jordan, a potential investor interested in registering a new firm has to wait three months, with half that time spent on a single procedure: inspection by the ministry concerned (World Bank 2003c). Increasing the cost and risk to business, such problems not only lower the quantity of new investment but also lower the quality and efficiency of the investments already made. They thus reduce growth as well.

Improving the inclusiveness and accountability of governance mechanisms in MENA will help in three ways: by reducing the scope for persistently arbitrary or distorted policies, by improving bureaucratic performance and thus reducing the uncertainties and costs of doing business, and by improving the delivery of public services for businesses to be productive.

First, good governance does not necessarily lead to good economic policies, but it does provide mechanisms—such as public debate on the effect of government policies—that help countries minimize persistent policy distortions. By ensuring public accountability of politicians and bureaucrats, good governance contributes to the effective implementation of economic policies that are conducive to growth. Transparency and contestability, the key principles of accountability, plus inclusiveness in the governance process, are essential checks against leadership and policies that may favor less-efficient businesses and the incompetent or greedy.

Second, better governance makes it easier to start new businesses and to run and expand existing ones. Accountable and capable bureaucracies help lower transaction costs (for entry, operation, and exit). Transparency and inclusiveness reduce the information asymmetries between business and governments, and thus reduce uncertainties and unpredictability in the application of government rules and regulations.

Better governance also increases the flexibility of countries to respond to economic shocks—as was evident for the Southeast Asian countries in the 1990s. The better the quality of their institutions, the faster they recovered from the regional crisis. The same pattern holds for MENA countries that are less affected by the oil cycle: their faster economic recovery since the mid-1990s can be associated with their better institutional quality. The lesson: good governance mechanisms facilitate the management of outside sources of economic volatility, such as oil prices.

Third, businesses operate in a commercial environment that depends on the satisfactory, timely, and equitable delivery of key public goods (such as safe, well-maintained roads) and on efficient and equitable enforcement of necessary public regulations (such as competition law and regulation of natural monopolies, as well as taxation and similar policies). Such a business environment can be ensured (1) by more inclusive participation of business, worker, and consumer interests in defining priorities for public services and in monitoring how well governments perform in providing them, and (2) by accountability mechanisms that help keep the officials, administrators, or other providers of those public services honest and able. And this environment can be further improved with good economic and regulatory policies formulated by accountable politicians.

Of course, it is possible that strong leadership can increase the economic well-being of a country—as in the Chile of Pinochet, the Singapore of Lee Kuan Yew, the Tunisia of Bourguiba, or the China of the past two decades. Such examples show that strong internal accountability mechanisms can, in some cases, mitigate the absence of strong external accountability. But strong leadership and strong internal accountability cannot permanently substitute for weak governance, as Indonesia demonstrates. Internal accountability works less well when issues become increasingly complex and variable—because welfare requires basic rights that are inherent in good governance, not just economic well-being; because citizen voice is needed to ensure equitable distribution of the gains from growth; and because complex services in an increasingly globalized world need a flexible flow of information that is best ensured by citizen participation. A case in point, again, is China, where the over-reliance on internal accountability channels led to difficulties at the onset of containing the SARS (severe acute respiratory syndrome) epidemic. Overall, there is an acute scarcity worldwide of examples of such competent, but unaccountable, leadership. This scarcity is testament to the fact that enlightened leadership with poor governance is a historical accident—as much, if not more so, in MENA countries as worldwide.

Weak Governance Has Also Limited the Quality of Public Goods and Services

Public service delivery has long been a key concern of all MENA governments. There have been some notable successes, both over time and in comparison with other countries at similar incomes. In Oman, gross primary school enrollments increased from just 3 percent in 1970 to 72 percent in 2000. In Lebanon, almost no children under 12 had DPT (diphtheria, pertussis, tetanus) immunizations in 1980—but 93 percent had been immunized by 1993. In Tunisia, there was less than one phone line for every 100 people in 1990—yet there is one line for every 5 people today. And between 1990 and 1999, the Arab Republic of Egypt built more than 18,000 kilometers of roads and the Republic of Yemen built almost 16,000 kilometers.

Still, there are significant gaps in public services in the region—especially defined in terms of outcomes—between the countries of the region and those with which they have to compete. To illustrate, despite progress, infant mortality in Egypt remained at 69 per 1,000 live births in 1999; in many other MENA countries, it remains above the worldwide average for their respective income grouping. Only the United Arab Emirates, one of the richest countries in the region, matches Hungary and Malaysia, with a rate of 8 per 1,000. Almost two in five adult males in Morocco are illiterate, and well over three in five adult females, which is on par with much poorer countries such as Mozambique or Pakistan.

Why are Egyptian bureaucrats so good at building roads, but so slow at eradicating illiteracy? Why are Lebanese administrators so effective at immunizing children, but so ineffective at drastically reducing infant mortality? And why has Tunisia been so successful at increasing the number of telephone mainlines, but not as effective in increasing access to the Internet, the tool of today's information age?

Clearly, the cause for those shortcomings in service delivery is not any lack of capability of the MENA administrators, as the region's score on the index for quality of administration attests. It is the thesis of this book that weak government performance stems from weak governance mechanisms, especially those for public accountability.

The quantity and quality of any public services delivered depend on the relationships and interactions among three parties: politicians or policymakers; service providers, whether bureaucrats in public service agencies or private vendors on behalf of government; and citizens, as clients, who are beneficiaries of the service and who act both individually and as members of civil-society intermediaries.

Public service agencies (such as public schools and clinics, but also regulatory bodies) are expected to provide the services they are responsible for: to teach children, to treat patients, to maintain roads, to assess and collect customs fairly and expeditiously, and to issue licenses according to appropriate rules. In short, they are expected to serve the client. The challenge that politicians and policymakers face is to motivate and monitor the service agencies. To accomplish this task, they need to design internal mechanisms of oversight and accountability that increase the information about services actually delivered (transparency) and to set out consequences for good or bad performance (contestability). In addition, they need to foster an ethic of service to the public and of stewardship of public resources, both of which are hallmarks of a truly effective service delivery organization.

How does this framework apply to the situation in MENA? Consider budget management—a central element in any public service delivery system. MENA governments have typically focused on traditional budget management: linking annual budgets to multiyear plans, using cost-benefit analysis, and putting in place financial controls. They have focused too little on the performance orientation of the system: arrangements such as the merit-based recruitment and promotion of civil servants who actually carry out the budget, the autonomy that high-performing line agencies need, and the competitiveness of salaries, each of which is indispensable in good internal accountability and performance management systems.

Politicians and policymakers must find ways to supplement such internal accountability systems through mechanisms for external accountability. This need is especially true for services that involve a large number of personalized transactions, such as teaching or issuing official papers, where centralized monitoring is neither practical nor effective. The officials can be helped in this effort by citizens who deal directly with agencies—citizens who can provide feedback on agency performance and can even participate actively in agency management. Put simply, the receiver of services has the best information on whether the quality of services was adequate or on whether the service provider failed to meet his or her needs. This is the first channel of external accountability—from the citizens, as clients, to the service providers.

But what if politicians and policymakers do not take their job of mandating and monitoring public service delivery seriously or are simply not in touch with the public interest? In those cases, citizens and citizen groups need channels to hold leaders accountable—in part through fairly contested elections but also through a wide array of other mechanisms to express their needs and concerns, such as interest groups, official consultations, independent research, and the media. This is the second channel of external accountability—from citizens to politicians and policymakers.

As noted above, it is in accountability that governance in MENA is weakest, especially but not only through the external accountability channels. Client voice and choice over service provision are conspicuously lacking, if not absent, in a region where client feedback mechanisms—either to the provider or to policymakers—are limited and often restricted.

Many innovations are being developed around the world to strengthen those accountability linkages, and a few are being tried in some MENA countries. But such experimentation, which is common in much the world, remains relatively rare and isolated in the MENA region. For example, Malaysia began to introduce performance-oriented budgeting in the late 1960s. Only now, three decades later, have some MENA countries begun to consider it seriously. Given the long gestation period to introduce such systems, the delay is all the more costly for internal accountability.

Client and business surveys, feedback mechanisms, report cards, polls, and other methods of giving beneficiaries a voice in service performance are common in other regions. But they are rare in MENA, a fact reflected in the scarcity of data on governance in MENA countries. Nor do clients have much choice in obtaining services, because the privatization of public monopolies is proceeding slowly. MENA is also the region with the most centralized governments—despite evidence that local governments can often deliver many public services, especially basic health and education, better. Local officials have more and better information about the needs of their communities, and local communities are more likely to be able to hold local leaders accountable. Finally, key external accountability mechanisms—such as the media and civil-society organizations—continue to be tightly controlled, if not discouraged, in many countries.

Bridging the Region's Governance Gap Is Both a Challenge and an Opportunity

Bridging the governance gap will be a challenge for both the governments and the people of the region. But it is also an opportunity, with potentially great rewards in sustained economic growth, social stability, and human development.

Men and women in the Middle East and North Africa are living today at a time of rising expectations—and growing frustrations. Economies are being strained by high population growth rates, which are among the highest in the world. That growth adds a rapidly increasing number of job seekers to the labor force. Aspirations race ahead, raising inevitable comparisons with other countries, which have been made easier by the global revolution in information flows. For those young men and women, the economy needs to create productive, income-generating opportunities through economic growth, and the government needs to provide services ranging from education to a good business environment. Good governance is a means to ensure growth and social improvement; it is also a fundamental dimension of human development itself.

Yet the MENA region proceeds on a profoundly fragile growth path. No country in the region has been able to move to a sustainable path—despite the enormous oil wealth of many of them, or perhaps because of that wealth. The gap in economic development, coupled with the gap in aspirations, puts progress in the region at risk.

The governance challenge is not selecting the "right" leaders or prescribing the "right" economic or social policies, important as they are. It is ensuring that the process of choosing, renewing, and changing leadership, as well as of conceiving, debating, designing, adopting, and implementing such policies, will give all the people—as both citizens and clients—an opportunity to express their preferences, to participate in the dialogue, and to hold the government accountable for acting in their best interest. Good governance cannot itself guarantee a particular set of "good" outcomes in terms of leadership and policies, but it is a sine qua non for minimizing the persistence of disappointing outcomes and ineffective policies and for moving toward better ones.

Exogenous factors—riches from hydrocarbons, instabilities caused by conflict or the threat of it, or interference stemming from geopolitical interests—have handicapped the emergence of the institutions of good governance in many of the region's countries. Worse, those factors often reinforce behaviors and governing arrangements that defy accountability and that put people at the mercy of government. Rising to the challenge of good governance will mean turning those handicaps into opportunities by acting on a wide array of entry points that can eventually lead to better governance—and with it, better economic performance.

Rising to the challenge of better governance is not solely, or even mainly, the responsibility of governments. The reason? Many in government (and many outside it) may resist the move to more inclusive and accountable governance. Better governance inevitably requires action by governments, but it also requires more active participation by the people. The governance challenge is thus a challenge for everyone in the region. Outside the region, governments and organizations also bear a responsibility to align their relationships with MENA countries more closely to the objective of helping them meet their governance challenge, rather than countenancing bad governance behaviors and institutions through self-interested aid and alliances.

Meeting the challenge is no simple matter, either technically or institutionally. Poor governance reflects the failure of institutions; yet the creation of better institutions itself requires the emergence of other institutions, notably active, inclusive, and responsible participation.

The uncharted transition will vary by country, but it is likely to be marked by compromises and halfway houses—such as the consociational democracy in Lebanon or the designated representatives of excluded groups in the Arab Republic of Egypt, Bahrain, and Morocco—that are designed to build institutions more representative of the people in the face of traditions and other institutions that limit inclusion. The transition to good governance also requires tolerance of compromises and mistakes, while the institutions required for good governance, like participation, gain capacity and credibility. Many fear that opening up channels of external accountabilities without capable civil-society institutions can lead to chaos; yet such fears are too often used to justify repressive, exclusive, and nonparticipatory governance, and they stifle the emergence of the very institutions needed for enduring stability.

One of the lessons of governance reform worldwide is that moving to inclusiveness, accountability, and participation takes time, because it involves changing traditions and confronting privileged interests. Universal suffrage was not common in developed countries until the mid-20th century—nearly two centuries after being enshrined as a concept in America and Europe. Performance-oriented budgeting was initiated as a means of increasing accountability and performance of government in the United States in the 1960s, and it is still a long way from being adhered to universally.

But there are grounds for optimism. Countries elsewhere in the world have gradually strengthened governance mechanisms without instability and with the reward of better economic performance. The governance reform in Eastern Europe was generally better than in the countries from the former Soviet Union because of more contestable political systems, which favored the growth and power of a wide array of citizen associations voicing support for reforms.

Within MENA, there are also grounds for optimism. Most constitutions enshrine the values of good governance. Governments remain strongly committed to providing citizens with good public services. The debate on governance in the region, hampered though it may be by censure and limited information, is a reality. There is evidence of some progress on many fronts throughout the region, albeit progress of variable strength and breadth, such as the meaningful local elections in the Islamic Republic of Iran and in Lebanon, the launch of e-government initiatives in most countries, the use of client feedback surveys in Jordan and in the West Bank and Gaza, the new parliaments in Bahrain and Morocco, the citizen participation in Aden's municipal management, and the national ombudsmen in Tunisia and Algeria.

Any Program to Enhance Governance Requires Attention to the Twin Values of Inclusiveness and Accountability, ...

Some broad principles—laid out in this book—should inform the selection and design of actions. Inclusiveness and accountability appear as essential components of any program of enhancing governance. For inclusiveness, basic rights—including the right to participate fully in the governance process, the right to equality before the law, and the right to equal treatment by government agencies—need to be guaranteed in every element of the program. For accountability, transparency and contestability should guide the process of designing the program and deciding its content.

Accountability requires both internal accountability mechanisms—roughly parallel to the index of the quality of administration in the public sector—and external accountability mechanisms—roughly parallel to the index of public accountability. The first depend on the initiative of governments, with impetus and pressure from the people. The second rely on the initiative of the people, with acceptance and accommodation by governments.

The program should target existing restrictions that limit inclusiveness and accountability, such as controls on the formation of citizen associations, high-level approval of candidate lists, and restricted access to information on government spending. It should also set up more active mechanisms for improving governance, such as legislating against discriminatory practices in the public sector, plus setting up a transparent monitoring and recourse system to assess adherence to new laws and to correct deficiencies.

... Starting with an Open Commitment by Countries ...

The first requirement is a public commitment to improve the inclusiveness and accountability of government and to increase transparency and contestability in the conduct of public affairs. This commitment should be a joint commitment of government (in all its branches) and of the people, both individually and through their civil-society advocacy and community empowerment organizations.

Formal declarations by governments serve notice of new directions in a visible and monitorable way. They gain in credibility when formulated in a participatory process that gives voice to citizen concerns and that builds a social consensus in which everyone feels he or she has a stake.

... To Formulate and Act on a Program to Enhance Governance ...

The commitment must be followed by a process with the participation of all in society to formulate a program to enhance governance. The aim would be to reach a consensus on key directions for enhancing governance, on actions to enhance inclusiveness and accountability across a wide array of governance issues and institutions, and on the definition of indicators that could be used to chart progress and to progressively adapt the program.

This process should set high standards for including all segments of society in the consultation and debate. It should ensure maximum transparency by making all deliberations public and by inviting debate in the media. And it should elicit a strong civic commitment and involvement. Such a process itself would make a strong contribution to strengthening public accountability.

... With Five Pathways to Good Governance: ...

The program to enhance governance could be elaborated along five pathways to good governance: (1) measures to enhance inclusiveness, (2) national actions to strengthen external accountability, (3) local actions to strengthen external accountability, (4) national checks and balances to strengthen internal accountability, and (5) administrative reforms to improve internal accountability (figure O.6).

The five pathways are interrelated. Inclusiveness, a value in its own right, is an indispensable ingredient in better accountability, especially external accountability. Internal and external accountability mechanisms are not substitutes; they reinforce one another. Stronger mechanisms for external accountability will reveal weaknesses in internal accountability mechanisms, while stronger mechanisms and capacity for internal accountability are needed to generate the information about what the government is doing, which is the basis for external accountability.

Any good action program needs to envisage measures along all pathways, even if there is a wide menu of appropriate measures for each. The elements of each national program and the specific mechanisms for implementing them will be matters for individual societies to decide consensually through consultation and debate.

FIGURE O.6

A Program to Enhance Governance

Inclusiveness

Enhancement measures

- Mandate universal suffrage for all elected posts.
- Reduce discrimination in laws and regulations.
- Broaden government consultative mechanisms.
- Encourage broad-based civil-society organizations.
- Monitor whether public service agency staff treat citizens equitably.
- Redress past exclusions.

Program to enhance governance

Internal accountability

National checks and balances

- Increase oversight authority and capability of parliaments over the executive.
- Ensure greater independence of the judiciary.
- Improve professional capacity of parliaments and the judiciary.
- Empower other independent oversight agencies, and mandate reviews by them.

Administrative measures

- Improve performance orientation, including monitoring of government budgets.
- Reform the civil service to enhance its service orientation and professional competence.
- Strengthen the resources and capacity of local agencies to design, adapt, and deliver public services.
- Ensure independence of regulatory agencies.
- Foster an ethic of service to the public in the civil service.

External accountability

National actions

- Mandate greater freedom of information and public disclosure of government operations.
- Invite external oversight to ensure open, fair, regular elections.
- Invite public debate on policies by representative civil-society groups.
- Generate, monitor, and disseminate data on governance quality.
- Encourage independent and responsible media.

Local actions

- Introduce feedback mechanisms, from clients to providers, and publish results.
- Increase competition among public service agencies—and with private providers.
- Move toward increased devolution to elected local authorities.
- Create opportunities for involvement of community empowerment associations.

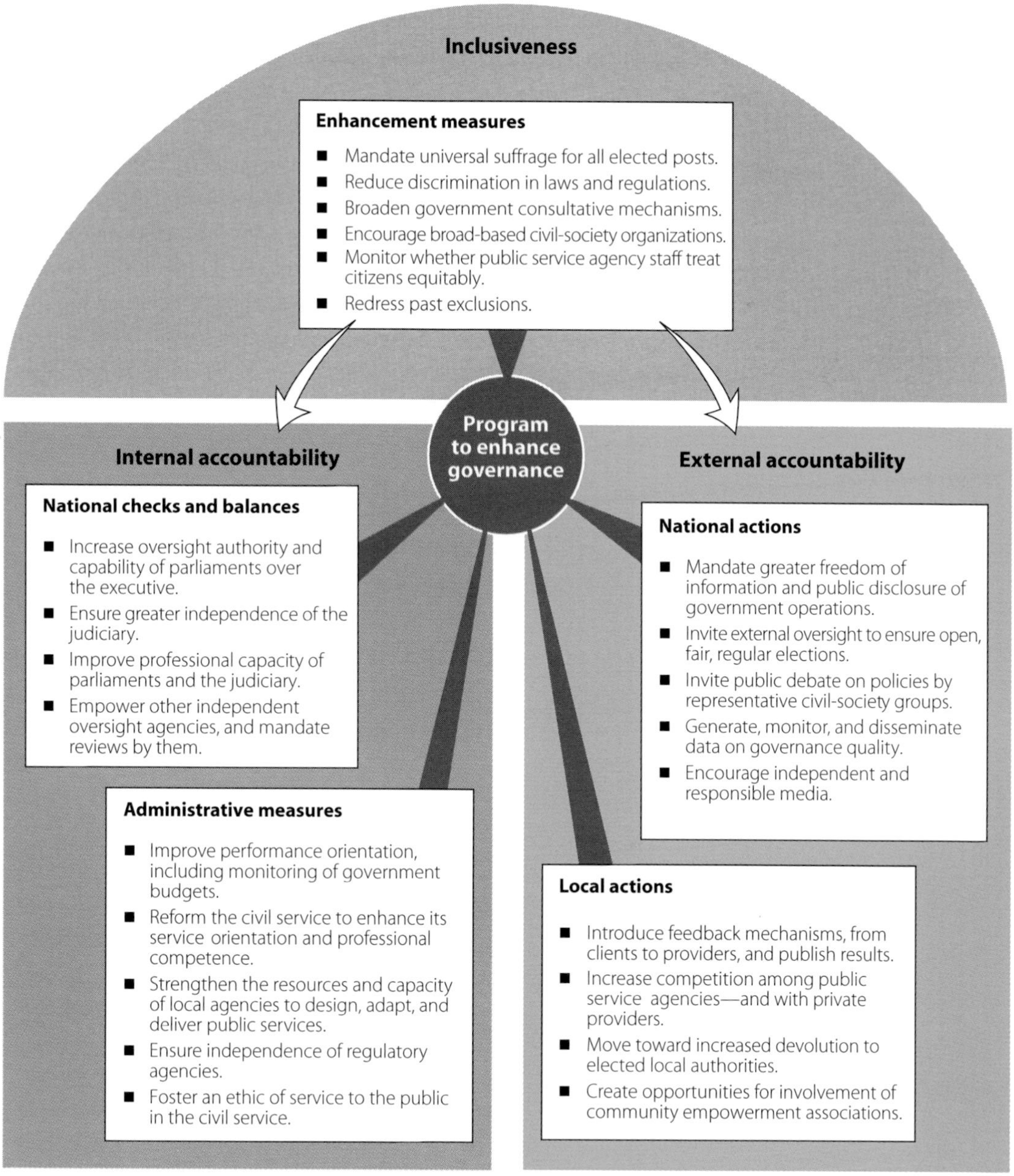

... To Enhance Inclusiveness, ...

The first step in enhancing inclusiveness is to adopt laws and regulations that widen and secure access to widely accepted basic rights and freedoms that include the right to participate in the governance process on an equal basis, plus the right to equality before the law, such as the right to be treated equally by government agencies. Broader public consultation, more freedom for the media, fewer restrictions on civil-society organizations, more equitable channels of access to health and education, and the end of discriminatory laws and regulations are examples of measures to secure inclusion. But laws may be little more than a declaration of intentions.

So, the second step is to establish mechanisms that can ensure that those laws and regulations are respected—mechanisms of internal and external accountability and, where necessary and possible, mechanisms that can help redress the consequences of past action.

... To Strengthen External Accountability Through National Actions, ...

Improving external accountability is critical in providing incentives for the governments to strengthen their structures of internal accountability. Actions on this level will determine whether a country's overall institutional environment supports good governance or not. A menu of actions includes the following:

- Widely circulate information—the currency of transparency—on what government is doing, and do it through laws that mandate greater public disclosure and access to information and a freer public debate.

- Increase contestability through open, fair, regular elections of public officials, a process supplemented by a variety of other forms of participation, such as broad official consultations and hearings on government policies, including citizen surveys and electronic feedback.

- Permit wider civil-society advocacy and participation, including citizen watchdog groups and investigative journalism. Such activism can be an important mechanism in exposing corruption as a symptom of poor governance.

- Institute better monitoring of the quality of governance and wider dissemination of data that measure that quality in a variety of dimensions, such as rule of law, press freedom, discriminatory practices, and control of corruption.

- Encourage an independent and responsible media.

... To Strengthen External Accountability Through Local Actions, ...

Improving external accountability typically requires greater citizen participation, mainly through the citizen–service provider link. But today in MENA, that accountability almost universally depends on the willingness of governments to accommodate such participation. Accommodating participation means governments would establish participatory mechanisms as they publish information on the rules, responsibilities, and performance of public agencies, and as they abide by the outcomes of electoral and consultative processes. Evidence worldwide shows that an active, informed civil society can claim greater participation, especially at the local level, as shown by the example of women demanding identity cards in the Arab Republic of Egypt. Local actions can also act as a powerful ally for governments seeking to improve their own internal accountability mechanisms. A menu of such actions by governments includes the following:

- Provide more reliable information on public service performance through surveys, feedback mechanisms, consultations, and similar mechanisms.

- Increase competition among service providers by giving clients greater freedom of choice (for example, through vouchers and sound regulation of alternative service agencies).

- Adopt policies to empower and to strengthen local governments, which are closer to the people and more able to involve them directly in public decisions and accountability.

- Facilitate the increased involvement of community empowerment associations, especially in the management and oversight of public services that must be tailored to specific communities and groups.

... To Improve Internal Accountability Through National Checks and Balances, ...

Improving internal accountability is primarily, but not only, aimed at enhancing contestability in the exercise of state power. It is done typically through a constitutional separation of power among the branches of government—especially to make it difficult for a powerful executive (the norm in MENA) to sidestep accountability obligations. A menu of actions includes the following:

- Strengthen parliamentary authority and capacity.

- Ensure the greater independence and capacity of the judiciary.

- Empower other independent oversight agencies within government, such as supreme audit organizations and ombudsmen.

... And to Improve Internal Accountability Through Administrative Reforms

Even without constitutional reform to establish checks and balances, even without elections and decentralized political power, and even without freer press and more public information, many administrative actions can strengthen accountability in agencies that provide public services. Among the most powerful mechanisms developed elsewhere are those focusing on the management of public sector performance. A menu of actions includes the following:

- Strengthen the performance orientation in public expenditure management, which itself requires actions to improve the flow of information and the quality of debate and dialogue within the administration, thus underlining the importance of an overall governance environment that supports transparency and contestability.

- Reform the civil service to make it more accountable for emphasizing results over bureaucratic action, for ensuring faithful implementation of policies, and for treating all citizens fairly and competently. One benefit would be better control of corruption by public officials through reforms to reduce opportunities for malfeasance, through stronger sanctions, and through an ethic of integrity and stewardship.

- Decentralize the functions of government to bring them closer to citizens, who have both a direct stake in performance (unlike a supervisory bureaucrat) and the first-hand information to assess performance.

- Ensure independence of regulatory agencies to avoid capture by either private-vested interests or officials within government who have a political agenda.

- Foster an ethic of service to the public and of stewardship of public resources to enhance civil servants' commitment to performance and to lower the costs of formal accountability monitoring and sanctions. Developing such an ethic requires vision and leadership from the top, as well as collaborative arrangements to build trust and mutual recognition between the citizens and the staff of public agencies.

In Sum: Follow Commitment with Action

There is no mystery to developing governance. It requires just two things: open commitment followed by action by all. If the people and the governments—the primary actors in governance—join together in the process, everyone in the region can have equal access to the fruits of faster growth, to better public services, and to a future replete with the attributes of human development. Those attributes encompass material well-being, wider choices and opportunities for people to realize their potential, and the guarantee of equality of treatment, freedom to choose, and full participation in the process by which people govern themselves.

Notes

1. Authors' calculations from World Bank data.
2. Authors' calculations from World Bank data; see appendix B.

Analytical Framework for Good Governance in the Middle East and North Africa

Every day, tens of thousands of interactions take place between people and government officials across the Middle East and North Africa—from Rabat to Riyadh, and from the towns of Tunisia to the villages of the Islamic Republic of Iran. Those governance interactions range from the simple (getting a driver's license or birth certificate) to the more complex (receiving education from the government or being regulated when operating a business). They can be smooth and rewarding—or wildly frustrating.

The challenge for both governments and people throughout the region is to expand the smooth and productive interactions and to minimize the frustrating ones—that is, to move toward good governance. The goal of good governance is to maximize the well-being of the public (in two words: human development) through promotion of strong economic growth and material satisfaction of basic needs, protection of basic rights such as liberty, and expansion and freedom of choice.

Because governance is multifaceted, it is difficult both to define and to measure. There have been many efforts to do so, each seeking to identify critical dimensions of governance and to assess its quality. Such dimensions range from the rule of law, to control of corruption, to public sector efficiency, to citizen voice, to democracy. Drawing on past work, this book uses a simple definition of governance—the process of exercising authority in the name of a constituency, including selecting and replacing those who exercise it. As an expository device, think of a circle with two parts: public governance, as the authority relationship between the government and the people, is represented by the arrows connecting the two (figure AF.1). "Government" and "people" are generic terms for an array of individuals and institutions. The government includes the king or president of a country, its parliament, and its top officials, but it also includes the local council. Essentially, the government is anyone who acts on behalf of the people in making decisions about public welfare. The people may be individual citizens or civil-society groups and other intermediaries, such as labor unions or newspaper publishers.

The Good Governance Relationship

If governance is the exercise of authority in the name of the people, good governance is doing so in ways that respect the integrity, rights, and needs of everyone within the state. Good governance re-

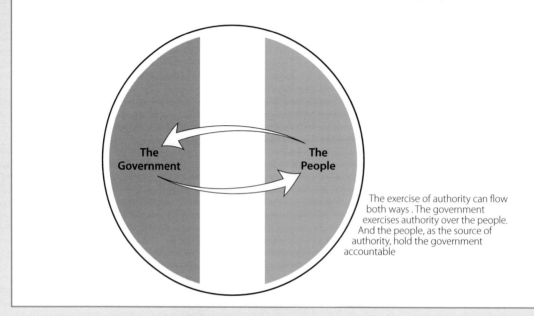

FIGURE AF.1

Public Governance Is the Authority Relationship Between the *Government* and the *People*

In this relationship, the *government* may be individuals or institutions, such as the president or parliament … or the local police officer or business registrar. The *people* may be individual citizens or may be civil-society groups and other intermediaries, such as labor unions or newspaper publishers.

The
Government

The
People

The exercise of authority can flow both ways . The government exercises authority over the people. And the people, as the source of authority, hold the government accountable

quires technically solid institutions and mechanisms that function effectively, but it cannot exist without respect for some core human values recognized and celebrated everywhere. Although the values are universal, the mechanisms that best translate them into practice vary from one setting to another.

Good governance rests on the two core values of *inclusiveness* and *accountability*.

- *Inclusiveness* means that all citizens are equally guaranteed certain basic rights, including equality before the law and the right to participate in the governance process on an equal basis. Conversely, it means the absence of exclusion and discrimination in all citizens' dealings with government.

- *Accountability* in a governance process means that those who are selected to act in the name of the people are answerable to the people for their failures, as well as credited for their successes.

These two universal values are particularly relevant in the Middle East and North Africa (MENA).

Governance is good when the process of forming and implementing rules is inclusive and the makers and implementers of the rules are accountable to the people. In the long run and on balance, a governance process that is both inclusive and accountable will generate good policies that further the welfare of the people and serve as a safety net against bad ones. It is a process, but one embedded with certain rights that are also the hallmark of development.

Inclusiveness

Virtually every national constitution in the MENA region enshrines the value of equality for all. Translated into governance, this value means that governance is good when the process includes all people living within the state—that everyone who has a stake in it and is affected by it has equal opportunities to participate in and benefit from it.

But people and entire communities can be disenfranchised by law, by tradition, or by their situation—not just when they lack the right to vote or receive services, but when legal rulings depend on money, or when bureaucrats spare no pains to help some importers clear customs while treating others with disdain. Such disenfranchisement weakens governance because some voices are not heard, some people's needs are not reflected in public decisions, and some people are denied easy access to the government services that others get.

Inclusive governance is the mechanism to define and to protect the basic rights of everyone, including providing remedies and recourse guaranteed by a rule of law. Rights include fairness and tolerance among the people themselves, and good governance means those rights are protected. Rights also include how governments treat the people, and good governance means that governments always treat everyone without discrimination and always ensure equal opportunities to access the services provided by governments. In most MENA countries, constitutions currently define basic rights as including access to key public services such as education and health; good governance means that everyone also has equitable opportunities to access those services (figure AF.2).

Finally, governance is better when officials and bureaucrats commit to an ethic of service to the public, to act in the interest of everyone—to uphold and advance the public interest.

Accountability

Upon his election as the first caliph, Abu Bakr spoke to the people: "I was chosen by you to lead you; if I do what is right, support me, and if I do what is wrong, then correct me" (Imam 1994; authors' translation). Translated into governance, his statement means that governments should exist to serve the people, that those who govern should represent the people, and, thus, that those who govern in the name of the people must be fully *accountable* to them. This sovereignty of the people is well enshrined in most constitutions across the MENA region. Although the value of accountability is simple enough in itself, the governance institutions and mechanisms to ensure it are complex, multifaceted, and constantly evolving in line with societal needs and pressures.

Accountability rests on knowledge and information (*transparency* in governance mechanisms), as well as on incentives that encourage those who act in the name of the people—government officials—to do so faithfully, efficiently, and honestly (*contestability* in the governance process). Because ensuring accountability in governance is so complex, multiple approaches have evolved to hold both governments and government officials more accountable.

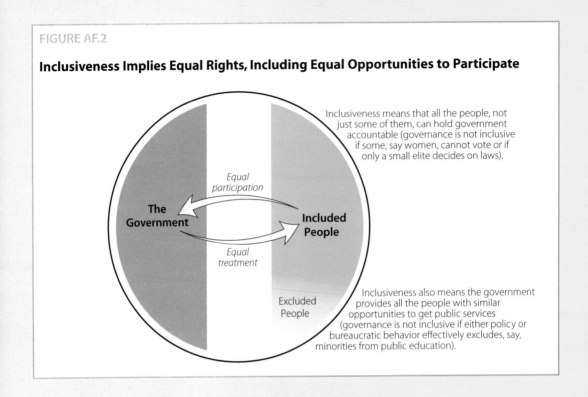

FIGURE AF.2

Inclusiveness Implies Equal Rights, Including Equal Opportunities to Participate

External accountability is when people hold the government accountable, such as when the residents in a village select their council representative (figure AF.3). But it also includes instances when the recipients of public services hold the service provider directly accountable. Holding government accountable happens when farmer communities manage the flow of public irrigation water—as happened in Tunisia and more recently in Egypt. It also happens where parents themselves are active in the operation of a school, as in the parents' councils that are active in most Egyptian schools.

Internal accountability is when the government—to protect the public interest—institutes various systems and incentives to govern the behavior of different agencies, such as separating powers and setting up independent checks and balances. The classic example of internal accountability is when the judiciary prevents the executive from overstepping its bounds. For instance, the Egyptian Supreme Constitutional Court—defying the executive—ordered parliament dissolved in 1986 after independent candidates were not allowed to run in the 1984 elections. In 1987, they were allowed to run in a limited way; since the 1990s, independents have faced no restrictions. In the wake of governance failures, both public and private, there is also a growing emphasis on ethics and integrity—the spirit of public service that flows naturally from inclusiveness, as an additional mechanism of internal accountability.

Although internal accountability is indispensable, such accountability itself is also considered by many to depend on sound mechanisms of external accountability. Government officials are more likely to worry about making internal accountability mechanisms effective when they face the public scrutiny that comes through the external accountability mechanisms.

FIGURE AF.3

Accountability Can Be Internal (by Checks and Balances within the Government) or External (by the People)

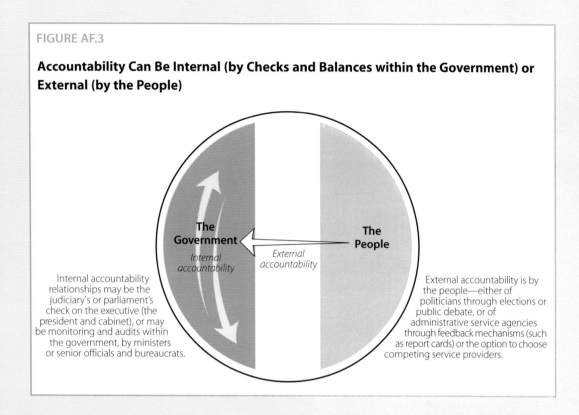

Internal accountability relationships may be the judiciary's or parliament's check on the executive (the president and cabinet), or may be monitoring and audits within the government, by ministers or senior officials and bureaucrats.

External accountability is by the people—either of politicians through elections or public debate, or of administrative service agencies through feedback mechanisms (such as report cards) or the option to choose competing service providers.

There are three key accountability channels in this framework (figure AF.4). The first is from the policymaker to the service provider (making teachers accountable to the minister of education, or a public health worker accountable to the minister of health). The second is from the client to the service provider (making teachers accountable to parents and students, or public doctors and nurses accountable to patients). The third is from citizens to policymakers and politicians (making a president or monarch accountable to the people, or a parliamentarian accountable to his or her constituents). The first channel is quintessentially one of *internal government accountability*—when one agency in the government functions to ensure that another one operates effectively. The other two linkages form the two essential channels for *external accountability*, whereby citizens' participation helps hold officials in government—those acting in the name of the people—accountable.

For an accountability relationship to be effective, the responsibilities should run in both directions. Consider the link between the service provider and the policymaker. The ministry of education, for example, normally provides the overall direction and the funding to hire teachers and to guide their work. In return, teachers promise to teach children effectively.

The relationship between citizens and politicians or policymakers can be direct (voting in an election, one-on-one discussions with a school teacher) or intermediated through a variety of formal and less-formal institutions. The formal institutions of governance include elected executives, parliamentary bodies, constitutional courts, independent audit agencies, public service agencies, and providers (that is, public bureaucracies in general). The people also create formal institutions to act as intermediaries between themselves and government: political parties, such as the Islah in

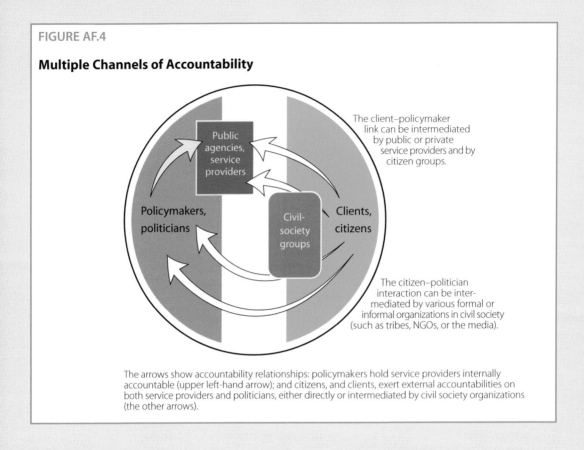

FIGURE AF.4

Multiple Channels of Accountability

The client–policymaker link can be intermediated by public or private service providers and by citizen groups.

The citizen–politician interaction can be intermediated by various formal or informal organizations in civil society (such as tribes, NGOs, or the media).

The arrows show accountability relationships: policymakers hold service providers internally accountable (upper left-hand arrow); and citizens, and clients, exert external accountabilities on both service providers and politicians, either directly or intermediated by civil society organizations (the other arrows).

the Republic of Yemen and the National Liberation Front (Front de Libération Nationale, or FLN) in Algeria; business associations, such as the Association of Commercial Bank Owners (*Jam'iyyat Ashab al-Masarif*) in Lebanon; faith-based organizations, such as the Foundation for the Disabled and Oppressed (*Bonyad-e Janbazan va-Mostas'afan*) in the Islamic Republic of Iran; labor unions, such as the Union Générale Tunisienne du Travail (UGTT) in Tunisia; and community empowerment and civic advocacy groups, such as Fathet Kheir in the Arab Republic of Egypt and Maroc 2020 in Morocco. These groups are typically complemented by a range of less-formal institutions. Personal connections (such as *wasta* in MENA) are an example of informal governance mechanisms as are the spontaneous community self-help efforts and street demonstrations that give voice to the disenfranchised. These less-formal institutions can better contribute to good governance when formal governance institutions are themselves solid. But they can also impede good governance by undermining sound formal governance processes.

Accountability and inclusiveness are distinct and complementary. Accountability is incomplete when some citizens are prevented from making their voices heard because they are excluded from governance processes. In the MENA region, governments sometimes argue that they act in the public interest, even when their actions are informed by listening to some citizens but not to others. But if they refuse to allow public debate and regular competitive elections, those governments may not be acting with the public's interest in mind.

Accountability mechanisms—especially external mechanisms that rely on public debate, independent scholarly research, and media reporting—can help ensure inclusiveness. Scholarly research can show how government subsidies benefit mostly the rich, not the poor, as is the case for gasoline subsidies in the Islamic Republic of Iran. Open and active media can spotlight the plight of the excluded, as is the case with the campaign in favor of land-mine survivors in Lebanon. It can also save lives. Nobel laureate Amartya Sen famously documented that there are no famines in democracies.

Making Governance "Good"

Governance as the "exercise of authority" is a neutral concept, one free of value judgments. But is the exercise of this authority "good" or "bad"? How responsive are governments to the needs of the people they serve, as they provide services such as public health and paved roads or as they protect the interests of consumers, entrepreneurs, or workers through the maintenance of law and order and sound regulation?

Putting "good" in front of "governance" invites a judgment about the quality of governance in a particular environment. Judgments are subjective by nature, and they are doubly subjective here. First, governance—the process of exercising authority—can take various shapes across countries and over time. Second, what one society considers to be "good" governance may be looked upon negatively by another. Or it may be judged critically by the same society at a later stage of its evolution.

For instance, the governance model that is predicated on the rule of a "just tyrant" (al-mustabidd al-'adil) has long epitomized good governance for many scholars and laymen in MENA, even if it is now anathema to most people across the region, as well as to people all over the world. It is possible that strong and good leaders can increase the economic well-being of a country, even when there is little transparency or contestability, as has been the case in the Chile of General Pinochet, the Singapore of Lee Kuan Yew, the Tunisia of Bourguiba, or the China of the past two decades. Such examples show that strong internal accountability mechanisms can, in some cases, compensate for the absence of strong external accountability.

But good leadership and strong internal accountability cannot permanently substitute for poor governance, for at least three reasons. First, there is more to welfare than economic well-being— and bad governance, by suppressing basic rights, lowers broader welfare. Second, without voice to ensure inclusiveness, even the economic benefits from strong leadership are unlikely to flow equally to all in society. Third, internal accountability works best when issues are simple and stable, but less well as they become increasingly complex and variable, as happens with development. In any case, the acute scarcity of worldwide examples of such competent, but unaccountable, leadership is testament to the fact that enlightened leadership with poor governance is a historical accident—as much, if not more so, in MENA countries as worldwide. Institutions of good governance cannot ensure good leadership; they, nevertheless, help minimize the duration of bad leadership and help preserve the gains of good leadership. Institutions persist; thus good leaders are mortal and often fallible.

There is likewise the temptation to evaluate a governance process by the policies and results it produces. Surely, the argument goes, if these policies are good (say, infant mortality rates have been decreasing), the governance process underlying policymaking and implementation must be "good" as well. But judging governance is necessarily about the quality of the processes of public policymaking and policy implementation, not about the quality of the resulting outcomes. There can be, for particular times and places, good policies with poor governance, as noted above; there can also be poor policies even with good governance, such as rent controls in the United States. In the short run, an inclusive and accountable governance process may not automatically lead to policies that maximize economic well-being, even if they maximize other components of welfare such as basic rights and freedoms. But such a process is more likely to limit the scope and duration of bad policies, both economic and otherwise, that restrain growth and curtail rights. On balance and over the long run, the positive causal relation between better governance and better policy does hold true.

Good governance is marked by the absence of corruption and the absence of abuse of public authority. Such corruption and abuse mean that people do not get equal treatment by government. Yet, corruption is only a symptom of poor governance, of the weaknesses in respecting the core values of inclusiveness and accountability. Therefore, controlling corruption is but one outcome of strengthening the governance processes.

Likewise, good governance is respect of democratic principles, which give sovereignty to the people. Yet, in its common manifestation through electoral politics, democracy may not universally achieve good governance, as worldwide experience shows. Democratic elections are a key, necessary mechanism of inclusive, external accountability, but elections themselves must be coupled with other mechanisms that give voice and choice to citizens and that ensure that within government itself there are strong channels of internal accountability, including separation of powers.

In summary, one way to take an objective view of good governance is to assess governance through criteria that are as universal as possible. Any exercise of public authority should be aimed at maintaining or increasing the welfare of the beneficiaries, where welfare means respect of basic rights as much as economic gain. For such "good" results to have more of a chance, the process of the exercise of public authority that leads to them has to be "good" itself. This process is where the quest for "good governance" begins (figure AF.5). Good governance can be viewed as the intersection of the four underlying principles of two core values (equal participation and equal treatment under inclusiveness, and transparency and contestability under accountability). Any of the four can help improve governance; only the four all together will ensure good governance.

Inclusiveness and Accountability Are the Values Underpinning Good Governance

Inclusiveness means that all those who have a stake in a governance process and want to participate in it—men and women, rich and poor, rural and urban—are able to do so on an equal basis, whether by voting, by contributing to consultations, or by overseeing local public service agencies.

Inclusiveness also means that governments treat everyone equally, that they protect the rights of everyone with equal vigor, that exclusion and discrimination are absent in the provision of public services by governments, and that everyone has equal rights to recourse and remedy if there is discrimination by public officials.

Accountability is based on the idea that people have the right to hold their governments answerable for how they use the authority of the state and the resources of the people.

Accountability needs transparency or full access to information—the people need to know about the functioning of the government, to hold it answerable, and governments need to provide access to such information.

Accountability also needs contestability—being able to choose among alternative political and economic entities on the basis of how well they perform. It also means recourse and remedy when government actions contravene basic rights—especially those of inclusiveness—or violate the rule of law.

CHAPTER 1

The Governance Gap
in MENA

Introducing Governance in MENA

Mona Masri, an 18-year-old living on the outskirts of Cairo, has encountered governance first hand while trying to get an identity card and a birth certificate (see box 1.1). Other such encounters range from receiving an education from the government, to being regulated when operating a private business. They can be smooth and productive—or they can be frustrating.

Good governance is about inclusiveness. Mona and the rest of her fellow villagers who did not have identity cards were excluded. They lacked the right to education and pensions—and the right to vote. Good governance is also about accountabilities, which depend on information (transparency) and recourse (contestability).

Mona suffered in part because internal accountability mechanisms were weak (see the analytical framework). One problem that Mona faced was the simple lack of information about procedures, which made it difficult for her to assert her rights. Another was the lack of recourse and possibility to contest dishonest behavior, such as that of the police officer. The community advocacy group that eventually got Mona her identity card acted as an intermediary to help her exercise external accountability. The residents in Mona's village also exercised external accountability directly by selecting their councilman, who became more accountable when more people, like Mona, were finally allowed to vote.

Because ensuring inclusiveness and accountability in the governance process is so complex, many approaches have evolved to expand and defend inclusiveness and to hold governments, and government officials, more accountable. This chapter examines those mechanisms in MENA countries and assesses their effectiveness.

Given the varied country experiences in the region, it is not surprising to find diversity in the quality of governance—both in inclusiveness and in accountability (box 1.2). Most MENA countries have universal

BOX 1.1

No Documents—No Identity

In January 1998, an 18-year-old woman named Mona al-Masri, from a village on the outskirts of Cairo, realized that she did not exist.

She wanted to enroll in literacy classes offered by the local authorities. And she wanted to start a small sewing business. But to manage it and to make it grow, she knew that she needed to do more than just barely be able to read and write her name.

Arriving at the class, Mona was asked for her identification card. She didn't have one. She had come to know that the lack of a card handicapped her in obtaining a variety of services—from inheriting property to receiving pensions when a husband or father died. But she had not known that it could exclude her from even such a basic right as education. In the eyes of the government, there was no such person as Mona al-Masri.

Back in her house, in a place without running water, electricity, or a paved road, she despaired about what to do. She asked everyone she knew how she could get an identification card. No one knew. Finally, she learned that she needed first to produce a birth certificate. She didn't have one. She was born at home, as were many in her family, and her parents never went through the process of registering her birth.

Mona and her mother steeled themselves and went to the local police station to obtain a new birth certificate. But they were not ready for what happened there. The police officer asked for Mona's identification card—and when she explained that she did not have one, he issued her a fine for not having the documentation required by law. Then, he intimated that if she needed a birth certificate, it could take many months for Mona to get one, with frequent visits needed to the police station. He could go out of his way to help her, of course. But that took time and effort on his part, and who would compensate him for the trouble?

Mona and her mother did not know the many steps to get the certificate, and they did not think they could afford to pay the officer for helping them. Then, Mona's mother recognized a distant kinsman, also a police officer, and appealed to him. With this *wasta* (personal connection), it took only a few minutes for the fine to be retracted and for the kinsman to promise to expedite the processing of the birth certificate.

Back home, Mona and her family thought about the next steps. Even when they received the birth certificate, how would they get the identification card? Once again, none of them knew the procedures for certain, and they didn't know where to start.

A neighbor suggested that they go ask the local councilman, setting off a round of laughter. Mona and the more than 400 other women in her village who did not have official identities could not vote—so the councilman cared little about their problems.

Two years later, Mona still had not obtained her identification card. And having started an unregistered sewing business, she was struggling to cope with its demands. When she wanted to buy a new sewing machine, for instance, she could not avail herself of the government's low-interest credit program because she was undocumented.

BOX 1.1 (continued)

Then Mona's life changed for the better. She met with the staff members at a civil-society organization that was working in some of Cairo's most underprivileged areas to help women overcome obstacles in obtaining official documents. With their help, Mona understood the steps required to get her identification card. In fact, taking Mona's new birth certificate, a representative of the organization filed a request for an identification card on her behalf. Within months, Mona al-Masri had an official identity.

Today, Mona runs a thriving little informal sewing business out of her home. She has even hired two other women to help her with the work. That accomplishment fills her with pride, but so do the electric lights in her house and the new paved road outside her door, services that came after the newly documented women in her village voted in the last elections. She repeats to herself the words she heard from one of these women, "It's a new life. I finally feel like a citizen of this country."

Note: The story is based on the actual situation described in Al-Hamad 2002, but the names have been changed.

---

suffrage, but some do not, and universal suffrage does not always mean competitive or fair elections. Most of the countries have parliaments, but not all do, and most parliaments have only limited power over the executive. Some countries, notably Lebanon, have a much freer press than others. Access to key public services, while generally good, varies in and across countries, and outcomes differ.

Each MENA country has a long and rich legacy that has marked individual political trajectories—from authoritarian rule to greater openness. Excluding the territory of the West Bank and Gaza, the region includes 11 "republics," while kings and emirs rule eight other countries. Morocco's ruling dynasty, the Alawis, achieved power in 1666, centuries before the Saudis and the Hashemites of Jordan.

Although generalizations are difficult, the quality of governance in MENA tends to increase with incomes, which is consistent with international empirical evidence. But MENA countries consistently have lower-quality governance than would be expected for their incomes. Thus, they have a governance gap with the rest of the world. The gap is widest for public accountability: not a single country in the region figures in the top half of the world's countries. And abundant natural resources in MENA countries are generally associated with lower public accountability.

What causes the governance gap in MENA? Exceptionally high oil and gas revenues have accrued directly to government coffers, thereby

BOX 1.2

An Analytical Framework for Good Governance

This book uses a simple definition of governance—the process of exercising authority in the name of a constituency, including selecting and replacing those who exercise it; it is the authority relationship between the government and the people. If governance is the exercise of authority in the name of the people, good governance is doing so in ways that respect the integrity, rights, and needs of everyone within the state. Good governance rests on the two core values of *inclusiveness* and *accountability*.

Inclusive governance is the mechanism that defines and protects the basic rights of everyone, including providing remedies and recourses guaranteed by a rule of law. Rights include fairness and tolerance among the people themselves, and good governance means those rights are protected. Rights also include how government treats the people, and good governance means that government treats everyone without discrimination and ensures equal opportunities to access the services provided by government.

Accountability in a governance process means that those who are selected to act in the name of the people are answerable to the people for their failures, as well as credited for their successes. Accountability rests on knowledge and information (*transparency* in governance mechanisms), and on incentives that encourage those who act in the name of the people—government officials—to do so faithfully, efficiently, and honestly (*contestability* in the governance process). Accountability can be both external and internal. *External accountability* is when people themselves hold the government accountable, as when the residents in a village select their councilman (figure 1.3). But it also includes instances when the recipients of public services hold the service provider directly accountable. *Internal accountability* is when the government, to protect the public interest, institutes various systems and incentives to govern the behavior of different agencies, such as separating powers and setting up independent checks and balances.

There are three key accountability channels: one from the policymaker to the service provider (making teachers accountable to the minister of education, or a public health worker accountable to the minister of health); another from the client to the service provider (making teachers accountable to parents and students, or public doctors and nurses accountable to patients); and the third from citizens to policymakers and politicians.

In sum, good governance can be viewed as the intersection of the four underlying principles of two core values: equal participation and equal treatment under inclusiveness, and transparency and contestability under accountability. Any of the four can help improve governance; only all four together will ensure good governance.

Source: Extracted from the "Analytical Framework for Good Governance in the Middle East and North Africa" in this book (pp. 25–33).

reducing the incentives of incumbent regimes to strengthen mechanisms of external accountability. Protracted conflicts have provided a rationale for coercive government institutions. And foreign interests—colonialism, cold war geopolitics—have often helped sustain incumbent regimes, thus favoring the status quo over reform.

Describing Governance in MENA

Inclusiveness in MENA

Inclusiveness, one of the two core values of good governance, is the translation in concrete terms of equality—a more abstract moral value. Sometimes referred to as distributive justice, equality is a universal value that underpins classical Greek philosophy and suffuses the precepts of the three monotheistic religions: Judaism, Christianity, and Islam. Of the three, Islam, the dominant religion in the region, places particular emphasis on equality by enshrining it in one of the five pillars of the faith: the *zakat*, or alms tax, requires all Muslims to share a percentage of their wealth with the poor and the needy.

Inclusiveness guarantees equal minimum rights to all members of society. Those rights, such as life, liberty, and equality before the law—including for those who govern, plus the right to participate in the governance process on an equal basis—are the rights fundamental to any society (figure 1.1). Inclusiveness means that the rights and interests of all groups—particularly women, ethnic and religious minorities, and any vulnerable group—are guaranteed and their concerns are addressed by governments.

Ensuring inclusiveness is a challenge to countries everywhere. Those with good governance typically provide mechanisms that give voice, recourse, and remedy to minorities and that protect their interests. But even without such mechanisms, there can be progress. For example, in 2001 the Algerian government recognized Amazigh as a second official language, after a decade-long struggle for legitimacy by the Berbers. By recognizing the cultural and linguistic heritage of the Berbers, the Algerian government sought to include them more fully in the national dialogue.

How inclusive is MENA when it comes to the right to vote? All countries that hold elections have adopted universal suffrage, except Kuwait and Oman. Despite a constitution that states "all people are equal in human dignity and in public rights and duties before the law," Kuwait does not give women the right to vote. Oman allows only part of the population to vote.

The right to vote is but one facet of weak inclusiveness. In MENA countries, women's participation in electoral bodies is also low. In

FIGURE 1.1

Inclusiveness Implies Equal Rights, Including Equal Opportunities to Participate

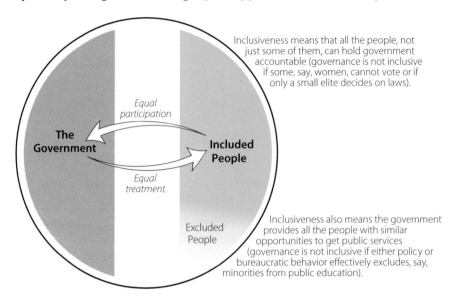

MENA legislatures, the average female participation stands at 6 percent, compared with 14–15 percent in Sub-Saharan Africa and Asia (figure 1.2). In local government, only 14 percent of council members are women, the second lowest proportion worldwide.

Even so, there has been progress. In 2002, Bahrain's *Shura* council set aside 5 of its 30 seats for women. Most recently, Jordan reserved for women 6 parliamentary seats out of a total of 116. In Morocco's 2002 elections, 35 women became parliamentarians after political parties agreed to a 10 percent quota for women in the lower house.

Representation can also be inclusive through consultation (*shura*). But scale and accompanying complexity make inclusive and accountable representation difficult to achieve solely through consultative mechanisms. In Saudi Arabia, which has 15 million nationals, the regular *Majliss* (assembly) gatherings can no longer ensure that individuals can have direct access to the ruling family, as they did earlier. Recognizing this problem, the government has created the Shura Council. Traditional consultative mechanisms and their credibility have also become stretched because the substantial oil wealth has increased the role and reach of the government and has raised the stakes for leaders to maintain their control.

Inclusiveness in governance also depends on whether all citizens have the right to form associations that promote their views and interests. Most MENA countries already allow labor unions and various professional associations, which are often invited to take part in high-level, government-sponsored economic and social councils, as can be seen in

FIGURE 1.2

Female Representation in MENA Parliaments Is Low

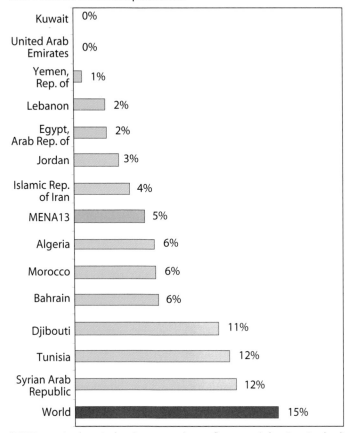

Share of seats in national parliament

Note: MENA13 includes all MENA countries shown in chart. Percentages shown reflect women's share in national parliaments, with both houses combined when applicable, rounded to the nearest percentage point.
Source: Based on Inter-Parliamentary Union 2003.

Tunisia and Lebanon. In addition, in MENA as elsewhere, formally organized civil-society organizations are promoting inclusiveness in the governance processes, especially for those outside professional organizations. But the right to associate is also closely monitored and is often controlled by governments.

Inclusiveness implies equitable and fair access to the services that government provides. Chapter 3 shows that MENA governments have broadened the definition of public goods and have made them widely available to the population, even if the scope and quality of services differ for many groups. Inclusion is weak wherever rural dwellers have fewer public services, thus leaving in its wake some of the highest levels of illiteracy among middle-income countries. Inclusion is weak when the government effectively controls the conduct of elections, as is the case in virtually all national elections. And inclusion is weak when nepotism, tribal affinity, patronage, or money determines who gets public services and who does not—plus who gets access to lucrative business opportunities and who does not. Yes, ensuring equitable treatment is a challenge worldwide, but the challenge is greater when there are few avenues for accountability, for recourse, and for remedies. In Egypt, the infant mortality rates for southern rural governorates are more than twice those in the four metropolitan governorates. And schools enroll 80 percent of children from the top income quintile, but less than 50 percent from the lowest quintile. The gender imbalance is clear across the region, particularly in education. In all MENA countries, enrollment rates are lower and dropout rates are higher for girls than for boys, even though in many countries more women than men are enrolled in universities (Eken, Schieber, and Robalino 2003).

Accountability in MENA

Accountability, the second core value of good governance, rests on transparency and competition—the right to know and the right to contest.[1] Accountability works through three interlocking channels. In the first, one level or branch of government seeks to hold another accountable. In the second, clients who receive services exert power over government agencies. And in the third, citizens exert power over politicians. The effectiveness of each channel depends on the flow of information and on the power or authority to impose sanctions.[2] The first is a form of internal accountability, while the second and third are forms of external accountability (figure 1.3).

Transparency. Access to information by all defines transparency. But most governments in the region either restrict access to official information or make no effort to publish it widely (Leenders and Sfakianakis 2002). In Algeria, the government has at its disposal a body of inspectors to oversee the functioning of public services. But it is hard to find out how this inspection body works and impossible to get the results of its assessments. Such lack of disclosure makes it impossible to highlight and correct mistakes—and possible to camouflage malfunctions (background paper, Mahiou 2003, p. 17).

But some countries are moving toward greater public disclosure. In Jordan, for instance, the parliament requires officials in the executive branch to disclose information about their personal assets. The Islamic Republic of Iran publishes its 1,500-page national budget in draft and in final form on the government's Web site and on a CD-ROM, and parliamentary budget debates are televised, as they are in some other coun-

FIGURE 1.3

Accountability Can Be Internal (by Checks and Balances within the Government) or External (by the People)

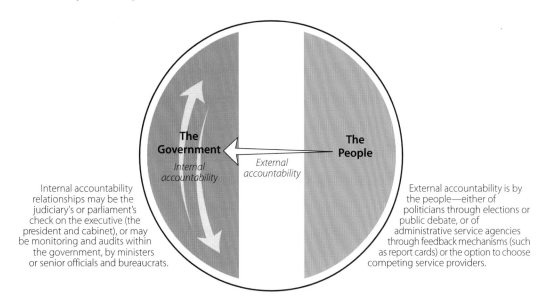

Internal accountability relationships may be the judiciary's or parliament's check on the executive (the president and cabinet), or may be monitoring and audits within the government, by ministers or senior officials and bureaucrats.

The Government

Internal accountability

External accountability

The People

External accountability is by the people—either of politicians through elections or public debate, or of administrative service agencies through feedback mechanisms (such as report cards) or the option to choose competing service providers.

tries in the region. Despite continuing harassment of the media, there is a general environment in which almost all Iranian government institutions feel obligated to explain their actions to the public. The press in Lebanon is vocal, and satellite television channels allow information to travel across previously impenetrable borders. The press in Algeria regularly publishes critical assessments of government actions emanating from the National Economic and Social Council, an organism itself created by government to represent society and to debate public policy. Several parliaments throughout the region have opened their doors to public hearings. The Arab Decision Project has an online database with the names, titles, and contact information of all ranking government officials and civil-society organizations in the Arab countries. The aim: to make institutional information about the Arab world easy for citizens to obtain (Arab Decision Project 2003).

Contestability. Regular, fair, competitive elections are the ultimate mechanism to hold government officials accountable in democracies. But they may need to be reinforced by other measures, such as by limiting the number and duration of terms and by allowing multiple candidates through an open vetting process. In most MENA countries that hold presidential elections, the only candidate is the incumbent president. In other elections, slates must often be vetted by the executive or, in the Islamic Republic of Iran, by the supreme leader.

But there are other ways to ensure contestablity for government posts and policies. Parliaments that have impeachment power and independent judiciaries that have the power to prosecute government officials can promote internal accountability by guaranteeing that no government official is above the law. Auditors-general, ombudsmen, and official investigative commissions help ensure accountability internally. And various mechanisms of civil-society oversight can help ensure accountability externally.

Internal Accountability Mechanisms: Checks and Balances. Nearly all constitutions in the region mandate the classic separation of government powers. Only Qatar, the United Arab Emirates, and Saudi Arabia do not provide for parliaments. In April 2003, Qatar held a referendum that approved its first written constitution that establishes a 45-member advisory council, two-thirds of which would be elected by popular vote.

But parliaments in MENA, which have a wide range of powers on paper, generally do not have as much authority in reality as do the executives. Likewise, even if the judiciary fairly upholds the rule of law for citizens, the judiciary in every country in MENA lacks the prerogative to question the executive.

Real power is concentrated in the executive: monarch, president, prime minister and cabinet of ministers, or governor (box 1.3). For example, Article 117 of the Syrian Arab Republic's constitution clearly states that "the President of the Council of Ministers and the ministers are responsible before the President of the Republic" not to the people (Syrian Arab Republic, Constitution of 1973). The constitution of Morocco makes the prime minister and the Council of Ministers "answerable to the Parliament but also to the King" (Morocco, 1996). Important issues, such as budgetary oversight, are mainly in the hands of the executive.

Constitutions often give the executive parallel power to create laws through executive decrees and regulations. Such parallel power manifests itself, for example, when the executive suspends parliament, as occurred in Jordan, Kuwait, and Bahrain. Between the fall of 2001 and the spring of 2003, when the Jordanian parliament was suspended, the executive proclaimed 110 temporary laws, including a new election law and a measure to reduce the number of municipalities.

A first glance at the constitutional authority granted to MENA parliaments generally shows an impressive range of authority, including control and oversight of the budget. And for the executive, most MENA constitutions stipulate that the cabinet can take office only with the con-

---

BOX 1.3

The Strong Executive in Egypt

The constitution of modern Egypt has always given the president a virtual monopoly over the decisionmaking process, devoting 30 articles (15 percent of the whole constitution) to presidential prerogatives. According to the constitution, the Egyptian president's powers are equivalent to those of the prime minister in parliamentary systems and to the president of the French Fifth Republic.

Article 73 of the constitution reads: "The Head of State is the President of the Republic. He shall assert the sovereignty of the people, respect the constitution and the supremacy of the law, safeguard the national unity and the socialist gains, and maintain the boundaries between authorities in a manner to ensure that each shall perform its role in the national action."

The presidential prerogatives—especially those related to the role of the president, the cabinet, and the legislature—envisage the head of the state as a referee among various authorities in the political system. Accordingly, the president is given the right to appoint and dismiss the cabinet, which comprises the prime minister, his deputies, the ministers, and their deputies (article 141).

Source: Saeed Ali 2003, background paper for this book, pp. 5–6.

---

fidence of a majority of the parliament. In most MENA states, such assemblies are elected and constitutionally bear primary responsibility for the legislative process. In a few countries, the parliament formally selects the head of state, but the head of state does not remain politically responsible to the parliament once selected.

This strong constitutional basis for parliamentary authority is rarely exercised. Few MENA parliaments have come close to voting "no confidence" for a minister or the entire cabinet. The frequent result is that the head of state and even the entire executive branch may operate without effective parliamentary oversight (box 1.4). Nor do most parliaments do much in drafting legislation.

To find the weaknesses of MENA parliaments, one must look beyond constitutions to the legal frameworks for executive accountability. First, the electoral process is often designed in a way that limits the possibilities for parliamentary independence. Second, parliaments often lack the resources to hold executive authorities truly accountable.

Even where they can establish some independence from the executive, parliaments generally cannot use it to control the legislative process. Most legislation proposed in MENA parliaments is initiated by individ-

Parliamentary Independence in MENA

If parliaments are to be an important source of internal accountability, they need to be independent of the executive and empowered to oversee it. In the MENA region, most countries have parliaments, with Egypt having the oldest continuous parliamentary tradition in the Arab world, dating from the popular assembly of 1866.

Today, the independence of MENA parliaments is generally limited, as is their constitutional or actual power to hold the typically strong executives accountable. In Egypt, for example, although a Supreme Constitutional Court decision in 2000 mandated electoral supervision by the judiciary rather than the executive, no other domestic or international monitoring has been permitted. And despite the constitutional reforms in 1980 that abolished the single-party system, every parliament has contained a massive majority of the president's own National Democratic Party.

In most countries, the head of state remains above parliamentary oversight, and parliaments do not initiate or control the legislative agenda or the contents of the budget. Yet, they do retain the power to question ministers, to ask for resignations, and to use the budget-approval process as an oversight tool.

There are signs of greater independence, as parliamentary reforms strengthen the systems of oversight and objectivity. Bahrain has recently moved to a parliamentary system. In Morocco, the government created an electoral commission, removing some aspects of elections from the strict control of the ministry of interior—similar to what occurred in Egypt in 2000. And Kuwait's parliament regularly questions government expenditures and is quite protective of constituents.

Source: Brown 2001b.

ual ministers or the cabinet, not by parliamentary deputies. In recent years, some MENA parliaments have augmented their institutional capacity in research and in drafting legislation. In the Islamic Republic of Iran, the Parliamentary Research Council, which is the research arm of the Majlis, prepared the first draft of a comprehensive law to reform public procurement.

Parliaments may have the authority to approve the state budget, but their review serves as an effective parliamentary oversight of the executive in only a few MENA countries. They have only a short period to review budgets, which are often vague and would require intensive work for anyone to ascertain their details. The result: parliamentarians have only limited influence over the outcome.

Nor do MENA parliaments have many direct links to public opinion. For example, in examining laws, parliamentary committees only rarely reach out to specific groups or the public. But some committees are moving toward public hearings to reach the public and selected constituencies that are interested in a topic or draft law. And some are forming direct links to the public by launching their own broadcasts and publications.[3] In Morocco, for example, the parliament set up investigative committees to inquire into financial wrongdoing involving one of the country's largest banks and the national social security agency. In Kuwait several years ago, parliamentarians launched a campaign by the name of *min ayna laka haza* ("where do you have this from?"), calling for the disclosure of financial information by the executive. Those efforts have helped show citizens that corruption in the public arena is a matter of concern to the whole population.

In MENA, the official standards for judicial independence and structures are close to international standards, but the systems vary greatly in the specificity that they give to judicial independence. A sophisticated and professional judiciary now exists in most MENA countries, and there is a strong sense of professional identity among many judges.[4]

If one assesses the judiciary's role in ensuring checks and balances on the executive, there is a tendency to focus on constitutional law. But the majority of disputes and administrative acts involve no constitutional controversies. Especially in MENA bureaucracies, judicial review of administrative acts is at least as important as judicial review of constitutionality. In many MENA countries, special administrative courts have broad authority to review legislation emanating from the bureaucracy and to ensure that administrative regulation and decisions comply with the law.

Despite the spread of administrative courts throughout much of the region, judicial independence is generally limited, and restrictions on jurisdiction are widespread (boxes 1.5 and 1.6). The separation between the judiciary and the executive is not clear. Executive authorities—presidents, kings, prime ministers, and justice ministers—have a tradition of appointing politically dependent judges. The executive in the Arab Republic of Egypt, represented by the minister of justice, continues to exercise considerable authority over the judiciary, especially the civil, criminal, and administrative courts. Other MENA countries show a similar inability to separate the ministry of justice from judicial affairs. So long as there is political interference in judicial proceedings, or the possibility of such interference exists, it is difficult to ensure equality before the law and even the rule of law.

In most MENA countries, the problem is not only that the judiciary lacks independence but also that the judiciary is not allowed to have exclusive power over judicial matters. The special and exceptional courts,

---

BOX 1.5

Judicial Independence in MENA

Constitutions in most MENA countries guarantee judicial independence, even if they lack specificity. The Arab Republic of Egypt, Morocco, and Lebanon each have a highly professional judiciary. Kuwait is developing one. More an objective than a fact, full judicial independence comes under continuing pressure from powerful executives. In most countries, the ministry of justice continues to hold significant authority over the financial and administrative management of the judiciary. In Egypt, there was a full-scale assault on judicial independence in 1969, partially reversed over the following two decades under the 1971 constitution. But unrest in the 1990s may have become a pretext for the executive to bypass normal legal and judicial channels, using state security and military courts. In Morocco, it is the king, along with the minister of justice, who heads the judicial council, and some cases are referred to military courts. In Jordan, there is no constitutional court.

Source: Brown 2001a.

---

the security services that bypass the courts, and the meddling within the jurisdiction of the courts are pervasive features in most MENA countries.

Internal Accountability Mechanisms: Institutional Arrangements. The executive branch of governments in the MENA region faces the complex problem of properly motivating service agencies—including government agencies and administrative bodies—to deliver services effectively. Because of pervasive problems with large and typically inadequately managed civil services, MENA governments have had problems in creating the institutional arrangements that can ensure the delivery of complex services to the people.

Part of the problem stems from the lack of contestability in the civil service itself. Personal connections and public employment imperatives that relate to social objectives have long dominated civil service hiring in the MENA region (box 1.7). In Egypt, long-standing government hiring practices to employ university graduates have resulted in a bureaucracy whose very size makes it difficult to monitor performance. The direct link between university education and a guaranteed job has recently been severed in Egypt. But there remains the overhang of a massive group of underpaid and unmotivated bureaucrats, whose assurance of jobs for life lowers contestability and, thus, accountability.

Weaknesses in transparency and, thus, in availability of information—even within the government itself—also compromise internal accounta-

---

BOX 1.6

Judicial Independence in Tunisia Is Lacking

The judiciary branch in Tunisia has recently been the object of serious criticism over its independence, neutrality, and relationship to the executive branch. Under the title "Judiciary Branch" (chapter IV), article 66 of the Constitution stipulates that "judges are nominated by decree of the President of the Republic upon the recommendation of the Higher Judiciary Council." Article 67 indicates that "the Higher Judiciary Council watches over the application of the guarantees granted to the judges in terms of nomination, promotion, transfer, and discipline," which means that the independence of the judges is actually predicated on the composition of the council.

This composition has been under fire for some time now. The absolute majority of the positions are filled by individuals linked to the executive in different ways. In addition to the president of the republic and the minister of justice (respectively the president and vice president of the Higher Judiciary Council), the council includes high-level bureaucrats and judges. Among those judges, some are public prosecutors, under the authority and payroll of the minister of justice. Others, while depending on the judicial body, have been nominated to sensitive posts by the executive branch. Only 6 of the 31 judges on the council are elected by their peers. Council decisions are taken according to simple majority rule; in case of equal distribution of votes, the votes of the president and the vice president prevail.

Moreover, it is still out of the question to honor the irremovability of judges, a principle considered by jurists the world over as a cornerstone of the independence of the judiciary. Without this elementary guarantee, judges are not immune from a transfer—from discipline disguised as promotion.

Even though judges enjoy autonomous status, their system of remuneration falls under the general basic principles of the civil service. In this system, remuneration is based partly on the judge's level, itself a function of seniority, and partly on the function each judge exercises. Positions that have specific functions attached to them are the most distinguished and give the holder the right to important benefits in kind and in prestige, all at the discretion of the president of the republic.

Source: Charfi 2003, background paper for this book, pp. 15–17.

---

bility. In general, countries across the MENA region exhibit a pattern of limited and reluctant transparency, which is reflected in the fact that it is the region with the least empirical data on the quality of governance.

Insufficient information hampers the effectiveness of administrative mechanisms—such as independent audit agencies, inspectors-general, and ombudsmen— that aim to ensure internal accountability. Moreover, these oversight agencies typically have insufficient resources and authority, and

---

BOX 1.7

Clientelism in the Bureaucracy Weakens Governance in the Syrian Arab Republic

In Syria, the predominance of clientelism over open competition for recruitment to the administration and the security apparatus of the government has generated a solidarity inside the civil service and has greatly reduced the accountability of politicians. Government posts are only very rarely perceived as carrying a responsibility that entails specific skills and requires an ethic of public accountability. Rather, they constitute a reward to those who made the right choice by enlisting in the ranks of the many political organizations of the Ba'th party and by displaying active support to its command.

Recruitment by political co-optation (for Ba'th party members) or by nepotism (for family or clan members) most likely eliminates the best-qualified candidates from the start. Because it aims to build and sustain a network most useful in the continual vying for power within the government, such recruitment favors those most disposed to exchange their political loyalty and services for the material privileges that come with government employment. Because the criterion for civil service recruitment and performance is loyalty to one's superiors and not professional competence, it is in the interest of neither the recruiter nor the recruited to ask questions about qualifications for the work or to worry about the quality of work performed subsequently.

In contrast to the mode of governance predicated on professional performance, under which public officials develop a sense of accountability and accept contestability, the mode of governance that is based on allegiance fosters a logic of redistribution and reinforces a sense of loyalty to leaders. As a result, it divides the population into two categories: the included and the excluded. Only individuals and social groups whose personal loyalty to the leaders is proven beyond doubt are granted access to administrative services by the loyal bureaucrats. For the excluded, everything carried out by the government, even the implementation of the law and the respect of the most fundamental human rights, is *makroma*, or generous gesture of good will on behalf of the leaders.

Source: Adapted from Ghalioun 2003, background paper for this book, pp. 10–11.

---

their assessments are not always disclosed to the public or acted upon.

In Algeria, the government set up a national ombudsman in 1995 to receive citizens' complaints and to present an annual report to the president. Most of the complaints were about bureaucratic unresponsiveness and lack of access to basic services (background paper, Mahiou 2003). But the authorities allowed the ombudsman's office to disappear. In Tunisia, however, similar approaches appear to have improved accountability between citizens and policymakers (box 1.8).

BOX 1.8

Improving the Relationship Between Public Organizations and Citizens in Tunisia

Tunisia's recent reforms to improve the relationship between citizens and public organizations are important in two ways. First, from an economic perspective, they try to reduce access costs to public services for citizens, although not necessarily for enterprises. And second, from a public management perspective, they try to improve the performance of public organizations.

A major part of this effort has been to rationalize the regulations and the paper burden imposed on citizens. There are far fewer regulations, and they are now harmonized across ministries. Administrative discretion has been a major target of the effort; what can be demanded from citizens is now clearly defined and published. Three new organizations report to the president's office either directly (the ombudsman) or through the prime minister's office:

The *Administration Ombudsman (Médiateur Administratif)* receives and evaluates complaints from citizens, instructs the appropriate agencies to follow up, and ensures that follow-up is adequate. The institution of the ombudsman has recently been expanded through the creation of regional branches across the Tunisian territory. The ombudsman submits an annual report to the president of the republic detailing the result of his work, the procedures likely to improve the functioning of the administration, and the changes to be introduced in the legislation to put these procedures in place.

The *Office of Citizen Relations (Bureau des Relations avec le Citoyen)* is a network of offices in each ministry, region, and public enterprise that receives citizens, directs their questions to the appropriate agency, and explains procedures. Reporting to a central office in the prime minister's office, the network offices also follow up on citizens' complaints processed by the ombudsman or brought directly to them. For instance, long-standing problems with identity papers dating back to naming procedures inherited from the protectorate era were solved by overhauling the regulatory framework, at the initiative of the Office of Citizen Relations. The central office has also recently been charged with managing relations with NGOs.

The *Supervising Citizen Team (Equipe du Citoyen Superviseur)*, established in the prime minister's office, supervises public agencies. Staff members pose as citizens and make anonymous visits to public agencies to ascertain the access to and quality of public services. Early experience shows that it is possible to limit administrative arbitrariness and to promote equal access to public services. But the feedback is not systematically used to improve the quality of public services and the productivity of public administration. Data on the use of the services and on citizen knowledge and comprehension of those services have been collected through surveys but are not available outside the public administration. Thus, the decline in the ombudsman's workload from 4,000 cases in 1996 to 2,500 in 1998 could be a measure of success—citizens' complaints have led to administrative changes—or a sign of failure—citizens stopped lodging complaints because the complaints serve no useful purpose.

Source: World Bank 2000d; and Charfi 2003, background paper for this book, pp. 20–21.

The lack of an explicit performance orientation in the internal budget processes of all MENA countries symbolizes the weak environment for internal accountability. Recent empirical work places MENA countries well behind comparators such as the Republic of Korea and Brazil when it comes to measures of internal accountability and of the performance orientation of budget management (Esfahani 2000). It is only recently that some countries, such as the Islamic Republic of Iran, have started moving toward a system in which explicit goals of public expenditure policy would be stated and performance toward the goals would be monitored.

External Accountability Mechanisms: Elections. A competitive and transparent electoral process ensures accountability in the governance process. Electoral laws typically provide for some guarantees of free and fair procedures. But leaders in MENA do not change. Although presidential elections take place in the MENA countries that are not monarchies, they often mean little in terms of real political contestability.

In some countries, the outcome of parliamentary elections is usually predictable, confirming the supremacy of the ruling party:

- In the 1995 elections in Tunisia, the ruling party won 484 seats; the opposition won 6. This result demonstrates the "weight of the executive in the preparation and holding of elections" (background paper, Charfi 2003, p. 9)

- In Syria, the ruling party is constitutionally guaranteed half the seats in parliament.

- Election rules are often tailored to favor specific results (for example, by having electoral boundaries and representational systems designed to disadvantage opposition candidates, as in Lebanon or more recently in Jordan) (background paper, Salem 2003, pp. 19–20; *The Economist* 2003, pp. 38–39). Urban areas, where opposition forces are often stronger, are frequently underrepresented.

- The ruling party or power may screen candidates, as in Syria. Lebanon, or the Islamic Republic of Iran, or may use its administrative powers to influence voters.

Indeed, in some countries the precise rules vary from one election to the next, leading opposition forces to charge that the rules are tailored to produce a specific result for the ruling party. The usual practice of using the ministry of the interior to supervise elections only strengthens doubts about their fairness. Rarely are international election monitors allowed; in Jordan's most recent election, monitors were banned and journalists were not allowed in voting stations. However, Egypt's most recent parliamentary elections were supervised by the country's relatively independent judiciary, and Lebanon allows candidates to place their own monitors in polling and counting rooms.

Perhaps more significant than electoral procedures is the general political climate. Political pluralism has been the exception in MENA, so that voters in parliamentary elections often face a restricted set of choices. Some countries effectively remain one-party states. Other countries have moved a few steps away from a single-party system without replacing it with full pluralism. In such countries, opposition political parties are allowed to operate but a single political party dominates—and with the full backing of the executive and much of the administrative apparatus of the government. Parliament is, therefore, generally dominated by the governing party or coalition, and opposition groups can only express themselves, generally with little effect on policy.[5]

Local elections in some MENA countries provide a more promising electoral picture. Perhaps national leaders are more willing to allow things to move at the periphery because changes there are considered unlikely to affect their position. Consider the 2002 local elections in Algeria, when the ruling party did not muster the support received in national elections. Several municipalities were won by opposition parties, thereby enhancing the credibility of the electoral process itself (background paper, Mahiou 2003). The 1998 local elections in Lebanon can be considered another success (background paper, Salem 2003, p. 20), as were the 1999 local elections in the Islamic Republic of Iran (background paper, Farhi 2003). In general, however, candidates at the municipal level are not likely to base their platforms on contesting the national executive.

External Accountability Mechanisms: Oversight by the Media and Civil-Society Intermediaries. Between the citizen and the government are many intermediaries that channel information to the public or that represent specific interests. Among those, the media act as one of the primary means to achieve external accountability. Despite the global information revolution, the media in MENA remain subject to considerable government control and restrictions. Some of the gains toward more press freedom achieved in the 1990s have proved to be fragile and easily reversed by governments capitalizing on international concerns to combat terrorism.

With a few exceptions, broadcast media in the region are under state control. Print media are usually freer but often are still highly partisan. And dominant newspapers are often careful not to take positions that could be regarded as excessively independent by the government or the head of state. In Egypt, the government, through the Ministry of Information, controls radio and television broadcasting, even though the country has begun to open its airwaves to privately owned television channels.

Some countries in MENA have press laws that impose penalties for breaching "red lines," particularly members of the press who criticize the head of state, the ruling party, or the army. A recent amendment to the Algerian code threatens journalists with up to one year in prison and fines equivalent to US$3,200 for libeling government and army officials. (Leenders and Sfakianakis 2002) In an October 2001 press law amendment, Jordan replaced the fines with prison sentences of between one and three years for criticizing the king and his family, harming the reputation of the state, and inciting people to go on strike or to hold illegal public meetings. The law also tightened restrictions on reporting and now imposes heavy fines on a broader spectrum of violations (Reporters Without Borders 2003). In other countries, strict security and defamation laws severely constrain press freedom and hamper the ability of journalists to scrutinize government officials and policies. In the Syrian Arab Republic, for instance, a new press law that subjects all forms of media to tight controls was passed in September 2001. Among other restrictive provisions, the law puts a ban on "propaganda publications" financed "directly and indirectly" with foreign funding and requires key staff members of newspapers to be approved by the ministry of information (Human Rights Watch 2002).

Although the private ownership of the media reduces direct government control, it by no means guarantees independence and accurate public debate. In Jordan, where much of the media are private, "government officials … use the press as they deem appropriate to enhance their public standing by selectively offering information that supports government viewpoints" (background paper, Khouri 2003). In Lebanon, most of the private television stations are partly or entirely owned by wealthy politicians or prominent government officials.

As a result of those various constraints, the public has increasingly been turning to satellite pan-Arab and foreign media, which national governments find more difficult to control. Arab satellite stations such as Qatar-based al Jazeera have become a popular source of opinions and facts on issues of public interest, often exposing corruption scandals and revealing information on poor governance.

Progress does exist in some countries. Morocco has launched a comprehensive media reform that seeks to liberalize, regulate, and promote the audiovisual media through the creation of a Supreme Audiovisual Council (*Haute Instance des Médias*). A royal decree and a legislative text have already put an end to the state monopoly in radio and television broadcasting. Despite continuing repression, the Iranian press echoes the vibrant debate between the country's reformists and its conservative elements and persistently requires government officials to defend their actions (background paper, Farhi 2003). Lebanon has also managed to maintain a long-standing tradition of press freedom, amid some internal and external pressures. In Algeria, the media play a vocal role in exposing government mismanagement, as illustrated by the criticism of government construction standards and recovery efforts following the recent earthquake.

Beyond the media, a variety of civic associations—women's associations, student groups, religious bodies, election monitoring groups, and human rights groups—provide channels for citizen advocacy and oversight. They raise awareness of corruption, illiteracy, and violence against women. They work for legal changes to broaden inclusiveness. To strengthen public accountability, they monitor the conduct of public officials and agencies. Civil-society organizations also manage and even deliver some public services to their constituencies. Their proximity to local populations enables them to identify citizens' needs. In fact, civil-society organizations are becoming a vehicle for citizen participation in MENA. As part of a global trend, myriad registered civil-society groups have emerged in MENA, rising from fewer than 20,000 in the mid-1960s to about 70,000 in the late 1980s. Those groups reflect a thirst to affect the quality of life in the society, as well as a growing disaffection for political parties (Norton 1996; Bayat 2002, pp. 19–20). In Jordan, for instance, about a dozen professional organizations representing lawyers, engineers, doctors, and others evolved as the leading nongovernment political forces in the country during the decades of martial rule and the suspension of parliament and restrictions on political activities (background paper, Khouri 2003, p. 24). In Morocco, civil-society organizations and the government have worked hand in hand to tackle corruption. Moroccan civil-society groups, particularly women's organizations, have for years advocated reform of the country's personal status code. During the Lebanese civil war, civil-society organizations provided the bulk of public services. In the Arab Republic of Egypt, Parliament Watch was created to monitor parliamentary activities. Not all of those civil-society groups are formal, and informal networks of discussion groups that interact with the governing elite are a traditional feature of some MENA countries (box 1.9).

Some MENA governments have association laws that impose cumbersome restrictions on the right to associate, laws ranging from constraints on accepting foreign funding to interdictions on dealing with political issues. In Egypt, the government proposed a new association law (law 153), which imposes greater restrictions on freedom of association, a subject of intense debate in the past decade. The Egyptian law was eventually deemed unconstitutional by the judiciary and overturned. Jordan, Morocco, and the Republic of Yemen have also enacted new association laws.

BOX 1.9

Informal Mechanisms of Participation in MENA

Two decades ago, understanding Iranian politics meant recognizing the significance of the *dawra* (circle), an informal group of individuals who meet periodically. These networks are formed through overlapping professional, religious, political, and economic ties. Cumulatively, they constrain the arbitrariness of the state and its exercise of authority. In the small monarchies of the Gulf states, where many residents are not citizens and lack basic political rights, men who have full citizenship participate vigorously in debates. In Kuwait, some of these debates occur in the *diwaniyyas* (discussion salons), which function much like the Iranian *dawra*. When the Kuwaiti parliament was suspended, the *jama'at ta'awuniyya* (neighborhood cooperative societies) served as important political platforms to express society's interests.

Source: Norton 1996.

Measuring Governance—How Does MENA Compare?

Because inclusiveness and accountability are broad, multifaceted, and dynamic qualities of the governance process, it is not always easy to identify proxies that measure them faithfully. Further compounding the difficulties of measuring governance in MENA is the lack of reliable data. Global research on governance has produced an array of indicators that covers all aspects and dimensions of governance, but very few include all MENA countries (see appendix A for details on indicators, sources, and aggregation methods). The empirical analysis in this book relies on three indexes that aggregate indicators from data sources that have a good coverage of the region (box 1.10)

When MENA countries are compared with the rest of the world in terms of their overall level of *governance quality*, they display consistently lower levels of governance quality than would be expected for their incomes—the governance gap. And for the richer countries in MENA, the difference from their peers—countries in the world with similar income levels—is particularly large.

Compared with the rest of the world, MENA countries score reasonably well when it comes to the *quality of administration* in the public sector—the efficiency of the bureaucracy, the strength of the rule of law and protection of property rights, and the control of corruption and quality of regulations. Although most MENA countries display slightly lower levels of administrative quality than would be predicted given their income levels, the average scores for the region are close to the world av-

---

BOX 1.10

Measuring the Quality of Governance in MENA—Not an Easy Job

Measuring the quality of governance is not an easy task, because governance has many facets and because quality can quickly change. Investigators typically rely on subjective indicators of governance that draw on the perceptions of international investors and observers and on in-house expert-opinion rating agencies. Ratings depend on an analyst's knowledge of a country or region. Often there is an implicit assumption that governance systems in OECD countries are the ideal to measure all others against. And often the measurement omits the power of well-funded interest groups in shaping and influencing policy.

Recent work tries to minimize the subjectivity bias in available governance indicators. Using a special statistical methodology, the authors aggregate a wide array of quantitative indicators to produce six broad governance indexes, clustered around three broad dimensions of governance:

- The process by which those in authority are selected and replaced.

- The capability of the state to formulate and implement sound policies.

- The respect for institutions that govern interactions between citizens and government.

There are considerable benefits from combining related indicators into a small number of aggregate indicators. First, the aggregate indicators span a much larger set of countries than any individual source, permitting comparisons of governance across a broad set of countries. Second, the aggregate indicators can provide more accurate measures of governance than individual indicators. For instance, if several independent sources point to a country as having good rule of law, the observation is more robust than if it were based on just one source.

Despite the limitations of these empirical measures, they do provide a valuable, if partial, perspective on the quality of governance, an important complement to more qualitative information about particular countries. They are often the only means available for comparing the quality of governance across countries in a systematic way.

Source: Kaufmann, Kraay, and Zoido-Lobaton 2002.

---

erage. For the countries within MENA, as in the rest of the world, levels of administrative quality and income levels tend to be positively associated: the richer countries in the region display relatively higher levels of administrative quality than the poorer ones.

Levels of *public accountability*—how well citizens can access government information and hold their political leaders accountable—are particularly low in MENA. When compared with other countries at similar income levels, MENA countries show a sizable average gap in public accountability relative to the rest of the world—irrespective of income levels. In fact, the gap in public accountability is particularly large for the oil-rich countries in the region. Equally striking is the lack of association between income levels and levels of public accountability in MENA.

Overall Governance Quality

The quality of governance generally increases with incomes in MENA—a worldwide pattern found in every empirical study on governance.

Overall governance quality, the quality of administration, and the quality of public accountability are measured by three indexes, respectively labeled IGQ (index of governance quality), IQA (index of quality of administration), and IPA (index of public accountability) (box 1.11). In the overall IGQ, upper-middle-income countries across the world have average governance quality about twice those of lower-income countries, revealing the broad relationship between governance and development. This pattern holds for MENA as well. But MENA countries stand out because their quality of governance is consistently lower than would be expected for their incomes.[6] In short, they have a governance gap (the average gap for MENA is shown by the vertical bar in figure 1.4).

What creates that gap? Is it symptomatic of weaknesses in internal accountabilities or in external accountabilities? Does it also reflect an inclusiveness gap? To answer these questions, the discussion turns to the two sub-indexes: the IQA (a proxy for internal accountabilities) and the IPA (a proxy for external accountabilities and inclusiveness in access to basic political and civic rights).

Quality of Administration

On average, MENA countries fall short of other countries at similar income levels in the IQA in the public sector (compare the two fitted lines in figure 1.5). And the gap widens for richer countries in MENA.

Within the region is a strong and positive association between IQA and incomes: countries with better-quality administrations have higher incomes, which is consistent with empirical evidence worldwide. Richer and more complex environments tend to provide more resources, greater capacity, and higher demand for capable public administrations with adequate internal accountability systems. But regional averages mask wide variation: 11 countries are in the bottom half of the distribution and 8 are in the top half (figure 1.6).[7]

Most MENA countries do not perform much worse in the quality of their administration than other countries at similar income levels, and several countries do better. In terms of the rule of law, the United Arab Emi-

---

BOX 1.11

Constructing Indexes of Governance for MENA

Data coverage for MENA countries is limited. The analysis for this book required adapting conceptual and methodological approaches and supplementing data with additional sources to construct three broad governance indexes:

1. The *index of governance quality (IGQ)* aggregates all indicators available for MENA and measures the overall quality of governance processes. It is separated into two broad indexes.

2. The *index of quality of administration (IQA)* assesses the capability of the public administration to formulate and implement the sound policies and the respect for institutions that govern interactions between citizens and government. Broadly, it measures the quality of governance according to the relative strength of internal accountability mechanisms in the public administration. It aggregates 10 indicators that measure the risk and level of bureaucratic corruption and black market activity, the degree and extent to which certain rules and rights are protected and enforced (for example, property rights, laws and regulations), the quality of the budgetary processes and public management, the efficiency of revenue mobilization, the overall quality of the bureaucracy, and the independence of civil service from political pressures.

3. The *index of public accountability (IPA)* assesses the process of selecting and replacing those in authority. It measures the quality of governance according to the inclusiveness of access to basic political and civic rights and the relative strength of external accountability mechanisms. It aggregates 12 indicators that measure the level of openness of political institutions in a country and the extent to which political participation is free, fair, and competitive; civil liberties are assumed and respected; and the press and voice are free from control, violation, harassment, and censorship. It also captures the transparency and responsiveness of the government to its people and the degree of political accountability in the public sphere.

Source: Data came largely from Kaufmann, Kraay, and Mastruzzi 2003.

---

rates (UAE), Kuwait, and Bahrain have very satisfactory protection and enforcement of private property rights, contracts are efficiently enforced by the court system, and expropriations are highly unlikely. But other countries do not always enforce private property rights because the outcome of judicial systems is not consistent and reliable. In terms of corruption in public administration, the region is below the median worldwide, again with variations across countries. Morocco and Tunisia are perceived to be countries with intermediate levels of corruption, for example.

FIGURE 1.4

MENA's Governance Gap Compared with the Rest of the World

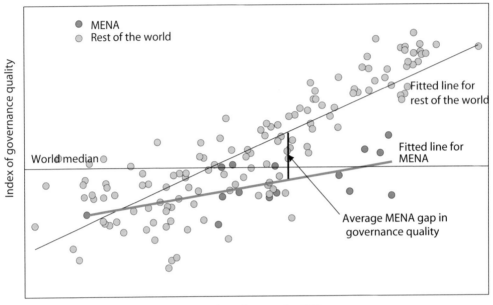

Log of per capita GDP

Notes: Refer to appendix B for the measurement of the governance gap. Data are insufficient to include Djibouti, Iraq, Libya, and the West Bank and Gaza.
Source: Authors' calculations, which are based on the index of governance quality, covering 173 countries worldwide.

In terms of the quality of regulations and their implementation, a higher proportion of firms recently surveyed in the region, when compared with other regions of the world, reported that they did not make new business investments because of the excessive burden of government regulations, which require senior managers to spend undue time on regulatory and legal compliance activities (World Bank 1997). The UAE and Bahrain have simple licensing procedures, with regulations fairly straightforward and often uniformly applied. The Islamic Republic of Iran, the Syrian Arab Republic, and Egypt have severe barriers to opening a business, complicated licensing processes, and cumbersome regulations (figure 1.7).

In some MENA countries, red tape and the proliferation of laws and regulations creates opportunities for corruption. Red tape creates many possibilities for extortion, and regulations encourage fraud and bribery. To avoid the complexity of administrative procedures and registration fees, private firms have to bear extra costs, relying on experienced intermediaries. And this extra cost opens an "inclusiveness gap," particularly

FIGURE 1.5

For the Quality of Administration, MENA's Governance Gap Is Narrower and Incomes Matter

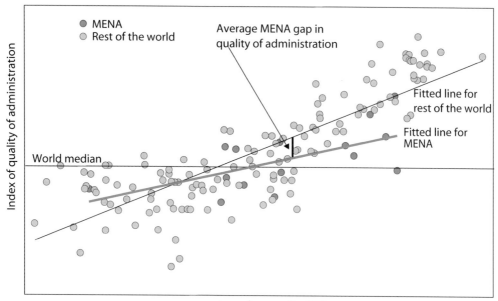

Notes: Refer to appendix B for the measurement of the governance gap. Data are insufficient to include Djibouti, Iraq, Libya, and the West Bank and Gaza.
Source: Authors' calculations, which are based on the index of quality of administration, covering 173 countries worldwide.

for small firms that cannot afford such costs and that have no choice but to operate outside legal boundaries, thus losing access to credit or government support services. Weaknesses in internal accountability mechanisms often impinge on the public administration's ability to maintain a good regulatory framework and to ensure the rule of law and control of corruption (box 1.12).

In terms of the quality of public sector management—the extent to which the budgeting system is comprehensive, credible, and linked to policy priorities; the financial management systems are effective; and the fiscal reporting is timely and accurate—there is also a wide variation within the region. Some countries have inadequate systems of budget reporting and monitoring and have delays in preparing public accounts. A few have stronger budget monitoring and control systems, with accounts more likely to be audited in a timely and professional manner. The same diversity is found in merit-based hiring and promoting of civilian central government staffs, although most countries have traditionally used civil service employment to generate jobs for young entrants to the labor force.

FIGURE 1.6

Within MENA, There Is Wide Variation in the Quality of Administration

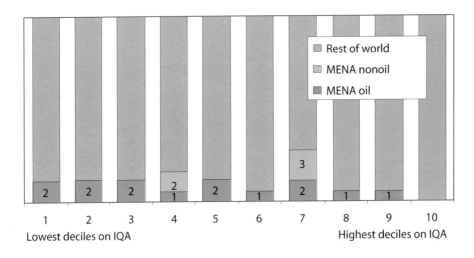

Notes: IQA is the index of quality of administration. MENA oil includes Algeria, Bahrain, the Islamic Republic of Iran, Kuwait, Oman, Qatar, the Republic of Yemen, Saudi Arabia, the Syrian Arab Republic, and the United Arab Emirates. MENA nonoil includes the Arab Republic of Egypt, Jordan, Lebanon, Morocco, and Tunisia. Data are insufficient to include Djibouti, Iraq, Libya, and the West Bank and Gaza.
Source: Authors' calculations, which are based on the index of quality of administration, covering 173 countries worldwide.

Public Accountability

Driving the governance gap between MENA and the rest of the world are the striking weaknesses in external accountabilities and in access to basic political and civic rights. All countries in the region, whatever their income, score well below the world trend (figure 1.8). MENA countries, regardless of income, also populate the bottom half of the world distribution (figure 1.9).[8] Indeed, some richer MENA countries score especially low on the IPA—with scores equivalent to those in some of the poorest countries of the world, even if they typically have marginally better scores for the IQA. Oil seems to be what matters: oil-reliant countries have the worst IPA scores. Having the substantial oil and gas revenues accrue directly to government budgets means that governments can maintain a deficient governance environment as long as they provide public goods to the population. In a situation of "no taxation, no representation," they face little pressure to improve governance to increase economic development.

For the region's resource-poor countries, the governance gap could be a reflection of vested interests—of established elites reaping private benefit from the status quo of weak governance. In such cases, where those elites control the governance process, there is little reason to ex-

FIGURE 1.7

Regulatory Quality Varies across MENA Countries

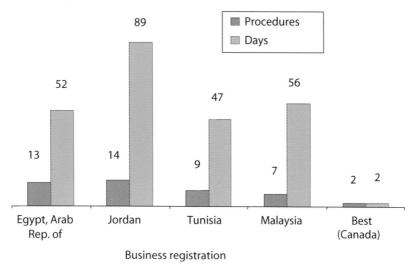

Business registration

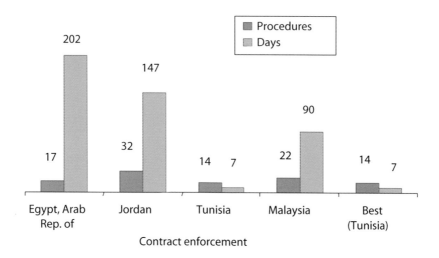

Contract enforcement

Source: World Bank 2003.

pect that higher incomes will increase the demand for better governance. One need look only at the regulatory capture in Latin America and the state capture in Eastern and Central Europe, for example, to see the power of business elites over government.

MENA countries exhibit systematic weaknesses in external account-abilities and in access to basic political and civic rights—albeit with some variation. Some are institutionalized autocracies, in which political rights are at best fragile, if not largely nonexistent; contestable political partic-ipation is restricted or suppressed. Others are one-party systems, with no

BOX 1.12

The Debilitating Impact of Administrative Regulations and Behavior— Examples from the Arab Republic of Egypt and Lebanon

Obtaining a construction permit is one of the most difficult bureaucratic procedures in Lebanon. For a foreign investor, the Investor and Development Authority of Lebanon will take care of the paperwork at a fixed cost. But the average citizen has to rely on specialist brokers, no matter how simple the case, because obtaining a permit involves five institutions and several departments within each. It can take up to a year to acquire a permit at prices almost twice the official rate.

Some stages may be undertaken for free, but the paperwork can be held up for years without money to speed up the process. "Because I refused to pay *baksheesh* (petty bribery), the employee could not find my land title," complained a Lebanese businessman. "Now I have to get a new land title, which will cost me $200, and I'm still not closer to getting a building permit."

According to a recent study published by the Lebanese Transparency Association, the roots of the regulatory burden in Lebanon are the result of citizens' lack of knowledge of their rights; lack of incentives by some civil servants who consider the *baksheesh* a bonus for efficient work; and weak appeal mechanisms, lack of internal accountability mechanisms, and the dissipation of responsibility when many public institutions are involved in issuing the same permit.

In Egypt, the ambiguity and lack of knowledge about relevant laws are exacerbated by the new laws issued frequently by the legislature, the binding presidential decrees issued by the executive branch, and other binding decrees issued by relevant departments. There are also inconsistencies between some of these laws and the way they are enforced. Such problems are made more severe because the process and debate leading to these laws are not transparent and because firms feel excluded from the process. Moreover, the new laws are often published only after a considerable time lag, or they are not published at all.

All these factors increase the likelihood that citizens and firms will lack familiarity with existing laws and regulations. Even when the laws are known, the monitoring and enforcement may be carried out by several different agencies, each with different criteria and methods for enforcement. So there can easily be substantial differences between the method prescribed by law and actual practice. And citizens and firms may be uninformed about one, the other, or both.

Sources: Fawzi 2002; Leenders and Sfakianakis 2002.

FIGURE 1.8

For Public Accountability, MENA's Governance Gap Is Wider, Irrespective of Incomes

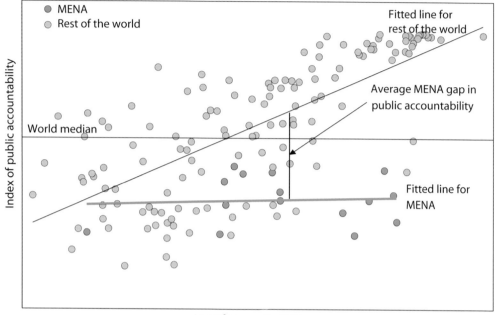

Notes: Refer to appendix B for the measurement of the governance gap. Data are insufficient to include Djibouti, Iraq, Libya, and the West Bank and Gaza.
Source: Authors' calculations, which are based on the index of public accountability, covering 173 countries worldwide.

opposition power and with severely restricted rights to organize in different political parties or other competitive political groupings. Still others are more democratic, with a coalition government and a parliament regularly elected by the people. One of the more common features among all countries of the region is the restriction of press freedom, as noted above.

The empirical analysis here clearly shows that MENA's governance is behind the rest of the world—and is farthest behind in public accountability and access to political and civic rights. The region as a whole ranks below similar countries in other regions, and even below all other developing countries as a group (figure 1.10). The pattern varies depending on whether countries are oil rich or not.

Why Governance Has Not Been Improving in MENA

The persistence of the governance gap in MENA has inspired a voluminous body of research (see appendix D). Generally, this research has fo-

FIGURE 1.9

All MENA Countries Have a Gap in Public Accountability with the Rest of the World

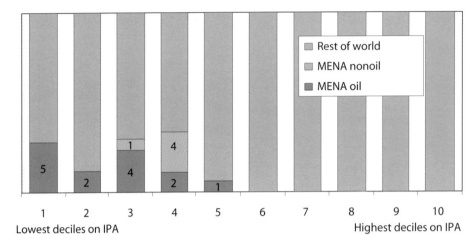

Notes: IPA is the index of public accountability. MENA oil includes Algeria, Bahrain, the Islamic Republic of Iran, Kuwait, Oman, Qatar, the Republic of Yemen, Saudi Arabia, the Syrian Arab Republic, and the United Arab Emirates. MENA nonoil includes the Arab Republic of Egypt, Jordan, Lebanon, Morocco, and Tunisia. Data are insufficient to include Djibouti, Iraq, Libya, and the West Bank and Gaza.
Source: Authors' calculations, which are based on the index of public accountability, covering 173 countries worldwide.

cused on geopolitics, conflict, and oil—to explain poor governance, especially low levels of internal and external accountability in MENA. None of these factors is unique to MENA, but their intensity and their cumulative effect have made it more difficult to improve governance processes in the region.

Geopolitics

For much of history, world attention has centered on this region. MENA was successively the cradle of civilization, the birthplace of three monotheistic faiths, the gateway to India and China for Europe, and the vessel holding two-thirds of the planet's known oil reserves. From the ancient spice and frankincense routes to the Suez Canal in more recent times—from the Silk Road of the Middle Ages to the oil pipelines today—the region lies at the center of a complex web of trade routes between east and west.

Its strategic commercial location astride three continents has made it a target of great foreign powers.

For roughly the last two centuries, the Middle East has been more consistently and more thoroughly ensnared in great power politics than any other part of the non-Western world. This distinctive po-

FIGURE 1.10

Compared with Other Regions, MENA Shows a Clear Governance Gap

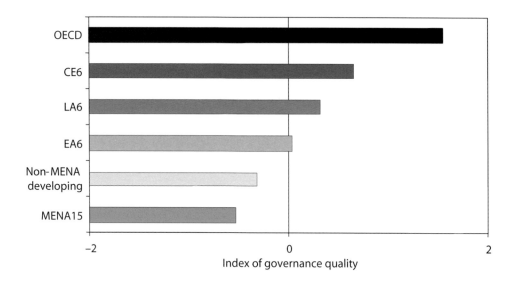

Notes: OECD includes Australia, Austria, Belgium, Canada, Denmark, Finland, France, Germany, Greece, Iceland, Ireland, Italy, Japan, Luxembourg, the Netherlands, New Zealand, Norway, Portugal, Spain, Sweden, Switzerland, the United Kingdom, and the United States. Central European countries (CE6) include Bulgaria, the Czech Republic, Hungary, Poland, Romania, and the Slovak Republic. Latin American countries (LA6) include Argentina, Brazil, Chile, Mexico, República Bolivariana de Venezuela, and Uruguay. East Asian countries (EA6) include Indonesia, Malaysia, the Philippines, Singapore, Thailand, and Vietnam. MENA15 includes Algeria, the Arab Republic of Egypt, Bahrain, the Islamic Republic of Iran, Jordan, Kuwait, Lebanon, Morocco, Oman, Qatar, the Republic of Yemen, Saudi Arabia, the Syrian Arab Republic, Tunisia, and the United Arab Emirates.
Source: Authors' calculations, which are based on the index of governance quality, covering 173 countries worldwide.

litical experience continuing from generation to generation has left its mark on Middle Eastern political attitudes and actions. Other parts of the world have been at one time or another more severely buffeted by an imperial power, but no area has remained so unremittingly caught up in multilateral great power politics" (Nathan Brown, as quoted in Henry and Springborg 2001, p. 3).

The interest of foreign powers has been domination and control, setting a bad example for governance and actively discouraging voice and accountability within the region. Even today, as external forces call for better governance in the region, some find a strong convergence of interest with regimes that provide secure access to strategic assets and that offer convenient alliances. Such strong foreign involvement has often hampered the development of more accountable and inclusive governance systems because foreign powers have generally found it more efficient to work with authoritarian regimes. More than ever, there is a tension, at least in the short run, between geopolitical interests and efforts to improve good governance.

Conflict—or Its Threat

Almost every MENA state over the past decades has been directly involved in some form of interstate conflict of varying intensities. From the western Sahara dispute to the war between Iraq and the Islamic Republic of Iran, to the Iraqi invasion of Kuwait, to the persistent Arab–Israeli conflict, interstate conflict has been a preoccupation of MENA political leaders. Wars and the threat of conflict tend to concentrate power in the hands of the executive, strengthening repressive governance and building up coercive organizations.

Military spending takes a larger share of national resources in MENA than in any other region (box 1.13). Enormous as military expenditures are, the issue is not simply that they have diverted resources from more productive uses. Equally important is the effect of large internal security and military institutions on governance processes. Because authoritarian regimes can use force to control political opposition internally as well as to defend against external enemies, those regimes reinforce government authority and control rather than promote inclusiveness, transparency, and contestability.

Even so, within the region, no clear relationship necessarily exists within the region between conflict or the threat of it and the weakness of political contestability.

Oil Wealth

The link between mineral wealth and governance quality in MENA, particularly when it comes to MENA's low levels of external accountability, has inspired a voluminous body of research. Recent empirical studies reveal that oil rents, controlling for incomes and population size, have a strong explanatory power in accounting for the weaker governance in MENA; variables measuring Islamic and Arab culture do not (Ross 2001; Sala-i-Martin and Artadi 2002.) Why? Because the substantial revenue from natural resources relieves a government from the need to tax, thus reducing its obligation to be accountable. In addition, a government is able to redistribute a significant share of its oil revenue through public employment and broad access to cheap public services. These two factors—no taxation and some redistribution—help mute demands for accountability.

Within MENA, the effect of mineral rents on governance quality is stark (figure 1.11). There is little difference in terms of the average quality of administration between the countries that rely significantly on oil or gas exports and those that do not. Oil-rich countries have as much interest as others in a strong administration, and more resources to achieve

BOX 1.13

Military Spending in MENA Is High

As a share of GDP, military expenditures in MENA, even excluding internal security spending, are the highest in the world, a trend that originates from the time most of the states in the region were established. In the 1990s, military expenditures averaged 6 percent of GDP in the MENA countries, down substantially from 17 percent in 1983, but still substantially above the world average of 2.4 percent. Of total public expenditure, MENA countries spent 19–20 percent on defense—as did the newly industrial Asian economies. Industrial countries and other developing countries spent about half that amount.

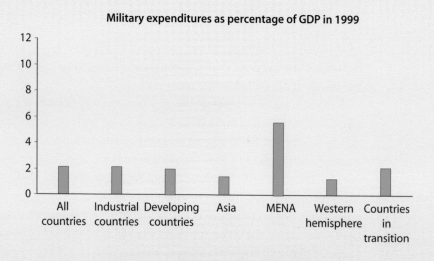

Military expenditures as percentage of GDP in 1999

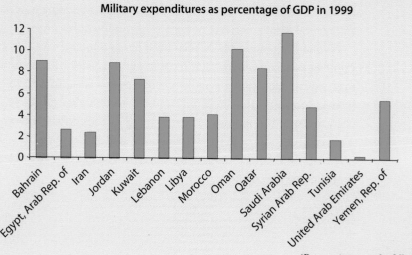

Military expenditures as percentage of GDP in 1999

(Box continues on the following page.)

BOX 1.13 (continued)

During 1995–99, Saudi Arabia and Oman spent 12–13 percent of GDP on the military, while the United Arab Emirates spent 0.5 percent of GDP on the military. In between were the Islamic Republic of Iran at 2.1 percent and Tunisia at 1.8 percent, the only other countries with data.

High spending in the region reflects both the prevalence of conflict, or the threat of it, plus the use of the military and the defense establishment to generate employment. High spending on the military has made the defense sector a powerful economic enclave that owns property, productive assets, and financial institutions—and a sector that can negotiate foreign and domestic loans and contracts.

Source: Data from International Monetary Fund 2003.

---

it. But for the index of public accountability, oil-reliant countries systematically score far below the nonoil countries.[9]

The presence of mineral wealth in a country may not cause a governance deficit but could make it more difficult for good governance institutions to emerge. Some resource-rich countries have high-quality governance institutions and have turned mineral resources into productive assets—Botswana and Norway are among them (box 1.14). In most MENA countries, the inflows of oil and gas revenues accruing directly to the government preceded the development of strong governance institutions—and raised the stakes for those already in power to hold on to it. Contrast that situation with Europe, where resource extraction and bureaucratic regulation went hand in hand as nation-building proceeded—and natural resources never dominated government revenues.

Nation-building in MENA has been discontinuous.[10] As in many developing countries, there were bloated bureaucracies with weak regulatory and technical capacity and with ineffective mechanisms to voice collective interests and to hold leaders accountable. Add to those characteristics big inflows suddenly going directly to the government. This combination of abundant resources and institutional deficiencies helps explain the persistence of the governance gap in the MENA region over the past two decades.

FIGURE 1.11

For MENA's Oil-Dependent Countries, the Public Accountability Gap Is Even Wider

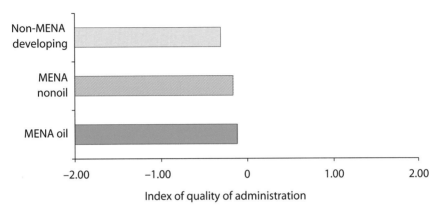

Index of quality of administration

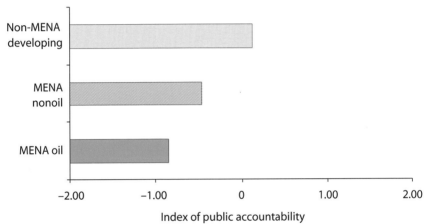

Index of public accountability

Notes: MENA oil includes Algeria, Bahrain, the Islamic Republic of Iran, Kuwait, Oman, Qatar, the Republic of Yemen, Saudi Arabia, the Syrian Arab Republic, and the United Arab Emirates. MENA nonoil includes the Arab Republic of Egypt, Jordan, Lebanon, Morocco, and Tunisia. Data are insufficient to include Djibouti, Iraq, Libya, and the West Bank and Gaza.
Source: Authors' calculations, which are based on the indexes of quality of administration and public accountability, covering 173 countries worldwide.

BOX 1.14

Botswana's Good Governance Helps Overcome the Resource Curse

A small, agricultural, predominantly tropical, land-locked nation, Botswana is very rich in natural resource wealth, with more than 40 percent of GDP from diamond revenues. Three things make the country special. First, unlike other African countries with abundant natural resources—such as Angola, the Democratic Republic of Congo, Sierra Leone, and Nigeria—it has had no civil war or intense infighting to control the revenues from diamonds. Second, despite its high dependence on mineral wealth, it has controlled corruption, thereby exhibiting the best African score on the Groningen Corruption Perception Index. And third, it has avoided the resource "curse." Botswana has had the world's highest growth rate since 1965: per capita income in Botswana grew at 7.7 percent annually between 1965 and 1998.

What explains the country's economic success? Good policies obviously, but those policies came from an underlying set of governance institutions that encouraged socially efficient resource exploitation, investment, and economic development. When institutions limit the powers of rulers and the range of distortionary policies they can pursue, good policies are more likely to arise. Effective restraints on political elites also reduce the likelihood of internal conflict, making it less attractive to fight to take control of the state apparatus.

The underpinnings of good governance can be traced to several factors:

- Botswana's precolonial tribal institutions encouraged broad-based participation and placed restraints on political elites. For example, political institutions such as *kgotla* ensured some accountability of political elites.

- Limited British colonial rule allowed the precolonial institutions to survive to the independence era.

- The political and economic security of the elites after independence was to some degree an outcome of the strong governance institutions that Botswana inherited from its precolonial period. The constraints those institutions placed on elites help explain why they did not use their political power to appropriate the revenue from diamonds starting in the 1970s.

- Postindependence political leaders built a relatively effective bureaucracy, relying in part on foreign experts and in part on the deep sense of public accountability.

- By the time the diamonds came on stream, the country had already consolidated a relatively participatory and accountable polity that supported efficient public institutions.

Source: Acemoglu, Johnson, and Robinson 2003.

Notes

1. There are other definitions of accountability. "Accountability has two dimensions: answerability, the obligation of public officials to inform about and to explain what they are doing; and enforcement, the capacity of accounting agencies to impose sanctions on power builders who have violated their public duties." (Schedler 1999). This definition is closely related to the one used in this book.

2. An ethic of service to the public and in the public interest also helps ensure good governance by putting a premium on good performance—irrespective of accountability mechanisms.

3. This section and the following one borrow extensively from the recent work on MENA judiciaries and parliaments by Brown 2001a and 2001b.

4. Brown 2001a notes that some problems that have arisen in other societies have not arisen in MENA. For instance, in some countries, judges lack independence because strong social pressures are put on them. Such social pressure can arise in MENA (for instance, with honor crimes) but it is less likely than in other settings (such as Latin America or even North America).

5. See, for example, background paper, Khouri 2003, p. 23; background paper, Salem 2003, p. 11; background paper, Mahiou 2003, p. 8; background paper, Charfi 2003, p. 25.

6. Figure 1.3 could also be read the other way. The MENA region, on average, enjoys an income "premium," with incomes higher than would be predicted by its low quality of governance, with much of this income derived from natural resource rents rather than from a productive investment and business climate created by good governance. (See remainder of chapter 1, plus chapter 2.)

7. Because of the diversity in the IQA within MENA, the average difference between the region and other developing countries as a group is statistically significant only at a confidence level of 75 percent.

8. This gap in the IPA between MENA countries as a group and other countries is always statistically significant, ranging from 95 percent to 99 percent confidence levels, and depending on the comparator group.

9. This difference in the IPA between oil and nonoil countries in MENA is statistically significant, with a confidence level of 95 percent. Both groups are below the scores for other developing countries as a group, with confidence levels of 95 percent and 99 percent for nonoil and oil countries, respectively.

10. An account of the diverse experiences of state-building processes in MENA countries and the different institutional legacies of transnational ideologies, colonialism and postcolonialism falls outside the scope of this chapter. See, among others, Anderson 1991; Ayubi 1995; Chaudhry 1996; Vandewalle 1998; Bellin 1994; Crystal 1995; and Richards and Waterbury 1996.

CHAPTER 2

Better Governance for Economic Development

"Although Europe is geographically near, in time and money terms for exporting my goods, I am farther away than an Asian firm," a Maghrebi businessman lamented recently (World Bank 2000a). His disappointment at being unable to reach his potential is reflected in the voices and attitudes of many of his peers in the region. They feel, despite the great strides over the past four decades, that the distance between potential and reality, and between MENA countries and their comparators, has been increasing.

That potential for development is sizable. Most countries in the region enjoy a strategic geographical location, a rich natural resource base, a demographic gift of an expanding pool of educated labor, and a dynamic and entrepreneurial population. And on the policy front, MENA governments have achieved macroeconomic stabilization. Fiscal and current account deficits have been reduced. Exchange rates are being corrected. And inflation has been brought under control. Substantial public investments in infrastructure and social services have, for the first time, brought roads, water, and health services to tens of millions of people in the region.

But there have also been disappointments in economic development (reflected in incomes and employment) and in human development (education, health, and other major aspects of quality of life). People in MENA countries today have incomes significantly higher than those in earlier decades—yet GDP per capita for the region has fallen by 0.8 percent a year since 1970. Tunisia's per capita growth of 3 percent during this period just matched that of Sri Lanka and barely exceeded the growth of Chile and the Dominican Republic. Tunisia's per capita growth was far behind the rates for, say, Malaysia (4.2 percent) or Indonesia (4.1 percent). And the Islamic Republic of Iran, Saudi Arabia, and the United Arab Emirates saw declines in their per capita growth, as population growth surged beyond increases in national incomes.[1] By the 1990s, unemployment had soared—almost a fifth of the male labor force in Egypt and a fifth of all laborers in Morocco, were unemployed.[2]

Similarly, great achievements in human development have been accompanied by grave letdowns. Although 90 percent of the population in Jordan is literate today, more than a third of Tunisian women and two-thirds of Moroccan women still do not know how to read or write. Just in the 1990s, infant mortality rates improved in the region by more than 20 percent—but they are still considerably higher than in Latin America, East Asia, and Central Europe. Access to water and sanitation is among the highest for developing countries, but the share of children under 12 months who receive DPT (diphtheria, pertussis, and tetanus) immunization is significantly lower than in other middle-income countries or in Latin America.

A key to economic development is economic growth, which has been elusive in MENA. This chapter tells the story of growth in MENA, particularly the link between growth and good governance. Chapter 3 includes a discussion of how public services, including those critically affecting social and institutional development, have been affected by governance in the region.

The Governance Gap and Development

Over the past two decades, the region has suffered from slow and volatile growth, a pattern common to both oil and nonoil economies. Why? A major reason is the governance gap, which has left a poor environment for businesses. So, for MENA to realize its growth potential fully, countries in the region have to redouble their efforts to offer better business environments, ones that encourage firms—large and small, domestic and foreign—to establish, to expand, and to operate with greater productivity.

These efforts entail action in each of the three main arenas of the business environment: the overall policy environment, the bureaucratic and administrative environment, and the commercial environment. And in each of these arenas, better governance can support growth by bolstering accountability and inclusiveness—growth caused directly by attracting new private investment and indirectly by improving the productivity of existing investments.

Numerous studies, for MENA as for other countries in the world, have documented the relationship between governance and private sector activity.[3] The influence of the quality of governance on growth works primarily through its effect on private businesses, which is the primary impetus for investment in today's world (figure 2.1). Businesses react to incentives, costs, and constraints—often summarized as the business environment or, more narrowly, as the investment climate. Those reactions are, in turn, influenced by the actions of the government in shaping and

FIGURE 2.1

Governance Improves Growth by Improving the Business Environment

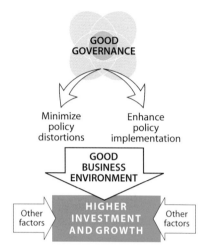

The quality of governance affects the business environment through economic, tax, and regulatory policy decisions.

The quality of policies is affected by the presence of inclusiveness combined with external accountability mechanisms—bad or discriminatory policies are difficult to maintain when there is external accountability by all.

Policy implementation depends on the quality of public institutions, including the bureaucracy. Better accountability structures, both internal and external, can lead to better institutional performance.

Other things being equal, a good business environment leads to more investment, which leads to faster growth.

implementing policies. What matters is the presence of good policies and the good administration of these policies. One without the other would still lead to ineffectiveness.

The twin facets of the quality of governance delineated in chapter 1—public accountability and the quality of administration in the public sector—are major influences on the quality of policy formulation and implementation. Weaknesses in both have constrained the quality and quantity of investments and, thus, growth in MENA.

- *Better governance reduces the scope for arbitrary government policymaking.* Although good governance does not always and in every case lead to good economic policies, it does provide mechanisms that help countries minimize the persistence of policy distortions. By ensuring public accountability of politicians and bureaucrats, better governance also contributes to the effective implementation of economic policies that are conducive to growth.

- *Better governance improves bureaucratic performance and predictability, reducing uncertainty and the costs of doing business, which, in turn, inhibit private investment or channel it into less-productive activities.* Better governance makes it easier to start new businesses and to run and expand existing businesses. It lowers transaction costs (entry, operation, and exit), reduces information asymmetries between business and governments, and lowers uncertainties and unpredictability. It does so by protecting and enforcing property rights, curbing burdensome administrative and judicial rulings, ensuring good regulatory quality, and improving access to affordable and reliable recourse to dispute resolution. By helping ensure more orderly public accountability processes, better governance also reduces political risk, which deters private investment.

- *Better governance contributes to the effective delivery of public goods that are necessary for productive businesses.* Businesses operate in a commercial environment that depends on many key public goods. And better governance helps ensure that such goods are available in a timely, equitable, and cost-efficient manner. Public goods that are essential for a good business environment include appropriately regulated public utilities (telecommunications, electricity, gas, water), a stable and prudently regulated financial system, and good quality health and education for an effective labor force.[4] Effective delivery of these goods boosts the productivity of investment and leads to faster growth.

The region's experience varies in these three areas. In many dimensions of bureaucratic performance and delivery of public services, several MENA countries are on par with countries at similar incomes (see the section on measuring governance in chapter 1 and the section on service delivery in MENA in chapter 3) but are below par in comparison with the better-performing economies of Asia, Eastern Europe, and Latin America. As chapter 1 has argued, public accountability is relatively weak in MENA, and that weakness has helped deter productive investment and thus growth.

The negative effects of the governance gap on growth are visible and quantifiable. But there are other costs as well, some of them difficult to quantify. Weak governance means that citizens' basic rights are restricted. That restriction weakens citizens' sense of civic engagement and their sense of control over their own destinies. That reaction, in turn, can breed apathy or, worse, cynicism, which can be destructive. Disenfranchisement, which comes with weak governance, generally means that the services of government, however limited, are not shared fully among those left out of the process. Although the full effects of the governance gap in MENA cannot be easily isolated, it has a negative impact on economic activity—and a negative impact on overall welfare.

Governance Deficiencies Are at the Root of Slow Growth in MENA

The MENA region benefited immensely from the sharp increase in oil prices that began in the 1970s and that continued until the mid-1980s. The oil windfalls and their spillovers led to an explosion of investment.[5] Growth in the oil-exporting countries was echoed in other parts of the region and was reflected in a sharp rise in worker remittances and in trade and capital flows. That rise led to a remarkable improvement in living standards. In addition, financial assets were accumulated abroad as national savings exceeded investment, especially in the oil-producing countries.

But as oil prices and production softened, the boom period soon faded, thus prompting a slowdown and, in many cases, a decline in growth rates in the 1980s. That slowdown left governments, which had also grown considerably in the previous decade, burdened with deficits and debt. Internationally, MENA countries have been confronted with an inability to compete in a globalizing world. Domestically, they have been contending with more youthful populations, high unemployment, collapsing productivity, and low levels of nonoil exports.

During 1985–2000, per capita growth in MENA averaged just 0.5 percent a year, a quarter of the average during 1960–84. East Asian economies, by contrast, have enjoyed sustained annual growth of 5 percent or more over the past 40 years (figure 2.2). Moreover, the growth in MENA has been unstable and volatile, more than five times more volatile than in East Asia (figure 2.3). Why has growth been so disappointing, particularly when compared with the East Asian economies? One major cause is the weaker governance environment in MENA countries.

FIGURE 2.2

MENA versus East Asia Shows Divergent Per Capita Growth

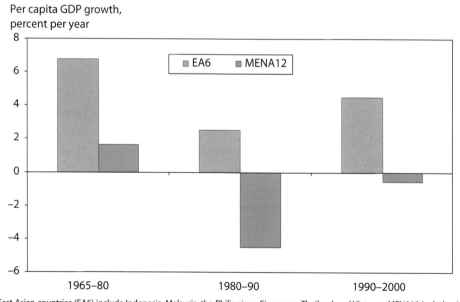

Notes: East Asian countries (EA6) include Indonesia, Malaysia, the Philippines, Singapore, Thailand, and Vietnam. MENA12 includes Algeria, the Arab Republic of Egypt, Bahrain, the Islamic Republic of Iran, Jordan, Kuwait, Morocco, Oman, Saudi Arabia, the Syrian Arab Republic, Tunisia, and the United Arab Emirates.
Source: Authors' calculations from World Bank data.

FIGURE 2.3

A 20-Year Growth Slowdown ... and a Record of Volatility

Annual GDP per capita growth (percent)

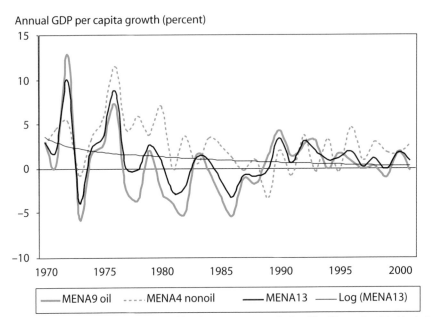

Notes: MENA9 oil includes Algeria, Bahrain, the Islamic Republic of Iran, Kuwait, Oman, the Republic of Yemen, Saudi Arabia, the Syrian Arab Republic, and the United Arab Emirates. MENA4 nonoil includes the Arab Republic of Egypt, Jordan, Morocco, and Tunisia. MENA13 includes all the above.
Source: Authors' calculations from World Bank data.

The Link Between Good Governance and Growth

Good governance establishes an incentive structure that reduces uncertainty and promotes efficiency, thereby contributing to growth. Without the creation, protection, and enforcement of property rights, the scope for market transactions is limited. Inadequate regulatory regimes undermine investment prospects. Corruption subverts the goals of policy and undermines the legitimacy of the public institutions that support markets. Without effective restraints on and incentives for public officials so they act on behalf of the public interest, the government's ability to provide growth-promoting institutions is severely hampered.

Empirical studies, including the one done for chapter 1, reveal a high positive correlation between good governance and economic performance.[6] But this finding is a weak basis for deciding policy, because correlations do not shed light on the direction of causality or on whether any other factor is a cause.

But more recent evidence has identified large causal effects running from governance to per capita incomes (Acemoglu, Johnson, and Robinson 2001; Hall and Jones 1999; Easterly and Levine 2002; Rodrik, Subramanian, and Trebbi 2002). Those studies reveal that the causal link running from governance to growth is stronger than the other way around. And the causal effect running from better governance to better economic performance seems to hold at the micro[7] and macro levels.[8] These findings have two implications. First, good governance matters for growth. Second, higher incomes do not necessarily lead to better governance. Good governance is not a luxury good that accrues automatically as countries become richer. (Appendix E has a more complete review of the analytical and empirical work on this issue.)

Growth in MENA: Sluggish, with Low Private Investment and Productivity

Economic growth in MENA countries has been slowing over the past two decades, while staying highly volatile (figure 2.3). How did the governance environment affect growth? First, the higher per capita incomes were the result of substantial oil and gas revenues and of indirect incomes through trade and remittance relationships with oil-rich countries. They were accompanied by high investment rates in MENA, but a lower payoff in growth than in the 1960s. Public investments still played a large part in total investment, unlike the situation in the rest of the world—partly because the governance environment did not encourage private investors. And these investments, especially public ones, were mostly inefficient—again for reasons of governance—and did not always yield better economic performance.

Investment rates in MENA were around 25 percent of GDP by the end of the 1990s (figure 2.4). That rate is higher than in Sub-Saharan Africa (18 percent of GDP in 1999) and Latin America (20 percent) and is on par with South Asia and with Eastern Europe and Central Asia. But it is behind the 30 percent seen in the fast-growing economies of East Asia. And it is much higher than in the 1960s, when the region enjoyed much higher growth rates. Clearly, the volume of investment was not paying off in sustained economic growth.

Private investment stands out. Private-to-public investment ratios in MENA have remained below world trends. For the region as a whole, the ratio has oscillated around 1.8 (figure 2.5). Although the reforms of the 1990s moved the MENA economies toward greater private investment, the overall private-to-public ratio remains well below the East Asian high-performing countries, which (with the exception of China) have about five times as much private investment as public investment.

Foreign investment has also been low. During the past two decades, foreign direct investment (FDI) in the MENA region accounted for only 0.8 percent of the total net flow of global FDI to developing countries. By contrast, FDI in the East Asia and Pacific region accounted for 59

FIGURE 2.4

High but Declining Investment Rates

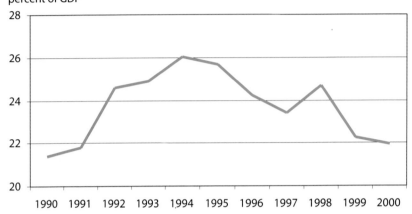

Note: MENA countries include Algeria, the Arab Republic of Egypt, the Islamic Republic of Iran, Jordan, Lebanon, the Syrian Arab Republic, the Republic of Yemen, and Tunisia.
Source: Authors' calculations from World Bank data.

FIGURE 2.5

The Share of Private Investment Is Low

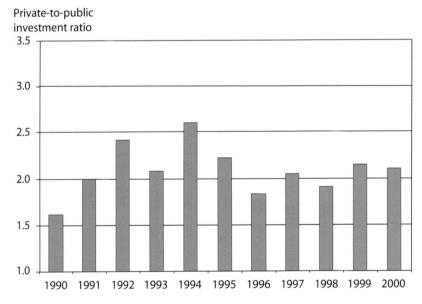

Note: MENA countries include Algeria, the Arab Republic of Egypt, the Islamic Republic of Iran, Jordan, Morocco, the Syrian Arab Republic, the Republic of Yemen, and Tunisia.
Source: Authors' calculations from World Bank data.

percent of total inflows to developing countries, on average. FDI flows also account for only a small percentage of gross capital formation in the region, about 5 percent in 2000. Compare that with Singapore, where FDI flows accounted for 26 percent.

The productivity of investment has been low as well, resulting partly from the low reliance on private and foreign investment and partly from the inefficiencies in public investment. Despite major public investments in telecommunications, the proportion of unsuccessful telephone calls is 35 percent in Tunisia, 50 percent in Lebanon, 57 percent in Morocco, and 60 percent in Jordan. And despite large public sector investments in building up the infrastructure in electricity, power distribution systems in MENA have losses equivalent to 13 percent of output, compared with just 5 percent in East Asian countries (Sala-i-Martin and Artadi 2002). And over the past three decades, MENA's overall productivity (measured by total factor productivity) has been declining (World Bank 2003e).

The Governance Gap Slowed Growth in MENA

Growth in MENA countries has been affected by many factors—particular policy environments, initial levels of development, and, most important, natural resource exports. But the pattern, level, and quality of investment have affected growth in MENA countries and have, in turn, been affected by governance.

In MENA, as indicated in chapter 1, the association between the quality of administration (measured by the IQA) and income appears strong and robust—countries with better public administration are exactly the ones with higher incomes. But the association between public accountability (measured by the IPA) and income is much less clear, a pattern that is consistent with worldwide trends (figure 2.6).

By encouraging investment and improving the effectiveness of the investment, the quality of administration has a direct effect on growth. Public accountability mechanisms, however, tend to interact with growth indirectly through their effect on the behavior of public and private agents in choosing the quality of investment and the public–private mix.[9] But overall, weak governance in the region is a cause of the sluggish growth, thereby hampering the public sector's ability to ensure a sound environment for investment and production. If one controls for income and natural resource rents, institutional quality has a strong and significant effect on GDP growth.[10]

Weaker governance in MENA costs 1.0 to 1.5 percentage points in forgone annual GDP growth. On average, improving the quality of institutions by one standard deviation—approximately equivalent to raising the average institutional quality in MENA to the average institu-

FIGURE 2.6

Incomes Are Positively Correlated with Governance Quality in the World and MENA

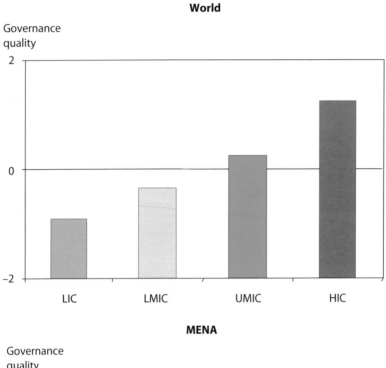

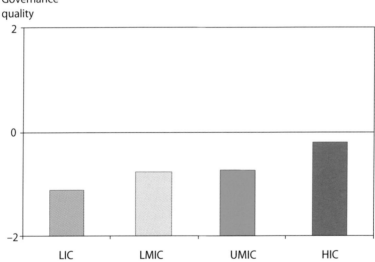

Notes: LIC is lower-income countries. LMIC is lower-middle-income countries. UMIC is upper-middle-income countries. HIC is high-income countries.
Source: Calculations for index of governance quality constructed for this book.

tional quality in a group of East Asian countries—would have resulted in an increase of almost 1 percentage point in average annual GDP growth for the region as a whole (figure 2.7).[11] This figure would rise to a 1.5 percentage point difference for the group of MENA countries with substantial oil and gas revenues. These findings are consistent with other analytical work on the subject.[12]

But governance does more than contribute to faster growth. It also sustains growth by making economies more flexible to adverse shocks. A good governance environment—securing and enforcing property rights, managing conflicts, and aligning economic incentives with social costs and benefits—is the foundation of long-term growth. And growth in a weak governance environment has proved either fragile (as in post-1997 Indonesia) or incapable of delivering higher-quality investments.

One lesson from the East Asian financial crisis is that good governance is critical in managing the adverse consequences of the initial shock. When governance is weak, the economic costs of external economic shocks are magnified by the distributional conflicts they trigger. Indonesia, lacking broad-based participation and accountability mechanisms, plus having relatively fewer developed systems of internal ac-

FIGURE 2.7

Better Governance Brings Added Growth

(1985 real per capita GDP = 100)

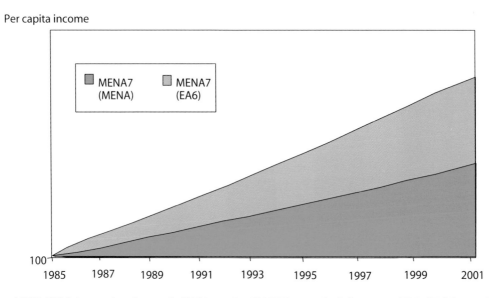

Notes: MENA7 (MENA) shows projected incomes for MENA7 countries with MENA's average level of governance. MENA7 (EA6) shows projected incomes for MENA7 countries if they had had EA6's average level of governance. MENA7 includes Algeria, the Arab Republic of Egypt, the Islamic Republic of Iran, Jordan, Morocco, the Syrian Arab Republic, and Tunisia. East Asia countries (EA6) include Indonesia, Malaysia, the Philippines, Singapore, Thailand, and Vietnam.
Source: Authors' calculations (refer to appendix C).

countability and administrative quality, eventually descended into chaos. But Malaysia's and Thailand's greater public accountability and their better-developed bureaucratic quality and internal accountability mechanisms proved much more flexible in coping with the shocks. They recovered much faster (Rodrik 1999). The responsiveness of growth to governance was smaller for MENA countries with higher-quality public administration (figure 2.8).

FIGURE 2.8

Better Administration Speeds Economic Recovery in East Asia and in MENA

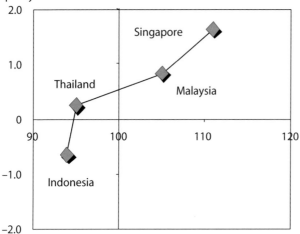

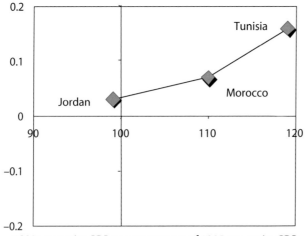

Source: Authors' calculations from the index of quality of administration constructed for this book and World Bank data.

The results raise an important question: If governance matters, through which channels does governance affect economic growth? Recent studies reveal that the quality of governance can affect growth through its effects on the level and quality of investments (Kaufmann, Kraay, and Zoido-Lobaton 2002; Page and Van Gelder 1998). Governance quality is positively and significantly associated with private investment. More important, the studies find a strong positive association between governance quality and investment productivity. Even controlling for relevant factors, governance quality remains positively and significantly associated with investment productivity.

Better Governance Improves the Environment for Productive Investment

Across MENA, the lower quality of governance affects growth because of the way it influences the behavior of business people and potential investors, both domestic and foreign. Investment climate surveys reveal that potential investors in many MENA countries face obstacles to entry and competition (cumbersome licensing processes, complex regulations, and opaque bidding procedures). Because the clients of international rating agencies—mainly foreign investors—pay for this information to help make their investment decisions, higher scores in governance quality indicators are expected to be associated with higher flows of foreign direct investment in those countries (World Bank 2003b; Banerji and McLiesh 2002; Sewell 2001).

In a recent survey in Morocco, about half the firms said that they had to hire intermediaries or to maintain full-time workers to deal with the bureaucracy (World Bank 2000a). In Jordan, an investor interested in registering a new firm has to wait three months, with half that time spent on a single procedure: inspection by the ministry concerned (World Bank 2003c). Increasing the cost and risk to business people, such problems lower the quantity of new investment and the quality and efficiency of the investments already made. They thus lower growth.

Better Governance Reduces the Scope for Arbitrary Government Policies

For business people, the economic policy environment obviously matters. But because businesses aim to operate over a longer period of time, what also matters is the process for making policies—so that everyone can anticipate the policy environment in the years to come, or at least can understand the rules of the game changing this environment. And just as important, businesses need to be able to understand the extent to which they can affect the course of the change because they are able to directly lobby and influence the process.

Research across countries has shown, on average, that more accountable regimes give rise to better policies. For trade and labor policies, more accountable governance systems create policies that are more inclusive. The trading systems benefit not only producers but also consumers and labor markets that allow new entrants to find jobs rather than just protecting the interests of insiders.[13]

In such situations, better policies persist for two broad reasons, as elaborated in chapter 1. First, the better availability of information (*transparency*) allows the private sector and social actors at large to monitor not just the policies themselves, but also the effects of the policies. Second, the private sector's ability to hold accountable those policymakers who make unfair or ineffective policies (*contestability*) deters policymakers from making policies that they know are bad, because they know they can be replaced with others who promise to reform those policies. In addition, public accountability can hold policymakers responsible for any failures in implementation. Still, good governance does not necessarily guarantee good policies (box 2.1).

BOX 2.1

Governance, Policies, and Growth—a Complex Link

Policies and the quality of governance interact in complex ways, making it difficult to identify their individual contributions to growth. Policy reforms can lead to improvements in governance quality. Some evidence suggests that greater openness to trade is conducive to better governance. For example, the European Union (EU) accession process may have contributed to stronger governance for countries in Central Europe. International trade agreements that promote openness may also encourage governance reforms by increasing the payoffs of transparency and by reducing internal barriers to starting new firms.

Causality can also run in the other direction—from governance to policies. Good governance, by providing mechanisms that reduce government's discretion in policymaking, lowers the likelihood of adopting persistently bad policies. Even when good policies are implemented, weak governance may undermine their positive effects on growth. For example, when financial regulation and supervision are weak, liberalization may encourage domestic banks to build up excessive risk.

Source: Appendix E.

In MENA, the problem is not just a lack of accountable processes—of complete and transparent information and of contestability. Businesses in many countries in the region also face the problem of a perceived lack of inclusiveness in access to systems for policymaking and for dispute resolution. In particular, small firms often feel disadvantaged relative to larger ones. A recent survey in the Arab Republic of Egypt, Bahrain, Jordan, Lebanon, and the Syrian Arab Republic found that small firms are at a disadvantage compared with large firms; the small firms in these countries complain that the regulatory and institutional framework lacks transparency and is inconsistent and inefficient (Mansour 2002). Large firms can alleviate some of these obstacles by producing needed services internally, but small ones do not have the organizational capacity or resources to cope with the obstacles.

Another recent survey of small entrepreneurs in the Republic of Yemen found that fewer than one in six firms believed it had any influence over the policy formulation. And well over half those surveyed thought that the major influences were social and tribal influences, key private players, or both (Banerji and McLiesh 2002). Larger firms thought that they had more influence than smaller ones. When they exist, such inequalities serve as a disincentive for smaller, less-influential investors to enter business. Given that smaller businesses have been the dynamo for growth in most countries outside the region in the 1980s and 1990s—from Poland to Malaysia—the bias toward large firms may have contributed to lowering MENA's growth below its potential.

Evidence on perceptions about grand corruption in the region suggest that large private businesses and wealthy individuals play a disproportionately large role in manipulating the system for their personal gain, a phenomenon often labeled as "state capture" (World Economic Forum 2002). This manipulation, or state capture, may range from the persistent awarding of large public sector contracts to a few well-connected groups, to actual change in laws and regulations that lower the costs or increase the profitability of such groups.

Such state capture lowers the effectiveness of investments (because the most efficient investors do not necessarily undertake key economic activities). State capture also deters new investors, including foreign investors, from entering the economies, because they are aware that the rules of the game are both unclear and biased. The situation particularly hurts small firms, because they cannot afford to buy favorable decisions.

State capture is attractive for some private and public entrepreneurs who can create effective networks to coordinate their interests. The lack of inclusiveness creates incentives for the excluded firms either to use bribes to bypass the restrictions—or to resort to informal businesses. Companies outside the corrupt network are hurt, because they cannot stop the network's practices.

But improvements in governance can help break exclusionary networks or can allow new, more inclusive ones to emerge (box 2.2). In Algeria, a rural development project that is government financed has encouraged the use of competitive procedures to allow for greater participation by small firms in public contracts (World Bank 2002a). Thresholds were kept low to encourage the use of small procurement lots, thus allowing small firms with limited means to compete for work. As a result, private sector involvement in the project, which ran at only 20 percent in the first year, rose to more than two-thirds of the cumulative financial volume by the fourth year. The greater involvement of smaller firms improved productivity through better activity design and lower unit costs.

BOX 2.2

Better Processes for Public Procurement Counter State Capture

The decision to purchase—Mar del Plata and public referendums
In public procurement, the purchasing decision is usually made in isolation from civil society but often in close cooperation with important business. This closed-door practice and lack of citizen involvement gives interested politicians leeway for making important purchasing decisions without considering the efficiency of spending. The only retributions they fear are the impacts that large scandals might have on elections or public opinion.

Mar del Plata, a city in Argentina, introduced a novel approach to important purchasing decisions: making the final decision binding on citizen approval. In 1995, the newly elected mayor called for a referendum on the construction of the 26 public works that would significantly improve infrastructure—a vital asset for a city dependent on tourism. Citizens could review the projects and then vote on them, along with an earmarked tax to be paid over four years for project implementation. The vote turned out positive, the project went ahead, and all 26 works were finished in time—months before the mayor was up for re-election, which he won overwhelmingly.

The tender documents—Morón and public hearings
The elaboration of tender documents is often another closed-door process. Interested companies and citizens generally are presented only with the final document, in which the specifications have been drafted in conjunction with the one company meant to win, making successful bids impossible for any other company. In Argentina, the waste collection tender is the largest tender awarded by municipalities. The waste collection industry is generally known as being a very strong and closed club that is extremely difficult to join and has secret ties between the companies and the mayor's office.

BOX 2.2 (continued)

To break this practice, the government of Morón, a municipality in the province of Buenos Aires, called for a public hearing to discuss the tender conditions on its draft waste collection contract. The draft tender required companies to show five years of existence to be eligible to bid. Many companies argued that this approach left out most companies. In the new tender, the requirement was lowered, allowing new companies to participate, including the one that ended up winning the award. The labor union demanded that whichever company won the contract should be obliged to keep the workers under contract at that time, a request that was taken into account in the final tender document. Expert advice established that the tender should be based on required specific outputs, not on inputs. Again, the suggestion was incorporated.

The results: stunning. The new company that was awarded the contract, and that was hardly known in Argentina, was operating in only two other municipalities. And the total contract value over four years was $13 million less than the previous contract, saving about 30 percent. The second lowest bid, from the former contracting company, was some $17 million higher than the winning offer. These savings show the benefits of breaking old, established networks and clubs.

The tendering process—using the Internet to deliver information
Difficult and scarce access to information on public procurement opportunities and to the relevant tender documents inhibits the participation of many companies in the public procurement process. The information tends to be highly disaggregated, in a great number of publications, making it difficult for interested companies to find it. And most information is incomplete and published too late. In Buenos Aires, tenders are announced, on average, only five working days before the closing date. The tender documents have to be obtained at the purchasing office, which can be far away.

A Gallup survey on the public procurement process in Argentina revealed that the majority of companies were interested in selling their goods and services to the Argentine government, but that most of them were not participating in the public procurement process. Why? Because the relevant information is not available in a timely and reliable way—and because the application process is often very tedious and costly. Companies also perceived closed access to contracts, which are awarded to a select group.

Experiences in Mexico and Chile, among others, are powerful examples of how the Internet can increase participation and lower prices in public procurement by providing timely and easy access to information on tenders, including the corresponding documents. In Canada, the number of suppliers has been increased 2.5-fold, and the prices fell 10–15 percent over the course of only three years; savings are likely to be higher in countries where corruption is more serious.

Source: Moreno Ocampo 2001.

Better Governance Reduces Uncertainty and Costs of Doing Business

Three main factors relating to the quality of public administration affect the quantity and quality of private investment. First, because investors are making long-term decisions, they need assurance that the rule of law will prevail, that just recourse is available for disputes, and that government policies are predictably decided and implemented. Second, although government regulation of many aspects of private business activity is reasonable and well warranted (in order to protect consumers, workers, and the general public), overregulation, long delays, high costs, and discriminatory treatment in implementing good regulations can deter investors from business activity. Third, the arbitrary application of the rule of law and overregulation can lead to bribery and extortion by the bureaucracy, thereby offering a further cost and disincentive for investment.

Rule of Law. Although many aspects of the business environment matter for investment, the security of property rights is probably the most important. No investors—domestic or foreign—are likely to risk assets if there is a high probability that they cannot be protected against arbitrary seizure and predation. So, investors demand a governance process that preserves—without discrimination—the right to private property, that ensures the equitable and consistent rule of law in protecting this right, and that incorporates external and internal accountability mechanisms against the use of the state authority to confiscate.

The formal establishment of property rights will have little effect on investment without effective incentives to respect and enforce them. A high-quality and reliable judiciary reduces transaction costs for businesses and sends positive signals to investors that the rule of law will be equitably and consistently protected and enforced. In a competitiveness survey in MENA, 70 percent of respondent firms indicated that "unpredictability of the judiciary presents a major problem" for their business operations and that "it is never, seldom, or only sometimes true that, in the case of changes in laws or policies affecting my business operation, the government takes into account concerns voiced either by me or my business association" (Fawzi 2002). The responses make it clear that private entrepreneurs in the region feel that laws and regulations—and the process of making, changing, enforcing, and applying them—are unfavorable for successful business operations.

The predictability of rules and regulations is also key for businesses, both in deciding whether to make new investments and in determining the returns on existing investment. Private businesses in MENA complain about the arbitrariness in the determination of taxable profits by tax administrators: "The central problem is that the criteria for tax assessment are ambiguous, and tax collectors enjoy unlimited powers." In Egypt, a survey found that the major obstacles to business reported by the respondent firms were the multiplicity of laws, the frequent changes in those laws, and their inconsistent application (Nugent 2002).

Of particular concern for businesses are the costs associated with litigation, as well as the long time it takes to resolve a dispute through the formal judicial system (figure 2.9). According to a study in Egypt, the clearance rate of commercial cases taken to the formal court system was only 36 percent, compared with 80 percent in Japan and 88 percent in Belgium (Galal 1996). At the same time, the average time needed for the minority of cases that were settled had increased from 2 years in the 1970s to more than 6 years in the early 1990s. Another study found the average commercial case takes 2 to 2.5 years to complete in Jordan and Lebanon—countries that have some of the best judicial systems and judges in the region (Anderson and Martinez 1996). Naturally, the longer it takes to resolve cases and the lower the resolution rate, the higher the firms' transaction costs.

Another problem is the inconsistent outcome of dispute resolution, which again increases risk and uncertainty for businesses and increases transaction costs. The higher such costs become, the more suppliers will

FIGURE 2.9

Some Court Systems in MENA Are Especially Slow

Number of days to enforce
a standard contract

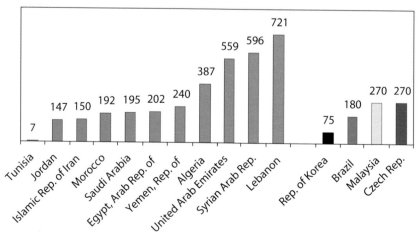

Source: World Bank 2003c.

attempt to pass them on to their customers by increasing prices. In many cases, this increase may raise the price so much that sales fall significantly, causing producers to exit the industry and preventing firms from entering.

Regulatory Quality. Overregulation can deter investment by raising the cost for starting up and operating businesses. Some procedures can be beneficial, but having numerous and cumbersome procedures can be unnecessarily costly for investors, both actual and potential. In several countries in the region, port and customs processing times impose important constraints on the competitiveness of firms that trade internationally (box 2.3), but there are some signs of improvement. Streamlining customs and port procedures has benefited domestic businesses in Morocco. In 1999, Moroccan firms spent fewer than two days on aver-

---

BOX 2.3

Reducing Red Tape in Lebanon

A good first step: reduce the costs of doing business
Registration, documentation, and customs procedures in Lebanon have been streamlined and simplified through computerization. The new procedures make importing much easier. Only three or four steps and four to five days are needed to release goods from customs. The procedures have been implemented at the Port of Beirut and the Beirut International Airport, which covers about 85 percent of the volume of goods that pass through customs. Many goods, about 41 percent, go through customs without being inspected at all.

The next step: strengthen internal accountability mechanisms
The reforms have reduced the discretion of officials, but poor incentive schemes for employees and weak oversight continue to result in corrupt behavior. Importers are assigned to a *vérificateur* and a chief inspector, who inspect the goods and assign appropriate tariffs. Problems arise because the importer lacks the ability to request another *vérificateur* or chief inspector in cases of dispute. If there is a dispute, the importer can use an expert to assess the value of a good. Importers often avoid doing so because the expert (often a competitor), can request a large fee for assessing the good, can delay the release of the good, or can increase the value of the good, thus resulting in higher tariffs. This system gives the *vérificateur* and the chief inspector enormous power over the importer and makes the customs procedures in Lebanon highly prone to corruption.

Source: Fawzi 2002.

age (the median is one day) to process their exports of finished goods through ports and customs. And it took three days on average to process imports through ports and customs (the median is two days). This performance compares very favorably with East Asian countries (box 2.4).

MENA entrepreneurs find that registering a business is a long procedure that involves too many administrations and is often very costly. In the Arab Republic of Egypt, as in much of MENA, a major obstacle for new investors and existing businesses is the cost of registering a business and enforcing contracts (figure 2.10). To avoid the registration fees and

---

BOX 2.4

Improved Regulatory Framework for Investment in Morocco

The streamlining of customs and port procedures seems to have benefited exports as well as imports of raw materials. Moroccan firms spent less than two days (median is one day) on average in 1999 to process their exports of finished goods through ports and customs. It took on average three days to process imports through ports and customs (median is two days). These performances compare very favorably with East Asian countries.

The overwhelming majority of manufacturers (82 percent) import inputs themselves rather than going through intermediaries. Labor regulations do not seem to be a burden on firms' activity. Three-quarters of respondents to a survey were happy with their current employment level. Only 25 percent of firms would reduce their staffing if there were no firing restrictions at all, so overstaffing caused by distorted labor market regulations does not seem to be a key problem. The state of law and order appears satisfactory. Recourse to legal institutions in case of breach of contract is frequent: close to half the firms surveyed went to court to deal with a recent contractual dispute with a client or supplier. One-third also use arbitration.

Exporting firms were asked whether they face difficulties exporting, either with customs or with harbor authorities. The overwhelming majority saw no or little difficulty. This result is a dramatic change in investors' perceptions. In March 1999, a survey of 556 exporting firms found that 31 percent perceived customs procedures as the most binding constraint on their activity, and 23 percent identified port procedures as their most important constraint. In March 2001, customs and ports procedures remained a serious difficulty for only 2 percent to 3 percent of firms and were a moderate difficulty for 5 percent to 6 percent of firms.

These findings suggest that inside Moroccan harbors, things are working very well, and measures are applied fairly. Contrary to findings in most developing countries, neither large nor foreign firms receive special treatment.

Source: World Bank 2000a.

FIGURE 2.10

Challenges for Business in MENA Shown by Lengthy and Costly Registration and Contract Enforcement

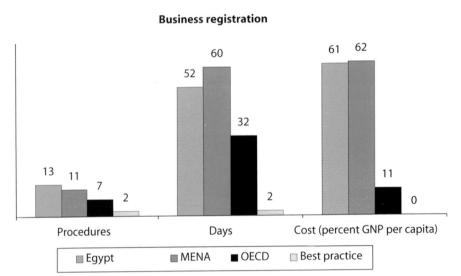

Business registration

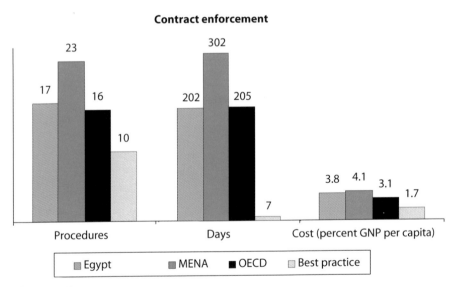

Contract enforcement

Note: Data as of January 2002.
Source: World Bank 2003c.

the complexity of administrative procedures, many private businesses have to bear extra costs so they can pay experienced intermediaries. And many businesses, particularly small ones, have no choice but to operate informally—missing out on the benefits of formal registration, such as better access to credit or government support services.

Control of Corruption. Corruption increases the costs of public investments, which reduces their productivity and lowers growth (Tanzi and Davoodi 1997). High levels of corruption are also associated with lower expenditures on operations and maintenance and with lower-quality public infrastructure. For private investors, corruption can increase investment and operating costs, as well as increase uncertainties about the timing and effect of the application of government regulations.

There are two broad classes of corruption in the public sector: "high-level" or "grand" corruption, where top-level policymakers subvert the governance process for financial gain (often by distorting the policy environment), and "low-level" or bureaucratic corruption. Both result from a failure of accountability structures, and both, as implied in figure 2.1, can worsen the business environment and growth.

High-level corruption is usually associated with a lack of transparency, insufficient contestability of the executive branch of the government, and inadequate checks and balances by the parliament and judiciary. In most MENA countries, a dearth of public accountability mechanisms make it possible to create policies that benefit only a small fraction of the population. This situation leads to a preference for personalized and often inefficient allocations of public resources (Keefer and Khemani 2003).

Low-level or bureaucratic corruption has its roots in inefficient public sector employment policies and in the lack of strong internal accountability mechanisms to improve the performance of public employees. Traditionally, MENA countries have had public sector employment policies that stress hiring and discourage firing. Public hiring practices may also have an element of informal relationships and nepotism, which weaken any internal accountability mechanisms that may exist.

Evidence on corruption (and tax evasion, which is often associated with corrupt bureaucracies)[14] suggests a considerable variance across MENA (figure 2.11). Greater transparency and effective sanctions (contestability) would reduce the scope for discretionary behavior, because they would provide open access to information and the legal means for holding politicians, bureaucrats, and private agents alike to account for their actions (Tanzi and Davoodi 1997).

In sum, by increasing the transparency of policy formulation and implementation, better governance will help improve the predictability of the design and application of rules and regulations. Better governance also involves better accountability—by providing opportunities for private investors to participate in the process, by ensuring standards of behavior of bureaucrats, and by expanding public oversight of administrative and regulatory performance. Better governance will also help reduce the costs of doing business, especially those costs arising from cumbersome regulations and procedures, from inconsistent or discretionary ad-

FIGURE 2.11

Large Variation in Corruption Exists in MENA

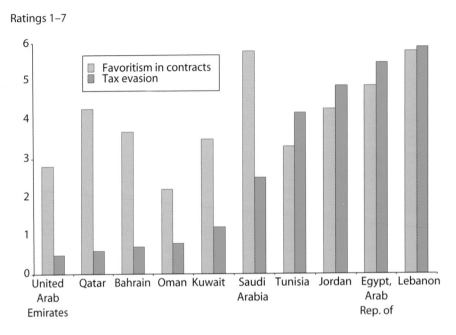

Ratings 1–7

Note: Scale for favoritism in contracts: 1 = favors well-connected firms and individuals; 7 = is neutral among firms and individuals. Scale for tax evasion: 1 = common in country; 7 = minimal in country.
Source: Results from surveys of local firms, World Economic Forum 2002.

ministrative practices, and from inadequate mechanisms of conflict resolution (box 2.5).

Better Governance Ensures Effective Public Services for Businesses

Productivity growth, and thus economic growth, will also depend on
how well governments can ensure an economic environment in which
the delivery of services that are essential for businesses is reliable and
effective. These services include an adequate infrastructure for trade
and transportation, a set of appropriately regulated public utilities, a
stable and prudently regulated financial system, and a healthy and educated labor force. Governments do not have to provide these services
themselves. But they do need to ensure that the provider—whether a
public official or a private investor—is doing so efficiently and inclu-
sively.

BOX 2.5

Corruption—Not a Synonym but a Symptom of Bad Governance

In the 1980s, when it was sometimes difficult for international observers to speak openly about corruption, the term "bad governance" was often used as a euphemism. Although "corruption" has now entered the lexicon of development, some confusion persists about the link between corruption and governance.

This book argues that governance is about the process of the exercise of authority. In that sense, corruption is among the manifestations of bad governance, not equivalent to the inadequate process itself. Corruption occurs, for example, when accountability mechanisms (foundations of good governance) are insufficient. But poor accountability mechanisms, implying bad governance, can also give rise to other unfortunate consequences—such as bureaucratic sloth and inefficiency, or sustained ineffective policies. But those consequences are not corruption.

There are two broad classes of corruption in the public sector. In high-level or grand corruption, top-level policymakers subvert the governance process for financial gain (often by distorting the policy environment). In low-level or bureaucratic corruption, bureaucrats demand personal payments or favors to ensure normal public service delivery. Both occur from a failure of accountability structures—and both can worsen the business environment and can hinder growth.

The specific accountability structures that can control each class of corruption are different. For high-level corruption, the best check is public (external) accountability through transparency and contestability (as measured in part by the index of public accountability). Some forms of internal accountability structures, such as empowered parliaments, judiciaries, or independent audit organizations, can also provide a check. In the typical MENA country, both types of structures are weak.

For administrative corruption, the best check is strong internal accountability structures (included in the index of quality of administration, or IQA). But here, too, accountability requires contestability—or a credible capacity of accounting agencies to impose sanctions. Again, in many MENA countries, such sanctions on the bureaucracy are weak—because employment policies in the public sector stress hiring and discourage firing, and because public hiring practices may have an element of informal relationships and nepotism.

Infrastructure. Better governance clearly increases the returns on existing investment in infrastructure. Recent studies show that greater accessibility to information, effective contestability mechanisms, and more direct user involvement will increase the rates of return of investments in physical infrastructure and human capital (Isham, Kaufmann, and Pritchett 1997).

Private entrepreneurs in the region complain about electricity supply and quality. In the Republic of Yemen, the number of days of power disruption averages 75 a year. In Morocco, the average is about 16 days a year. Algeria averages about 16 outages a year, 70 percent of them lasting up to five days. The problems are particularly severe for smaller firms (figure 2.12). In such instances, the lack of adequate and reliable infrastructure substantially increases the cost structures of firms, because it makes them diversify the sources they use for key inputs—such as buying generators to ensure against electricity blackouts or wells to mitigate an unreliable water supply.

FIGURE 2.12

Poor Public Infrastructure Forces Businesses to Spend on Private Alternatives

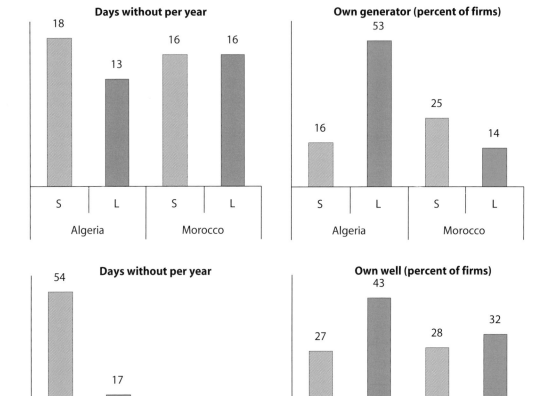

Note: S = small firm; L = large firm.
Source: World Bank 2000a; World Bank 2003b.

Human Capital. Private entrepreneurs face another important constraint on investing and expanding their businesses in MENA—the mismatch in skills between what is demanded by investors and what is available. If investors cannot hire a highly qualified and trained labor force, their investments will not be productive—and growth will suffer.

Migration traditionally addressed this problem. But as labor markets in the region have become flooded with new entrants, there is political pressure to provide jobs for the domestic laborers and to lower the reliance on foreign workers.[15] To meet this challenge, MENA countries have to gear up their educational systems both to improve basic educational attributes and to equip the labor force with skills appropriate for the modern world.

As chapter 3 will discuss, countries that have weak governance—especially underdeveloped accountability structures—are less likely to have effective, efficient, and inclusive delivery of public goods and services that are so essential for productive businesses and, thus, economic growth.

Notes

1. Authors' calculations from World Bank data 1970–2000.

2. Unemployment data in Egypt are from 1990 to 1998 and were in the 1998 Egypt Labor Market Survey. Unemployment data in Morocco are from 1995 to 1999 and were in the 1999 Morocco Living Standards Survey.

3. For the effect of the rule of law—and more specifically the security of property rights—on investment, see North 1981; Knack and Keefer 1995; Calderón and Chong 2000; Easterly and Levine 2002; and Rodrik, Subramanian, and Trebbi 2002. See also Jimenez 1984 for the effect of titling on investment. The effect of the rule of law on economic performance is the one that is best documented and supported by the empirical evidence. Causality problems cloud estimates of corruption and bureaucratic capacity on development; see Keefer 2003. Similarly, although the effect of participation (through greater inclusiveness) has been the subject of substantial attention, analysis has suffered from a lack of theoretical and empirical precision that clouds interpretation. This shortcoming is particularly true for the democracy and development literature (see De Haan and Siermann 1996; Przeworski and others 2000).

4. This list of public goods includes some goods that do not fit the strict definition of goods that are nonrivalrous (the use by one does not decrease the ability of others to use them) and nonexclusive (people cannot be prevented from using them). Some goods—like telecommunica-

tions—can also be delivered by the private sector. But for reasons of monopoly, governments have long provided them, a trend that is changing in the Middle East and North Africa, as elsewhere. (See also box 3.1.)

5. Increases in public investment reached more than 90 percent in the 1970s (Page 1998).

6. Kaufmann, Kraay, and Zoido-Lobaton 2002 reflect the breadth of the concept of governance in their efforts to devise systematic measures of governance. From 17 sources, the authors take some 194 different measures of governance, and divide them into 6 categories: voice and accountability, political stability, government effectiveness, regulatory quality, rule of law, and control of corruption. Yet, in their subsequent paper (Kaufmann, Kraay, and Mastruzzi 2003), they highlight the difficulty of aggregating these governance measures because good performance on some dimensions does not imply good performance on others. Recognizing this problem, in their analysis of the effect of governance on growth, they focus only on the rule of the law, which is strongly associated with growth.

7. See Langseth 1997 on public service delivery in Uganda and Yao 2001 on the effects of civil service reform in Shunde, China. Norton 1998 finds that countries scoring high on security of property rights fare better on longevity, literacy, child nutrition, and access to health services. Narayan 1999 shows that participating in local and national decisions helps improve the welfare of women and their children.

8. The research of La Porta and others 1999; Kaufmann, Kraay, and Ziodo-Lobaton 2002; Acemoglu, Johnson, and Robinson 2001; Engelman and Sokoloff 2002; Easterly and Levine 2002; and Rodrik, Subramanian, and Trebbi 2002, show the importance of governance quality for growth.

9. It may also partly reflect the shortcomings in the available empirical measures of public accountability, which are imperfect proxies of the dimension of governance that they try to measure.

10. Note that although "governance" here is proxied by measures of institutional quality derived from the dataset of Sachs and Warner 1997, they do not exactly match the indexes developed in chapter 1 of this book. However, they have a large overlap with the index of quality of administration (IQA), including some elements that measure internal accountability. In fact, to the extent that the analysis does not include broad measures of external accountability (for which MENA countries usually have low scores), it can be argued that the calculated growth effect of better governance may be even larger than shown.

11. The set of MENA countries used in this analysis excludes the Gulf Cooperation Council (GCC) countries, for which data were not available. However, when data are adjusted for incomes, GCC countries

have similar administrative quality (measured by the IQA) as the other countries, on average, so their absence from the sample is unlikely to bias the results.

12. For example, a recent empirical study (Elbadawi 2002) compared several MENA countries with those of East Asia and found that a key reason for the difference in growth rates is the quality of administration. The higher quality of administration in East Asia countries (Hong Kong [China], Indonesia, Malaysia, the Republic of Korea, Singapore, and Thailand)—controlling for all other factors—contributed to a growth rate about 1.2 percentage points higher than that of five diverse MENA economies (the Arab Republic of Egypt, Jordan, Lebanon, Morocco, the Syrian Arab Republic, and Tunisia) and almost 1 percentage point higher than that of the oil-exporting economies (Bahrain, Kuwait, Libya, Oman, Qatar, Saudi Arabia, and the United Arab Emirates).

13. See, for instance, Banerji and Ghanem 1997 on the effect of political regimes on trade and labor policies. For a cross-section of countries, regimes that were more democratically accountable had, on average, more open economies with more flexible labor markets that did not favor insiders. Other research has posited the opposite view—especially as it relates to growth-friendly policies. A good summary of the classic literature is Landell-Mills and Serageldin 1992.

14. Tax evasion is corrupt behavior by private agents and thus is not strictly a case of public agents "using public resources for private gain," the common definition of corruption. However, to the extent that bribing public employees (for example, tax inspectors) facilitates such behavior, it is an aspect of corruption.

15. A more detailed analysis of labor market issues is in World Bank 2003e.

CHAPTER 3

Better Governance for Social Development

More than economic growth, development revolves around improvements in overall human well-being beyond increases in income. Human development itself has many dimensions—ranging from enjoyment of basic human rights to better access to key social goods, such as education and health. Most governments in MENA, in line with their constitutions, provide a broad range of social and other public goods—in essence, so they can promote social development.

In this arena, there have been some astonishing rates of improvement:

- In Oman, gross enrollments in primary schools increased from just 3 percent in 1970 to 72 percent in 2000.

- In Lebanon, almost no children under 12 had DPT (diphtheria, pertussis, and tetanus) immunizations in 1980, but 93 percent were immunized by 1993.

- In Tunisia, there was less than one phone line for every 100 people in 1990, but 1 in 5 people have a phone line today.

- Between 1990 and 1999, the Arab Republic of Egypt built more than 18,000 kilometers of roads and the Republic of Yemen built almost 16,000 kilometers.

MENA countries have also had successes when compared with countries that are outside the region and that are at the same level of development. Dropout rates and class sizes in primary school are comparable, if not better. The provision of water and sanitation is also comparable, which is remarkable given the overwhelming scarcity of water in the region.

Against these successes, however, stand many examples of lagging performance. Even after large investments in education, 50 percent of the adults in Morocco and more than 40 percent in Egypt were still illiterate in 2001. Indeed, with the exception of Jordan and Lebanon, illiteracy rates remain disquietingly high in the region, even among youths who should have received schooling in recent years. In Saudi Arabia, which has a GDP per capita of more than $8,000, infant mortality was still 23 per 1,000 live births in 2001, worse than in countries at similar per capita incomes, such as Malaysia and Argentina, and even in poorer countries such as Sri Lanka.

Infrastructure is also disappointing. In Cairo, a resident who applies for a fixed telephone line from the state-owned telephone monopoly may have to wait more than a year to get the service installed. For those residing in other parts of Egypt, the wait may be four to five years. In Tunisia, despite huge strides in telecommunications in the past 10 years, there were only 96 Internet hosts in 2001—one for every 100,000 Tunisians, a drop in the bucket compared with the 64,000 hosts in Malaysia.

This unevenness in the delivery of public services in MENA is puzzling—both within sectors, such as health, and across sectors, such as health and education or telecommunications and water and sanitation. Why have MENA governments done well in some areas of human development and not so well in others? What are the key deficiencies? And why have some countries done systematically better than others?

This chapter addresses those questions. At the core of the discussion is the basic tenet that social development is a challenge of governance, because the performance of the public sector—so important in ensuring social goods—depends fundamentally on the quality of governance. And the quality of governance depends in large part on having governance structures matched to the varied requirements for delivering different types of public goods. It is in the mismatch between structures and requirements that the solution to the puzzle can be found.

A related issue is the appropriate role for the state (box 3.1). What goods and services should the state be providing? And what criteria should be used in making that determination? Once it is decided that the public sector should intervene, the resulting challenge is one of governance: how to design and maintain systems that deliver many services in the best way possible.

This chapter focuses on four important groups of public services: education, health, telecommunications, and water and sanitation. The main messages are as follows:

- As elsewhere, MENA countries have done well in delivering standardized services, but poorly in delivering more complicated services for which outcomes are more difficult to monitor.

- Contrary to common perceptions, the weaknesses in service delivery stem more from problems in governance than from technical weaknesses in capacity. In particular, weak accountability mechanisms permit weak performance, especially as the public good or service gets more complex.

BOX 3.1

Deciding When Government Action Is Needed

Economic theory offers a decision tree for assessing whether and how governments should intervene in economic and social affairs. These decisions also determine the nature of key governance issues in these interventions, notably the delivery of public goods.

The first decision is whether the problem is actually one that governments should seek to solve—that is, whether the question involves provision of public goods or reflects the presence of other problems requiring government authority, such as externalities, incomplete markets, asymmetric information, or the regulation of natural monopolies. For example, when a farmer withdraws water from a stream or aquifer in an arid area, there will be less water for other users, which is a negative externality. Food processing companies always have more information about ingredients than do those who buy the goods, thereby creating information asymmetries that governments can remedy. Citizens acting individually cannot provide national defense, thus making it a public good.

In the realm of problems requiring government intervention, public goods merit special attention so that decisions on government intervention are based on sound analysis. Pure public goods have the unique characteristics of *nonrivalry* in consumption and *nonexcludability* in supply. The property of *nonrivalry* ensures that the consumption by one citizen of the public good will not decrease the consumption level for any other citizen. Radio broadcasts or ensurance of clean air are examples of non-rivalrous public goods.

The property *of nonexcludability* means that, in providing a good to one consumer, it is impossible or impractical to exclude another consumer from securing its benefits as well. Thus, it is impractical to allow consumption by some and to exclude others. Most public roads are an example, as is the control of epidemiological diseases.

Other services—most important among them being those for basic health and education—are not public goods (they are neither nonrivalrous or nonexcludable), but societies may decide to have government provide these services anyway. The logic is often that of externalities and of market failure—if it is agreed that healthy and educated individuals benefit society collectively (that is, there are positive externalities beyond the benefits accruing to the individual)—or that of equity. Only with government intervention would everyone have equal access to basic health care and education.

Once it is agreed that government intervention is appropriate, the next decision is whether intervention requires the use of public resources—or simply the issuance and implementation of regulations that influence private action. To illustrate, a government may adopt regulations that require private insurance companies to cover all applicants irrespective of risk, thus inevitably raising the premiums paid by those who are good risks. Or it may instead fund a government insurance scheme or a social safety net for the uninsurable, as in the Islamic Republic of Iran.

(Box continues on the following page.)

BOX 3.1 (continued)

When government spending is decided to be the appropriate intervention, the next decision is whether the government administration should provide the public good directly—or whether it should simply finance the provision of the public good by nongovernmental service providers. Road maintenance is a typical public good, especially where it is difficult to organize all road users themselves (for example, through toll roads) to take on that responsibility. Governments traditionally fund road departments, which handle maintenance through a force account. Increasingly, however, governments are financing nongovernmental contractors to do this work. In education, the choice between publicly funded government schools and cash vouchers that allow parents and students to attend nongovernment schools is another example.

The decision at each stage determines the type of governance arrangement required to optimize delivery of the public good.

Sources: Stiglitz 1998; McNutt 1999.

- Addressing these deficiencies will require more effective accountability mechanisms for each of the major players in service delivery—between the policymakers and the service providers (stronger internal accountability), between the providers and their clients (more direct, external accountability through wider choice and direct participation by clients), and between the citizens and the policymakers (stronger external accountability).

Service Delivery in MENA: Commitment and Achievements

Overall Outcomes Show Improvement over Time ...

In areas ranging from education to health care, as well as from water and sanitation to broader infrastructure services, the MENA region has progressed tremendously over the past decades.

In education, the average number of schooling years has increased significantly, for both girls and boys (figure 3.1). Net enrollment rates for primary schools increased by almost 10 percentage points in the past two decades, reaching an average of 82 percent in 2000 (World Bank data). Youth illiteracy rates in the region came down by almost 20 percentage points between 1980 and 2000 (figure 3.2).

In health, infant mortality rates have declined from an average of 94 deaths per 1,000 live births in 1980 to 37 in 2000 (figure 3.3), outstrip-

FIGURE 3.1

Years of Schooling Are Up Significantly

(average years of schooling in MENA)

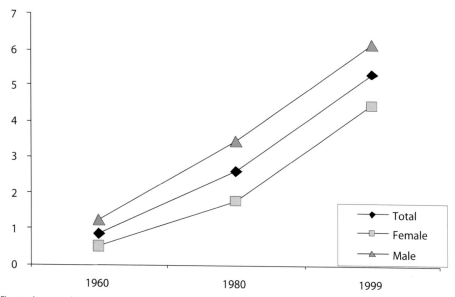

Notes: Figures show population-weighted averages for those countries with available data for persons of ages 15 and older. Similar patterns are found for simple averages.
Source: Authors' calculations from Barro and Lee 2000b.

ping the average for middle-income countries around the world. There has also been a rapid expansion in immunization rates, especially in the 1980s (figure 3.4).

The story is much the same for water, all the more remarkable because the region is the most water-scarce in the world. In 2000, on average, almost 90 percent of the urban population and 71 percent of the rural population in MENA countries had access to an improved water source. The access to improved sanitation facilities is even better, at 96 percent in urban areas and 73 percent in rural areas. The improvements have been remarkable (for example, the proportion of Egypt's rural population that has access to improved sanitation facilities rose from 79 percent in 1990 to 96 percent just 10 years later) (World Bank data).

In infrastructure services, there has also been considerable progress. Perhaps the greatest recent achievements were in promoting competitive mobile phone services. In 1990, not a single country in the region offered competition among mobile phone providers. By 2001, competitive mobile services were offered in many countries: from Egypt and Morocco to Jordan, Lebanon, Oman, the Republic of Yemen, and Saudi Arabia.[1] The change for fixed phone lines has been less dramatic, but there has still been good progress. The Islamic Republic of Iran, Mo-

FIGURE 3.2

Youth Illiteracy Is Down by 20 Points

(youth illiteracy rates, ages 15–24, percent)

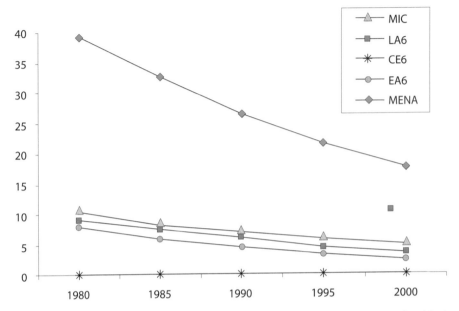

Notes: Figures show the population-weighted averages for those countries with available data. Similar patterns are found for simple averages. Middle-income countries (MIC) include all middle-income countries for which data are available. Latin American countries (LA6) include Argentina, Brazil, Chile, Mexico, República Bolivariana de Venezuela, and Uruguay. Central European countries (CE6) include Bulgaria, the Czech Republic, Hungary, Poland, Romania, and the Slovak Republic. East Asian countries (EA6) include Indonesia, Malaysia, the Philippines, Singapore, Thailand, and Vietnam. MENA includes Algeria, the Arab Republic of Egypt, Bahrain, the Islamic Republic of Iran, Jordan, Kuwait, Lebanon, Morocco, Oman, Qatar, the Republic of Yemen, Saudi Arabia, the Syrian Arab Republic, and the United Arab Emirates.
Source: Authors' calculations from World Bank data.

rocco, Oman, and Tunisia more than quadrupled the number of their phone mainlines over the past two decades. In the Islamic Republic of Iran, for instance, there were 23 phone mainlines for every 1,000 people in 1980 but 149 in 2000. On average, MENA countries had twice as many phone mainlines in 2000 as in 1980.

... Because of a Strong Commitment by Governments

Governments in the region have all identified the delivery of basic public services as priorities in their development agendas. The priority is also evident in the large amount of resources spent on financing those services.

For example, education for all has been regarded as a fundamental right of citizenship by all governments after independence, with commitments making their way into laws and constitutions (table 3.1). Public provision of free education has been widespread, and most countries in the region provide basic education to children. Primary education is

FIGURE 3.3

Infant Mortality Is Down by Almost Two-Thirds

(infant mortality rates, per 1,000 live births)

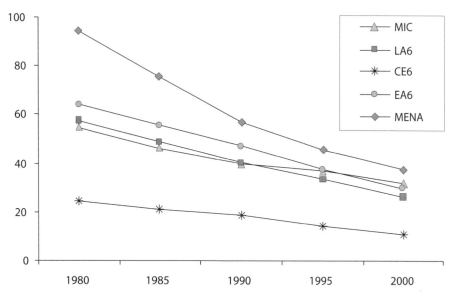

Notes: Figures show the population-weighted averages for those countries with available data. Similar patterns are found for simple averages. Middle-income countries (MIC) include all middle-income countries for which data are available. Latin American countries (LA6) include Argentina, Brazil, Chile, Mexico, República Bolivariana de Venezuela, and Uruguay. Central European countries (CE6) include Bulgaria, the Czech Republic, Hungary, Poland, Romania, and the Slovak Republic. East Asian countries (EA6) include Indonesia, Malaysia, the Philippines, Singapore, Thailand, and Vietnam. MENA includes Algeria, the Arab Republic of Egypt, Bahrain, the Islamic Republic of Iran, Jordan, Kuwait, Lebanon, Morocco, Oman, Qatar, the Republic of Yemen, Saudi Arabia, the Syrian Arab Republic, and the United Arab Emirates.
Source: Authors' calculations from World Bank data.

compulsory everywhere, and lower secondary education is compulsory in six countries (Algeria, Egypt, the Islamic Republic of Iran, Jordan, the Republic of Yemen, and the West Bank and Gaza) (World Bank 1999b).

Some countries of the region have made major efforts to promote girls' education in rural and poor areas, as is the case in Egypt, the Islamic Republic of Iran, Morocco, the Republic of Yemen, and Tunisia. Community schools are targeting girls' education in remote areas, fostering critical thinking and creativity, and improving skills as the basis for lifelong learning (box 3.2) (World Bank 2002e).

The new wave of education reforms in MENA goes beyond increasing its quantity to emphasizing improvements in curricula and teacher training. Jordan, for instance, is developing the Educational Reform Program to improve the quality of basic and secondary education—not only through building schools and hiring educational staff, but also through helping develop students' cognitive skills. The goal is to give the country the skills and knowledge-intensive work force it needs for its increasingly complex economy (World Bank 2002b).

FIGURE 3.4

Immunizations Are Expanding Rapidly

(DPT, percentage of children under 12 months)

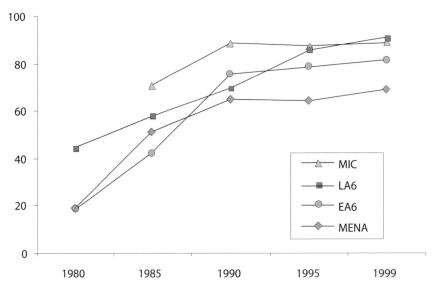

Notes: Figures show the population-weighted averages for those countries with available data. Similar patterns are found for simple averages. Middle-income countries (MIC) include all middle-income countries for which data are available. Latin American countries (LA6) include Argentina, Brazil, Chile, Mexico, República Bolivariana de Venezuela, and Uruguay. East Asian countries (EA6) include Indonesia, Malaysia, the Philippines, Singapore, Thailand, and Vietnam. MENA includes Algeria, the Arab Republic of Egypt, Bahrain, Jordan, Kuwait, Lebanon, Morocco, Oman, Qatar, the Republic of Yemen, Saudi Arabia, the Syrian Arab Republic, and the United Arab Emirates.
Source: Authors' calculations from World Bank data.

Governments have also committed to improving health services, controlling communicable diseases, and making water and sanitation available to much of the population, if not all of it. For example, the first phase of Egypt's Comprehensive Health Reform Program commits the government to improve primary health care. This program is being implemented by introducing cost-effective primary health care services—as well as necessary emergency and basic curative care services—across the country.

The strong commitment to providing public goods is evident in the public subsidies to consumer staples. MENA governments spend a substantial share of budgetary resources on subsidies. For food subsidies alone, the spending has, in some cases, reached almost 4.5 percent of GDP (table 3.2).

In many countries worldwide, policies and proclamations remain just that—nice-sounding words on paper. But as the food subsidies suggest, in the MENA region those words have been backed up by substantial funding, thus reflecting governments' commitments to service delivery. On average, countries in the region spend almost $117 per capita on health services, the third highest among the low- and middle-income regions,

TABLE 3.1

Constitutional and Legal Provisions for Education in MENA

Country	Constitution	Law/act
Algeria	November 28, 1996 • Education is a right • Basic education is compulsory • State provides free instruction at all levels	1976 laws on educational reform • 9 years of basic education are compulsory and free
Egypt, Arab Rep. of	May 22, 1980 • Education is a right • Primary education is compulsory • State provides free instruction at all levels	Law No. 233/1988 • 8 years of basic education are compulsory
Iran, Islamic Rep. of	October 24, 1979, amended July 28, 1989 • Obliges the government to pursue free primary and secondary education for all, and to facilitate and expand higher education	
Jordan	As amended through January 8, 1984 • Elementary education is compulsory and free in government schools	1994 Law of Education and Instruction • 10 years of education are compulsory and free
Lebanon	No statement in the 1926 constitution, as amended in 1990	1998 Law • Elementary education is compulsory • 6 years of basic education are compulsory • Public education is free at all levels
Morocco	Revised 1996 • Education is a right	
Syrian Arab Rep.	March 13, 1973 • Education is a right • 6 years of primary education is compulsory • Public education is free at all levels	
Tunisia	No statement in constitution as amended in 1998	Education Reform Law in 1991 • Basic education defined as 9 years
Yemen, Rep. of	November 1994 • Education is a right • Primary education is compulsory	1992 Education Law • Defines compulsory education as 9 years, but because of present financial constraints, only 6 years of basic education are currently compulsory

Source: World Bank 1999b.

just after Latin America, Eastern Europe, and Central Asia (World Bank 2002e). In relation to GDP, health expenditures in the MENA region are similar to the average for middle-income countries worldwide: 2.7 percent in 2000 (figure 3.5). For education, MENA countries have allocated almost 5 percent of spending in 1998, higher even than the amount in some of the world's leading middle-income countries (figure 3.6).[2]

Most countries in the region have a wide array of other social safety net programs—for family and school allowances, public works, cash transfers, unemployment insurance, utility subsidies, and school nutrition (van Eeghen and Soman 1998).

BOX 3.2

Community Schools in Upper Egypt—Bringing Education to Girls

In Upper Egypt, a particularly deprived region of the country, poor families who cannot afford to educate all their children favor their sons. In many hamlets, fewer than 15 percent of the girls attend school. In 1992, the Ministry of Education and UNICEF introduced girl-friendly community schools, expanding educational choices and fostering different attitudes toward girls' education. Now 200 community schools operate in some of the most conservative parts of Egypt, with girls making up 70 percent of the students.

The model relies on active learning. Contents of the government curriculum are transformed into activities, such as cards and games, and are enhanced with subjects suited to local interest, such as health, environment, agriculture, and local history. Using stones for counting, toothbrushes for painting, and so on, children are encouraged in self-directed activities and in learning-by-doing in small groups.

The results are very encouraging. The pupils of the first four community schools took the ministry's standardized third-year exam, and they all passed with flying colors. The child who scored highest in one of the districts (Manfalout) was a girl from a community school. Within communities, more profound changes are seen: 12-year-olds are convincing their parents that the girls should postpone their marriages until they graduate. Slowly, girls are gaining a voice in areas far from the city walls.

Source: Zaalouk 2001.

TABLE 3.2

Food Subsidies, 1995

Country	Algeria	Egypt, Arab Rep. of	Iran, Islamic Rep. of	Jordan	Morocco	Tunisia	Yemen, Rep. of
Percent of government budget	2.9	4.6	9.5	3.8	5.5	4.5	16.3
Percent of GDP	0.9	1.3	2.9	1.4	1.7	1.7	4.9

Source: World Bank 1999a.

A Mixed Record in Public Services Delivery

The significant achievements of MENA countries, as well as the considerable efforts and resources devoted to the provision of public goods and services, are marred by continuing disparities in delivery:

- First, there is uneven performance across different types of services—with successes in health, for example, but shortcomings in education.

- Second, there are enduring gaps with other middle-income countries—in literacy rates, for instance, or in the quality of infrastructure regulation.

FIGURE 3.5

Health Spending Is on Par with Other Middle-Income Countries

(public spending on health, 2000, percentage of GDP)

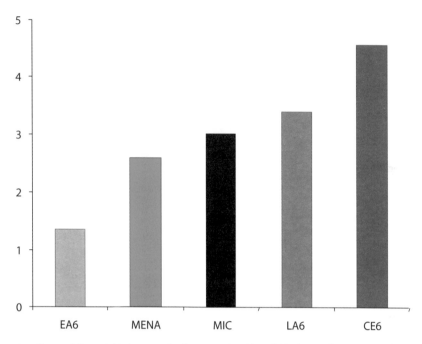

Notes: Figures show the population-weighted averages for those countries with available data. Similar patterns are found for simple averages. East Asian countries (EA6) include Indonesia, Malaysia, the Philippines, Singapore, Thailand, and Vietnam. MENA includes Algeria, the Arab Republic of Egypt, the Islamic Republic of Iran, Jordan, Kuwait, Morocco, Oman, Saudi Arabia, and the Syrian Arab Republic. Middle-income countries (MIC) include all middle-income countries for which data are available. Latin American countries (LA6) include Argentina, Brazil, Chile, Mexico, República Bolivariana de Venezuela, and Uruguay. Central European countries (CE6) include Bulgaria, the Czech Republic, Hungary, Poland, Romania, and the Slovak Republic.
Source: Authors' calculations from World Bank data.

- Third, there is differential access to services within countries—marked, for instance, by inequalities in telephone lines or, more broadly, by poverty rates between rural and urban areas.

Consider the differential performance of MENA countries in delivering health and educational services. In health services, many of the countries have generally been more effective than their peers elsewhere in the developing world. On an efficiency index, they score more than 80 percent on average (of the maximum potential), while other middle-income countries score only 70–75 percent on average.[3]

One can also compare infant survival rates (the inverse of infant mortality) and public health expenditures. Most MENA countries— Egypt, Lebanon, Oman, Syria, and Tunisia, and, to a lesser degree, Bahrain, the Islamic Republic of Iran, and Morocco—are more efficient than their peers in the rest of the developing world. They have managed with lower

FIGURE 3.6

Education Spending Is Even Higher than in Some Leading Middle-Income Countries

(public spending on education, 1998, percentage of GDP)

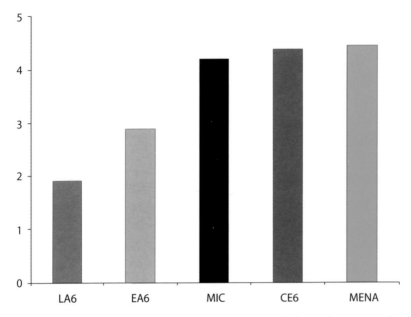

Notes: Figures show the population-weighted averages for those countries with available data. Similar patterns are found for simple averages. Latin American countries (LA6) include Argentina, Brazil, Chile, Mexico, República Bolivariana de Venezuela, and Uruguay. East Asian countries (EA6) include Indonesia, Malaysia, the Philippines, Singapore, Thailand, and Vietnam. Middle-income countries (MIC) include all middle-income countries for which data are available. Central European countries (CE6) include Bulgaria, the Czech Republic, Hungary, Poland, Romania, and the Slovak Republic. MENA includes Bahrain, the Islamic Republic of Iran, Jordan, Lebanon, Morocco, Oman, Saudi Arabia, the Syrian Arab Republic, Tunisia, and the United Arab Emirates.
Source: Authors' calculations from World Bank data.

spending to achieve infant survival rates at or above what would be expected for countries at their incomes (figure 3.7). Most MENA countries in the sample are in the northwest or northeast quadrants and are efficient or overachievers. Only two countries, Djibouti and Saudi Arabia, appear to have spent more and gotten less.

Spending on public education, by contrast, appears to be less efficient. Spending for primary education is relatively high, yet by such measures as the illiteracy rate, MENA countries are not doing as well as their comparators. Only two countries, Jordan and Lebanon, have literacy rates above what would be expected at their income. The remaining MENA countries either have underachieved (spent less and achieved less—Bahrain, Oman, Qatar, the Syrian Arab Republic, and the United Arab Emirates) or, even worse, have been inefficient (spent more but achieved less—Algeria, Egypt, Kuwait, Morocco, Saudi Arabia, the Republic of Yemen, and Tunisia). Of countries in the sample, only Lebanon can be classified as efficient—achieving more with less (figure 3.8).

FIGURE 3.7

In Health Spending, Most MENA Countries Are Efficient ...

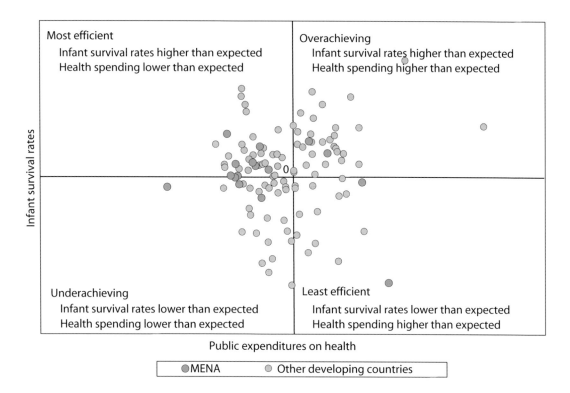

Notes: The x-axis measures differences between actual public expenditures on health and predicted expenditures. Predicted rates are derived from world trends. They represent the public expenditure rates that would have been predicted given countries' income levels. Similarly, the y-axis measures the difference between actual infant survival rates and predicted rates. The distance from the country point to each one of the axes measures the size of these differences. Accordingly, the northwest quadrant reflects the "zone of greatest efficiency," followed by the northeast, then the southwest, and finally the southeast quadrant—the "zone of greatest inefficiency."
Source: Authors' calculations from World Bank data. Data are insufficient to include Djibouti, Iraq, Libya, and the West Bank and Gaza.

Part of the explanation for this pattern lies in the strong emphasis on higher education, which is much more costly per student in general and noticeably more costly in MENA countries, therefore consuming a substantial share of the education budget. But the fact remains that unit costs of educating elementary and secondary school students in MENA countries tend to be significantly higher than in other countries. Spending by the government on each secondary school pupil in MENA countries is, on average, roughly twice as high as in other middle-income countries—nearly $700 PPP-adjusted 1985 international dollars, compared with about $350 in other developing countries. And it is about a third higher for each primary school pupil (calculated from Barro and Lee 2000b).

Similar observations apply to welfare services. Governments spend enormous amounts on food subsidies, which serve as social safety nets to

FIGURE 3.8

... But in Education, MENA Countries Are Either Inefficient or Underachievers

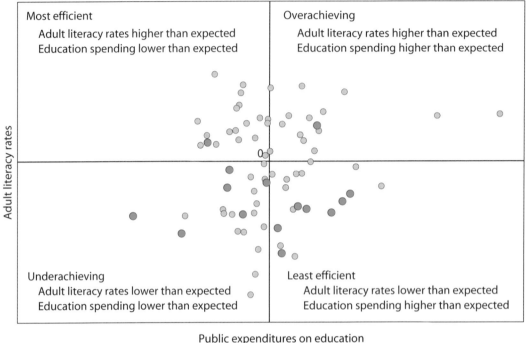

Public expenditures on education

● MENA   ○ Other developing countries

Notes: The x-axis measures differences between actual public expenditures on education and predicted expenditures. Predicted rates are derived from world trends. They represent the public expenditure rates that would have been predicted given countries' income levels. Similarly, the y-axis measures the difference between actual adult literacy rates and predicted rates. The distance from the country point to each one of the axes measures the size of these differences. Accordingly, the northwest quadrant reflects the "zone of greatest efficiency," followed by the northeast, then the southwest, and finally the southeast quadrant—the "zone of greatest inefficiency."
Source: Authors' calculations from World Bank data. Data are insufficient to include Djibouti, Iraq, Libya, and the West Bank and Gaza.

ensure that minimum food consumption is available to a typical household (table 3.2). Yet, in some MENA countries, malnutrition among children remains fairly widespread. Several MENA countries have had difficulty identifying the needy and targeting the necessary services. That difficulty has led to expensive programs that are not fully effective and that deprive the government of the resources to deliver better services in other areas (van Eeghen and Soman 1998; World Bank 1999a and 2002e).

Reviews of the social safety net programs typically indicate large leakages. The most needy are often excluded. And some programs, such as utility or fuel subsidies in the Islamic Republic of Iran are regressive in their distributional consequences—the rich get the most benefits because they are the largest consumers of subsidized goods (World Bank 2003d). Some programs are more effectively targeted, such as cash transfers to unemployed poor in Jordan and the public works programs in Morocco and Tunisia.

The regulation of private activities, rather than directly providing or financing public intervention, is a public good—and one that is poorly developed in most MENA countries. Rather than relying on private providers that operate within a regulated environment, governments have typically financed and provided services directly through public agencies. And few governments have emphasized regulation that protects certain areas of public interest, such as competition policy or environmental and consumer protection. When regulation is pursued in the public interest, it is most often in the social arena, especially through labor laws to protect workers in the "formal" sector (which usually benefit employed workers at the expense of unemployed workers and small business owners).

This limited experience with regulatory arrangements has led to multiple problems, each impeding growth (see chapter 2). Poorly designed regulations permit excessive bureaucratic discretion and corruption. Weak regulatory laws do not ensure that regulatory agencies can function independent of outside interference—either from the government or from certain elites. The technical capacity for sound regulation is limited. Those weaknesses partly reflect governance problems, including poor transparency (to foster dialogue) and insufficient accountability structures (to minimize capture by the social, political, or business elite).

It comes as little surprise that, in regulation, MENA countries lag behind countries with comparable incomes. This lag is nowhere more evident than in the private provision of infrastructure services, a situation that demands capable and independent regulators. Despite the achievements in mobile telephony, the number of mobile telephones per capita in MENA countries—at one line for every 10 people—lags significantly behind that in comparator countries. As the experience in other countries suggests, private markets can provide mobile phone systems much more easily than fixed phone lines, if a minimally effective regulatory regime can facilitate entry and operation, including interconnections (Koshi and Kretschmer 2002). The lethargic growth of mobile telephony in MENA countries points to weak regulatory frameworks and institutions, although some countries have begun a process of reform (box 3.3).

Governance Matters for Public Service Delivery

Why do MENA countries seem to do better in some services than others? What accounts for the uneven quality and costs across public services? Can institutional reforms improve the delivery of services that

BOX 3.3

Regulating Telecommunications in MENA

The Arab countries that are implementing reforms in telecommunications have taken steps to restructure (and often privatize) the incumbent operators, to introduce competition in some market segments, and to update regulatory frameworks. The leaders—Algeria, the Arab Republic of Egypt, Jordan, Mauritania, Morocco, and Saudi Arabia—have set up independent regulatory authorities. Oman and Tunisia have decided to establish such authorities, and Bahrain and Lebanon are considering doing so.

Despite fairly strong legal foundations, the new authorities face big challenges as they struggle to establish their credibility and to exert their authority. The problems include the lack of a clear mandate to enforce decisions free of political interference, the scarcity of professional and financial resources to ensure sufficient capacity, and the limited adoption of transparent regulatory processes including consultation with operators and users. In this long process, Egypt, Jordan, and Morocco have already updated their laws in a second round, so that they refine the structures and functions of their regulatory authorities.

Source: Mustafa 2002.

now are of poor quality or are provided at high cost? The answers lie in the institutional arrangements governing relationships among those in the delivery chain of public services.

An Accountability Framework for Governance and Public Service Delivery

Public service delivery involves complex interactions among three parties:

- Politicians, policymakers, and others who formulate public policies—the president or king, the parliament or cabinet.

- Service providers—both the public administrative bureaucracy that implements policies and the frontline providers, such as teachers, police officers, doctors, and road workers.

- Clients as beneficiaries of services and citizens as the ultimate repository of state authority.

The relationships and interactions among these three sets of actors constitute three critical dimensions of governance: between citizens and politicians, between politicians as policymakers and service providers, and between service providers and citizens as clients (figure 3.9).[4]

FIGURE 3.9

Multiple Channels of Accountability

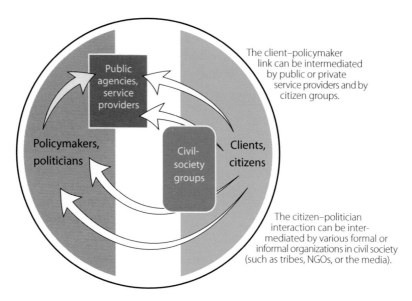

The client–policymaker link can be intermediated by public or private service providers and by citizen groups.

The citizen–politician interaction can be intermediated by various formal or informal organizations in civil society (such as tribes, NGOs, or the media).

The arrows show accountability relationships: policymakers hold service providers internally accountable (upper left-hand arrow); and citizens, and clients, exert external accountabilities on both service providers and politicians, either directly or intermediated by civil society organizations (the other arrows).

In an ideal world, service providers respond adequately and promptly to the needs of citizens, who are the clients of the service. But in reality, some providers do not—especially when citizens have weak leverage over them and thus have difficulty holding them accountable for their performance. This problem is the same in MENA as in the rest of the world. Enhancing accountability for performance is, thus, a fundamental governance issue in the delivery of all public services. And solutions vary depending on where accountability is weak in the relationship chain. The two principles underpinning accountability—transparency and contestability (or competition)—are tools that governments and the people can use to improve accountability.

Typically, accountability for good service delivery remains an internal issue for governments. Even if policymakers are responsive to citizen demands, they do not actually provide the services. Instead, they rely on a wide array of service agencies and staff—units of government ministries, semiautonomous agencies linked to ministries, local government units, or private contractors and firms. Policymakers might lay out policies and the guidelines for implementing them, but will need others to actually handle the implementation, just as lawmakers need courts, judges, and police to ensure that laws are enforced. Policymakers thus confront the complex problem of properly motivating service agencies to deliver services effectively, to make sure there is a real effect, and to do so efficiently and at relatively low cost (see the arrow in the upper left segment of figure 3.9).

Citizen leverage—external accountability—can supplement and reinforce internal accountability mechanisms. That leverage is partly indirect; it comes through real or potential pressures that citizens can exert on policymakers, who in theory should be accountable to the citizens for making sure that government performs (see the two arrows in the bottom half of figure 3.9). But the pressures that citizens can exert through policymakers put them at least two steps away from service agents in the accountability chain. This route depends on the effectiveness of internal accountability mechanisms that are within government and that link policymakers to the service agencies (the upper left arrow).

Citizens can also exercise leverage directly on service providers (see the two arrows in the upper right segment of figure 3.9). Although it puts the citizen just one step away from the provider (a shorter route than the political one), that leverage requires greater transparency and good mechanisms for contestability (or competition). The leverage could be achieved through an effective feedback mechanism, which typically depends on the initiative of the service agency to establish a system for finding out what clients think about service quality. Or it could involve a choice of service agencies—if clients can send their children to private schools, can visit private clinics, or can subscribe to private mobile phone carriers. By establishing systems that improve the accountability link between citizens and service agencies, policymakers can use this external accountability system to strengthen internal accountability systems.

The quality of the accountability links depends on the information gaps between the various actors. For example, the quality of elections depends on how much the voters know—and thus on the quality of information and debate in the public domain. Even without elections, informed citizens are better able to build a case and to apply pressure to hold government and policymakers accountable. Information also enables citizens to articulate their needs and concerns to governments. When information is restricted, information gaps deter citizens from communicating with policymakers. And, even when information is widely available, its effective use typically requires groups that intermediate between citizens and the government.

Intermediation is vital in the accountability chain between citizens, politicians, and service agencies. (This intermediation is represented in figure 3.9 by the arrows passing through the rectangle representing civil-society organizations.) Citizen leverage will inevitably depend on the work of the media and organized civil-society organizations, such as nongovernmental organizations (NGOs), interest groups, and religious organizations. Those groups can monitor government performance, organize complaints, and advocate on behalf of citizens. For example, the Institute for Democracy in South Africa's Budget Information Service helps build the capacity of citizens to participate in budget analysis. Advocating pro-poor budgeting, the institute has been a pioneer in launching children's and women's budget initiatives that have been replicated worldwide.

But forming such groups and linking them in powerful coalitions must deal with collective action problems when interests are not wholly convergent (Olson 1965). Moreover, effective intermediation requires an enabling legal environment that secures the ability to advocate, share information, and carry out activities. Where organized accountability mechanisms are lacking, when civil organizations are discouraged, and when public information is tightly managed, some citizens may feel they have no option other than to express their voice through demonstrations, which in extremes can degenerate into violence. This approach is not an acceptable accountability mechanism; it reflects weaknesses in alternative, more civil mechanisms.

The Link Between the Politicians or Policymakers and the Service Agencies

Explaining the Link. Structuring an effective arrangement of internal accountability that governs the relationship between policymakers and service agencies is a challenge. Systematizing and regularizing implementation requires laws, rules, and procedures to structure and guide the relationship between policymakers and providers. These laws, rules, and procedures (sometimes called institutional arrangements) define the accountability arrangements between the two parties. Their effectiveness depends on the establishment of a system that will allow policymakers to monitor the performance of service agencies.

Monitoring is easier when clients and the services they require are simple, standardized, easily observed, and homogenous. And monitoring can be achieved centrally, as with immunizations, primary school classes, and electricity generation. But it is more difficult and costly when services are tailored to each client, involve individual and discretionary transactions with each client, and have no precise link between service delivery and effect. For those services, it is hard to formulate simple indicators of effectiveness (such as whether means-tested food subsidies went to the poorest, whether a patient in a rural clinic actually received the right care and medicine, whether a fourth grader can read at the level expected, or whether a police officer effectively patrols a neighborhood).

So, the effectiveness of internal accountability mechanisms depends not only on the effort and capacity of the policymaker but also on the nature of the service (World Bank 2003h). As illustrated earlier in this chapter, health outcomes in MENA are generally better than education outcomes because results in education are typically more difficult to measure and, thus, to monitor than are those in health. For similar reasons, outcomes in telecommunications have tended to be poorer than in water and sanitation.

Because internal monitoring is inherently difficult and expensive, especially when performance indicators are tough to define precisely, governments often enlist the help of citizens. Governments may ask consumers to rate agencies through feedback surveys. Or they may require that agency budgets and performance records be publicized. These tactics combine both internal and external accountability mechanisms to strengthen the capacity of policymakers and to hold providers accountable for their performance.

Examining the Link in MENA. Given the important role of government in delivering public services, a key question is whether the internal accountability arrangements (the rules, procedures, requirements, restraints, and the like) enhance or impede actual service delivery. Because of data constraints, it is difficult to assess the effect of these arrangements on service delivery. And in the MENA region, data on agency performance are typically less available than in other countries. So the effectiveness of internal accountability must be, in part, inferred by examining internal arrangements, especially as they relate to the people who govern budget formulation and execution.

Because budgets translate policymakers' priorities into policies, programs, and projects, an analysis of the institutional arrangements that govern the budget process opens a window onto the accountability link between policymakers and service agencies. Indexes that measure the effectiveness of budgetary arrangements show that good budget management correlates highly with good governance overall, both in MENA and in key comparator countries (box 3.4). The causality runs in both directions. More effective budgetary arrangements contribute to better quality governance. And the better the overall quality of governance, the more likely that accountability arrangements related to the budget process will be effective.

Worldwide, countries that score higher on the quality of public administration (a reasonable indicator of the overall quality of public sector governance) will tend to perform better in service delivery outcomes. The better the quality of public administration, the better the service delivery outcomes: lower infant and maternal mortality, higher immunization rates, higher life expectancy, higher youth literacy, and better access to telecommunications (figures 3.10 and 3.11). For instance, countries

---

BOX 3.4

Quantifying the Effectiveness of Institutional Arrangements in the Budget Process

The effectiveness of institutional arrangements promoting the allocative and operational efficiency of a budgeting system can be assessed by experts, responding to standard questions. Allocative efficiency refers to the alignment of budgetary allocations with the strategic priorities of the country. Roughly speaking, it addresses the following question: Are budgetary resources being allocated to the "right" things ("right" being based on strategic priorities)? Operational efficiency refers to the cost-effectiveness of service delivery: Given the resources allocated to a service, is the service being provided at a reasonable quality and cost? A good budgeting system promotes both allocative and operational efficiency.

The overall assessment relies on several categories of institutional arrangements, including those that tighten the link between planning and budgeting, enhance cost-benefit analysis, emphasize performance in agency management, ensure predictability in budgetary flows to agencies, and strengthen budgetary and financial accountability (of line agencies to policymakers).

Performance orientation covers arrangements such as merit-based recruitment and promotion, autonomy of line agencies, and competitiveness of salaries. Accountability structures include ex post reconciliation of budgets and spending, competitiveness in public procurement, auditing, performance measurement, public availability of information on spending, and explicit sanctions for misuse of funds. Each of these arrangements is evaluated by experts and assigned a score, usually normalized from zero (not effective) to one (highly effective). The effectiveness index for performance orientation is the average of the scores for each of these arrangements. The average of the indexes for each of these performance categories constitutes the overall effectiveness index for allocative efficiency. For operational efficiency, a similar process of evaluating effectiveness along several dimensions and then averaging the scores across categories is used.

The results can be used to compare governments on their relative effectiveness in budgetary management and to identify weaknesses within a government's budgetary system.

Sources: See Campos and Pradhan 1997; Esfahani 2000.

---

that have public administration of a quality above the world average tend to have, on average, youth literacy rates 15 percentage points higher than do countries with lower quality. Similarly, the approximate number of months that applicants must wait for a telephone line goes as low as 7 months for countries with above-average quality of public administration, compared with about 55 months for those with below-average quality.[5] When countries in MENA are divided into those with an index of

FIGURE 3.10

Good Governance Matters for Health …

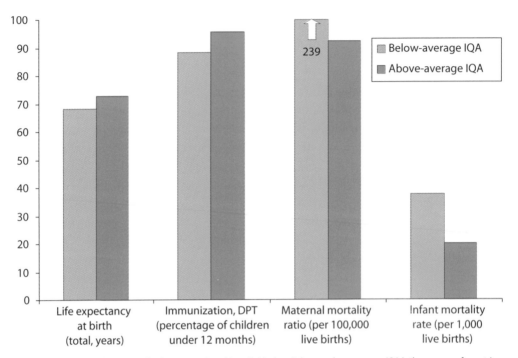

Notes: Figures show the simple averages for those countries with available data. Below- or above-average IQA is the average of countries scoring lower or higher than the overall MENA average on the index of quality of administration.
Source: Authors' calculations from World Bank data.

the quality of administration (IQA) in the public sector below the region's average and those above, the same relationships prevail.[6] Not surprisingly, good governance matters to public sector performance.

In short, while many facets of good governance account for this positive relationship, one of the key mechanisms is an effective budgeting system. Better budgeting systems make for better service delivery outcomes.

How well do the budgeting systems in MENA countries function? Some insights can be gleaned by comparing several MENA countries with Brazil, Indonesia, and the Republic of Korea. MENA countries compare well in linking planning and budgeting, using cost-benefit analysis, and managing budgetary flows. But they score considerably lower in the performance orientation of budgeting and the strength of internal accountability (figure 3.12). These weaknesses result in inadequate attention to and monitoring of program implementation—and, consequently, in service delivery performance that is only average. Within MENA, countries that have an above-average IQA tend to have better performance and internal accountability systems, and those that have a below-average IQA have worse systems. Countries that have an above-average

FIGURE 3.11

… And for Education and Infrastructure Services

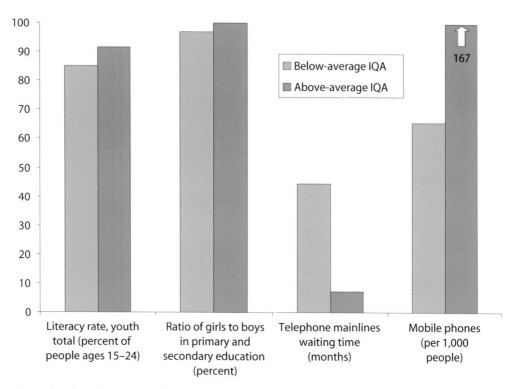

Notes: Figures show the simple averages for those countries with available data. Below- or above-average IQA is the average of countries scoring lower or higher than the overall MENA average on the index of quality of administration.
Source: Authors' calculations from World Bank data.

IQA are 10 percent more effective on performance orientation and 5 percent more effective on internal accountability within their budgetary systems, compared with those that have a below-average IQA.

The budgeting system may be a central mechanism for ensuring internal accountability, but it is only as effective as the civil service that administers it. Countries around the world face the problem of motivating civil servants to perform. So, the quality of the civil service, the degree to which it is managed to maximize performance, and the degree to which it respects an ethic of stewardship and public service will enhance or weaken the budgetary system. The problems are typically compounded when civil services are large. For MENA countries, the stereotypical civil service is overstaffed and undermanaged, a legacy of using government employment as a reward and as a solution to weak employment opportunities in the private sector—and of assuming wide-ranging responsibilities to deliver public services.

FIGURE 3.12

Performance Orientation and Internal Accountability Are Low

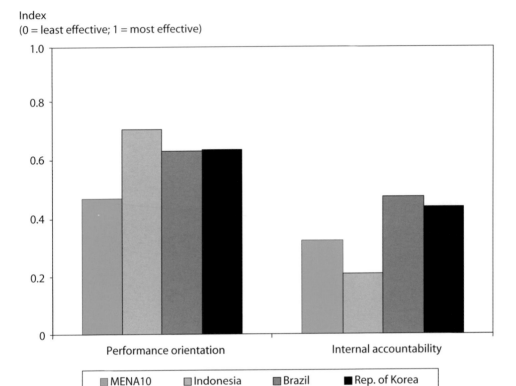

Note: For definitions, see box 3.4. MENA10 includes Algeria, the Arab Republic of Egypt, the Islamic Republic of Iran, Jordan, Kuwait, Lebanon, Morocco, the Republic of Yemen, Tunisia, and the United Arab Emirates.
Source: Authors' calculations from Esfahani 2000.

Strengthening the Link. Governments around the world have sought to strengthen internal accountability mechanisms, and the rich bureaucratic history in the MENA region shows it to be no different. Typically, however, efforts to strengthen accountability have focused on increasing levers of control, aiming to minimize poor behavior rather than reward good performance. But over the past 30 years, the art of performance-oriented budgeting—to strengthen internal accountability through the budget process—has been developed and tried in several countries, mostly in the Organisation for Economic Co-operation and Development (OECD). And many developing countries have introduced elements of such systems (box 3.5).

Performance-oriented budgeting builds on traditional mechanisms of accountability, including competent internal accounting and auditing departments, independent financial audit and oversight agencies, access to government information on budgets and bureaucratic performance, and strong (and public) parliamentary debate. But it takes these further by

BOX 3.5

The Move to Performance Budgeting

To improve the efficiency and stability of their budgets, countries around the world are implementing medium-term *performance budgeting*, which incorporates the notions of managing the budget according to given medium-term objectives, with a greater flexibility, an increased transparency, and a greater accountability for outcomes. Performance budgeting, at its core, infuses budget formulation and execution with more accountability (making budget managers responsible for the performance of their organizations), more transparency (tracking both the use of funds and their effects), and contestability (making subsequent budgets dependent on achieving results and tying managerial incentives to performance).

Elements of medium-term program-based budgeting were included in budget systems in OECD countries in the 1960s. Among the first to attempt this type of budgeting was the United States, with its Planning, Programming, and Budgeting System (PPBS). Back then, performance in budgeting—as it is known today—was still very much in the background. By the 1980s, however, performance in budgeting had come to the forefront. The most prominent examples, which explicitly brought together many components of what constitutes performance budgeting today, were the budget management systems of Australia and New Zealand.

In Australia in the early 1980s, budget reform was a response to an emerging fiscal crisis—and to perceived inadequacies in the links between policies, programs, and the resources allocated to their implementation. The budget reform had three parts: explicitly incorporating the existing medium-term framework of "forward estimates"; using a high-level committee—the Expenditure Review Committee—to manage the annual budget process; and introducing a "running costs" system for line managers, which gave them substantial autonomy and flexibility in managing their budgets. By the end of the 1980s, the deficit of 4 percent had been converted to a surplus of 2 percent. The government had significantly reoriented expenditure to reflect its core strategic priorities, and the incentives for efficient and effective use of resources had been considerably strengthened.

Among developing countries, some elements of a performance-based system were introduced in Malaysia as early as 1969. And several African countries have launched similar, if less well-advanced, programs (Ghana, South Africa, and Benin, among others). But the major changes came only with the introduction of total quality management in the late 1980s and early 1990s, which transformed the work and performance management culture in the public sector—and, in 1989, with the introduction of a performance budgeting system popularly known as the modified budgeting system. That system lets managers manage flexibly in producing mandated outputs and matches this flexibility and authority with greater accountability.

(Box continues on the following page.)

BOX 3.5 (continued)

As a result of this system, fiscal and financial discipline in Malaysia has improved, even compared with the tight, detailed control by the treasury and other central agencies that existed before the reform.

These innovations take several years to implement and should be considered part of a systemic process. Their implementation works best when policymakers search for synergies between budget reform and other institutional reforms in government (such as civil service management, decentralization, or devolution).

Governments also have to pay attention to the reform of complementary financial management institutions that are essential to the success of budget reforms. Such reforms include budget classification and accounting systems, transparent public procurement rules, capacity for internal and independent external audits, and capacity and transparency in monitoring and evaluation. Implementing these reforms requires new administrative capacities, but the nature of these reforms, which focus on increased accountability, also provide incentives to managers for building this capacity.

Sources: Rasappan 1999; Hofman 1998; World Bank 2003f.

---

focusing on obtaining value for money and on obtaining results, rather than focusing mostly on probity in spending money.

This wave of interest in more modern budget management techniques has not bypassed the MENA region, even if the experience is more recent and limited. Several Gulf countries—notably Bahrain and Qatar—are working on the design of a performance-oriented budget system. The Islamic Republic of Iran is in the middle of a multiyear budget reform program that aims to put in place the fundamental budget mechanisms needed for a performance-oriented system and to introduce a performance orientation in budget preparation and execution. Other governments—including those in the Arab Republic of Egypt, Jordan, and Morocco—have expressed interest in such systems, though all are in the early stages of conception and reform.

Irrespective of the quality of public budgeting, it is the actual expenditure of funds that ultimately determines the effectiveness of the budget programs—expenditures on both goods and services procured from outside government and civil service staff. One of the ways that governments in other regions have sought to increase efficiency and to reduce fraud in procurement is through the use of information technology—e-procurement. These systems help increase competitive bidding and transparency in the process, to lower transaction costs, and to save governments substantial sums (box 3.6).

BOX 3.6

Greater Accountability in Procurement

Public procurement is traditionally an area where lack of transparency, poor competition, and inefficient public processes are legend—around the world. In short, public procurement is a governance challenge.

Many governments have sought to strengthen governance in their procurement through the use of information and communication technologies. For example, both Chile and the Philippines began to pilot e-procurement systems in 1999–2000. In both cases, the electronic system posts public tenders online, automatically notifies all companies registered to bid on the specific goods or services, provides them instant access to relevant bidding information and documents from the agencies, and publicizes the results, including the winning bid, rationale, and amount of the award.

In the first year of operation, both systems posted impressive results in terms of increased transparency, lower transaction costs, better cooperation between government and the private sector, and less corruption. Both governments intend to extend the system to all public agencies. In Chile, the government expects to save as much as 5 percent annually in its procurement, which in MENA countries would translate into as much as 0.5 percent of GDP. The gains are the result of greater transparency and greater competition in the process governing public procurement.

Sources: Orrego, Osorio, and Mardones 2000; Granados and Masilungan 2001.

If performance-oriented budgeting provides a framework for better governance, the functioning of the civil service will determine how much of the potential "good governance dividend" (in better development outcomes) can be realized. One of the most difficult of all areas of public sector reform, improvement in civil service administration stands out as a key element in improving internal accountability mechanisms (box 3.7).

Several MENA countries are in the midst of major programs of civil service reform, even if progress is limited (as it is many countries worldwide). The programs in the Republic of Yemen, and to a lesser degree in Jordan, illustrate how such reforms aim to improve the accountability of the civil service by making recruitment more competitive, by linking promotion and grading to some assessment of performance, and by improving training opportunities.

In the mid-1990s, Morocco initiated a comprehensive review of its public administration, aiming to improve efficiency while also making its public wage bill more sustainable. The reform has focused on modifications of staffing profiles (redefining jobs, aligning recruitment and mak-

---

BOX 3.7

Public Administration Reform

Public administration reform aims to improve the efficiency of managing public resources. It is generally driven by a mix of economic imperatives (cost reduction) or human resource management (better service delivery). The shape of reform depends on the more pressing of these imperatives. In the developing world, the initial push toward administration reform measures was economic—in Africa in the 1980s and early 1990s, for example. In recent times, more effort has been placed on improving human resource management and improving service delivery. Malaysia, Botswana, and Singapore stand out as examples of making human resource management an integral part of reforms.

Experience in the MENA region (in Jordan, Morocco, the Republic of Yemen, Tunisia, and other members of the Gulf Cooperation Council) is widespread but remains in the early stages of implementation. Because the region's wage bill is the highest in the world, saving public funds should provide an important incentive for reform.

But the social nature of much public sector employment in the region puts a strong emphasis on human resource considerations. Thus, rather than focusing on downsizing, program design typically focuses on simplifying service procedures, introducing performance measures into personnel management, strengthening training and career planning, developing codes of conduct, and improving records management.

International experience indicates that the success of public administration reform depends very much on six factors:

• High-level political commitment to reforms

• A coherent long-term vision shared by civil servants

• Selectivity and phasing of reforms

• Measures to help those hurt by the reforms

• Stamina to carry out long-term reforms

• Technical capacity to implement the reforms.

Sources: Commonwealth Secretariat 2002; Schiavo-Campo and Sundaram 2000; World Bank staff.

---

ing it more transparent, and improving in-service training), management flexibility, staff mobility, performance-oriented evaluations and promotions, and simplification of pay systems. Despite the decade of reflection, most reforms remain to be designed and implemented, a process that may take another decade.

Reducing the size of the civil service may be necessary for fiscal reasons. That reduction could improve the overall working environment for those who remain. But reduction is unlikely, in itself, to improve performance unless part of a policy of making it easier to reduce the tenure of nonperforming civil servants.

An important complementary strategy to strengthening accountability is building a strong ethic of public service for the civil service. A peer-based value system that places a high premium on and that measures one's value to and respectability within the group—in terms of serving the public interest—can create strong incentives for civil servants to focus on delivering socially desired outcomes. This system not only reduces the cost of monitoring but also may be an indispensable adjunct to any sanctions-based system of performance management (which is a typical element of most civil service reforms).

To illustrate the power of a strong public service ethic, the state of Ceara in Brazil was faced with a very serious fiscal crisis in 1987 that led to a significant deterioration of services. To address this problem, the state government infused a sense of mission in some key programs and their workers. Publicity campaigns were launched, and awards and recognition were introduced for well-performing civil servants. The community was tapped to help push this effort. The result: dramatic improvements in the quality and coverage of the services throughout the state.

The Link Between Service Agencies and Client–Citizens

Internal government accountability systems, no matter how effectively designed and implemented, can never ensure adequate accountability because the people are excluded from that linkage. So, one of the most effective ways for policymakers to increase the accountability of service agencies is to rely more extensively on external accountability mechanisms, notably by empowering clients to demand better services. This philosophy follows from a key tenet of modern management theory: the customer is always right.[7] Successful organizations are the ones most attentive to what their clients want and need. Not only are citizens best able to judge the effectiveness of most public services—especially those in the economic and social domain—but also they are at the interface with the service agency and, thus, in an immediate position to assess.

Explaining the Link. Policymakers can empower clients by giving special weight to clients' views in monitoring and evaluating service agencies, by giving them a more direct role in managing the service provider, and by giving them wider choices among service agencies. For example, governments can survey citizens who use a public service to gauge their satisfaction. Governments can establish agency oversight or management committees that include users of the agency's services. They can also facilitate the emergence of competing agencies and can give vouchers to citizens allowing them to choose among those agencies.

Even when policymakers do not actively enlist citizens in ensuring agency accountability, citizens—individually, but more commonly through civil-society organizations—can take the initiative independently to lobby for better or different performance from a service agency.

Examining the Link in MENA. In MENA, the move toward stronger, more direct accountability of providers to their clients has only begun. That condition reflects the generally weak climate of overall public accountability in most countries in the region, the highly centralized governments based on a powerful executive branch, the tradition of central planning and a strong socialist ethic that government should provide for the people, and the limitations on more active civil-society organizations.[8] Governments have typically not sought to enlist citizens in ensuring better agency performance.

Even so, experimentation to strengthen the link between clients and providers has begun across a limited array of services and countries—with a limited array of techniques. The king of Jordan, disguised as a commoner to allow him to experience public services as Jordanian citizens do, is but one famous illustration. But many of these experiments have been initiated from the top, rather than from civil society, mainly because the latter's maneuvering room and capacity are more limited.

Accountability for public service delivery rests ultimately with the government—central or local—regardless of whether others are contracted to deliver services. Countries throughout the world have been decentralizing service delivery responsibilities to local governments in the past couple of decades in order to tighten the accountability link between government and citizens—and to deliver services that better reflect local needs and preferences. In MENA, this move toward decentralization has been slower than in most other regions. But efforts are under way to move service delivery closer to people through political decentralization (involving local elections) or deconcentration (empowering regional representatives of the central government, or "administrative decentralization"). With political decentralization, accountability shifts from the service provider–central government link to the service provider–local government–citizen link. In either case, service delivery can be improved if accountability is clear and based on performance.

Some central governments have made openings toward local elections, as in the Islamic Republic of Iran and Lebanon. Although still shy of decentralizing authority for key public services, several countries, such as Morocco, are moving toward greater administrative deconcentration, which puts the management of centrally controlled services closer to the clients. Greater administrative decentralization is also well under way in the Republic of Yemen. Some municipal governments have been given additional latitude to improve the delivery of some public services.

Client feedback surveys are rare, although some countries in MENA have begun to experiment with them, including Jordan, Morocco, the Republic of Yemen, and the West Bank and Gaza. Regardless of the complex set of intergovernmental relations that determine the precise nature of decentralization or deconcentration, client feedback surveys have enough scope to improve accountability among governments, service providers, and citizens—and the quality of service delivery.

Most countries in the region have launched e-government initiatives, which are designed primarily to improve the interface between the government as a service provider and the citizen as a client. Those countries have the highest rates of Internet subsidy in the world and fairly high scores on global indexes of e-government efforts. But as one translates those initiatives into better service delivery, two key ingredients seem to be missing: Little attention has been paid to client services, and government transparency is generally weak. The region seems caught in a low-level equilibrium. Without action to improve the overall governance environment, it is unlikely that e-government, as a technological tool, will live up to its potential to further improve accountability, despite subsidies.

Strengthening the Link. More governments in the developing world are attempting to solve the accountability problem in service delivery by relying more extensively on external mechanisms for the links between client–citizens and service providers. New forms of interaction establish a more direct and stronger accountability link between the two. These new forms can be classified into three categories:

- More regular, reliable, and cost-effective information flows.

- Increased competition in service provision to give clients more choice.

- Increased involvement of citizens directly in the management of public service delivery systems, say, through participatory processes.

IMPROVING THE FLOW OF INFORMATION. First, the flow of information between citizens and policymakers will enable citizens to articulate their needs and concerns so that service agencies can better respond to them. The past decade has seen the flowering of innovative approaches to generate information that agencies need to improve their service—or that policymakers need to enhance their oversight of agencies.

The main tool has been surveys, which can be categorized as report card or citizen-based surveys, surveys of business enterprises, or public expenditure tracking surveys. Report cards enable citizens to rate the quality of services received, thus enabling providers to elicit regular feedback from the users of their service (listening to their "voice"). Such surveys provide a fairly independent and inexpensive way to monitor the general effect of the services they offer. They have been used effectively in a number of countries worldwide (box 3.8).[9]

A key lesson from client surveys is that they function best when there is (1) high-level commitment by government officials to act on the surveys and (2) widespread publicity of results. They rarely solve the service problems, but by objectively highlighting problems from the client's perspective, they open the door to dialogue. And by shining a public spotlight on agency performance (often relative to other agencies), they increase the incentives for agency managers to act. In Latvia, the local housing authority received a favorable rating of roughly 10 percent, compared with the 30 percent favorable rating of the social benefits office. Both ratings were poor, but the local housing authority should have been particularly embarrassed.

Enterprise surveys target the business community and generally attempt to obtain the community's assessment of the general business environment and to identify barriers to investment and operations. Perhaps the most extensive use of this tool has been in the Eastern and Central European region. There, a comprehensive multicountry survey (the Business Environment and Enterprise Performance Survey) helped identify major governance impediments to private sector development—such as bribery and inefficiency in customs and in tax administration, inefficiencies in regulation and infrastructure, and corruption in the judi-

---

BOX 3.8

Citizen Surveys in Bangalore

In 1994, a civil-society group introduced report cards that rated user experiences with public services in Bangalore, Karnataka, a city that had failed to address low-quality and corrupt services. Widely publicized by an active press, the report cards gradually opened a dialogue between service agencies and user groups that eventually led to deeper monitoring and corrective measures by the city. By 1999, the quality of some services had improved substantially. The process is being replicated in other Indian cities, as well as in other countries as diverse as the Philippines, Ukraine, and Vietnam.

Sources: World Bank 2003h.

BOX 3.9

Public Expenditure Tracking Surveys

In 1996, the Ministry of Finance in Uganda launched a public expenditure tracking survey to monitor the flow of budgeted per-student capitation grants from the central education ministry budget to primary schools. Through the survey, the ministry discovered that, in 1994, school districts got less than 20 percent of the nonwage budget that had been allocated to them for primary education. Most of the leaked funds were embezzled or used for purposes unrelated to education. The government began publishing in local newspapers and on the radio the monthly budget transfers to school districts. School administrations were required to post notices on all inflows of funds actually received. Within five years, the share of grants actually received had risen to 80 percent, with the greatest increase in school districts with the best access to newspapers.

True, the improvement coincided with a massive government commitment to primary education and a large increase in overall public funding. But the power of public information is evident. The campaign worked because the information enabled high-level government officials to know when and where lower-level bureaucrats were shirking responsibility or engaging in malfeasance. Similar surveys have been launched in several other countries in Africa.

Source: World Bank 2003h.

---

ciary.[10] Those surveys can be fine-tuned for a particular country so that more focused problem areas can be identified.

Surveys provide clients only with an opportunity to furnish information. The initiative for action remains with the government agency. But when the surveys are published and when the information fuels public debate, governments often have little choice but to act on the information. And outcomes can improve tremendously, as they did following the public expenditure tracking surveys in Uganda (box 3.9).

Surveys give voice to citizens, but responsibility for initiating the surveys and for acting on their results remains with the government. One way of enhancing the flow of information about public services, while monitoring citizen feedback, is the wider use of e-government. This electronic approach is especially useful when government agencies provide regulatory or licensing services to citizens, such as registering vital statistics and issuing permits and approvals. E-government helps reduce corruption (by reducing the discretionary role of bureaucrats and by increasing the transparency of the transactions), speeds up the services, and generally enables the agency to become more responsive (box 3.10).

BOX 3.10

Promoting VOICE in India—Online Delivery of Municipal Services

In Vijaywada, a city of 1 million in Andhra Pradesh, India, citizens (70 percent of whom were literate) were facing many difficulties in dealing with the municipal government. Obtaining a building permit or death and birth certificates required several trips to municipal government offices. The issuance of certificates often was delayed, with the intent to extract a bribe. But complaints about poor services could not be filed easily, and officers were inaccessible.

Things changed after the federal, state, and municipal governments collaborated to set up the Vijaywada Online Information Centers (VOICE) in 1998–99. Citizens can now go to any of the five Internet-enabled kiosks that have been set up in different parts of the city and get public services or information—or they can file grievances against public officials. Those who have a private Internet connection can also connect to the Web server and retrieve information.

There have been tangible benefits to the citizens and to the municipal government. Corruption has been reduced. Services are quicker. And the municipality has become more responsive. In just under a year, the system issued 15,000 birth and death certificates, 2,100 building approvals, and 224,000 demand notices for taxes. Nearly 7,700 grievances were registered, of which 97 percent were resolved. Nearly 700 suggestions have been sent in by citizens.

The commissioner can view these statistics by ward and department, making monitoring more effective. All internal processing of applications is now screen-based, generating greater efficiency. For example, the rent calculation for billboards is automatic and transparent. The system tracks advertising agencies that have not renewed contracts, and those with outstanding debts are sent timely notices.

Source: Kumar and Bhatnagar 2001.

PROVIDING GREATER CHOICE AND COMPETITION. Second, the accountability of providers to clients can be enhanced through competition by giving the clients the power to choose the best among alternative service agencies. As in markets, greater competition generally leads to better outcomes—lower costs and better quality. In Lebanon, public hospitals were shunned for many years by the majority of the population, who preferred the better-equipped private clinics. This trend caused the Lebanese government in recent years to invest more in bringing public health care up to private hospital standards.

In education and health, several governments have experimented with innovative ways of generating competition among service providers, even when the service remains funded by the government. One wide-spread experiment is a voucher system. In this arrangement, the government gives eligible clients vouchers, which they can then use to obtain a particular service from any accredited provider—public or private. Providers redeem the vouchers for cash. Through this system, users of a service are given the opportunity to choose among several providers, and the revenue of providers depends in part on how many vouchers they earn. Therefore, a form of competition is infused among the providers. In Colombia, a voucher program targeted to poor families increased the supply of secondary education and, thus, the competition among providers (box 3.11).

Often governments do not finance a public service—they simply regulate its provision because of various market failures or public interest

---

BOX 3.11

Colombia's Targeted Voucher Program for Secondary Education

Voucher programs can increase the supply of education by enticing nontraditional providers to cater to—and compete for—the "business" of the poor. In Colombia, the government established a targeted voucher program for secondary school students. Every year, vouchers were awarded to students through a lottery. A winner could use his or her voucher to attend any of the private schools participating in the program, about 50 percent of the private schools in the targeted areas. The participating schools were predominantly of average quality and charged low fees. Voucher recipients at those schools typically came from the poorest students in the community.

The program has significantly improved outcomes. Voucher recipients now complete more years of schooling than those who did not win vouchers and are less likely to repeat grades. They are 13–15 percentage points more likely than those without vouchers to finish the eighth grade, primarily because of reduced repetition. This achievement translates into a 25 percent increase in secondary school completion rates.

This type of targeted voucher scheme can be a cost-effective way to increase educational attainment and achievement in countries that have a weak public school system and a well-developed private education sector. The program can improve outcomes by enabling lottery winners to attend private schools (which may be better than public schools) and by giving stronger incentives for voucher recipients to devote more effort to school (because failing a grade disqualifies them from keeping the voucher). In Colombia's program, this incentive reduced work outside school, lowered repetition, and raised attainment and achievement.

Source: Patrinos 2002.

concerns, such as minimizing abuses in natural monopolies (utility companies) or maximizing economies of scale. In such cases, good economic regulation should maximize the overall benefits and gains to society, while protecting consumers from potential abuses from monopolists and protecting investors from political influence and interference. Good regulation has three key precepts:

- Independence from the operator and sector policy setter.

- Accountability through transparent decisionmaking, clear rules and procedures, and consumer and investor participation in decisionmaking and monitoring.

- Autonomy in financing, sanction power, and staff selection.

In MENA, more often than not, infrastructure services—for power, water, telecommunications, and transport—are publicly owned monopolies whose accountability to consumers is small and whose performance is inadequately regulated and monitored by independent public agencies. Investment climate assessments in the region show service to be poor. Businesses report long delays in establishing connections for power, water, and telecommunications. The quality is often also poor with low coverage, and brownouts are common in the power sector. Offsetting these problems in many MENA countries are uneconomic tariffs that encourage wasteful consumption and do not provide for investment resources. Moreover, many MENA infrastructure providers are inefficient users of scarce capital and labor resources. Urban water utilities typically account for only half the water provided, and electricity distribution losses are typically about 15 percent.

Expanding choice in this context typically means allowing multiple providers of a service to compete with the state-owned company—within a regulated environment that allows competition while protecting public interest. Good regulation is a key in ensuring optimal economic efficiency in the infrastructure sector.

In MENA, there are examples of emerging regulators. The Moroccan telecommunications regulator was one of the earliest and most effective. In 2002, the International Telecommunication Union observed that "it was North Africa's most independent regulator, which inspired confidence in investors." In Jordan, strong regulators are emerging in all the main infrastructure sectors, with the telecommunications regulator the most advanced. Most MENA countries have a telecommunications regulator, and about half have a power sector regulator. The key challenges for virtually every MENA regulator are to establish independence, autonomy, and accountability.

ACHIEVING MORE DIRECT CLIENT PARTICIPATION IN PUBLIC SERVICE DE-LIVERY. A third means to improve the accountability link between service providers and citizens is to decentralize the delivery of public goods—especially when quality depends on adapting the service to specific client needs and relying on immediate, localized monitoring, as is the case with primary health and schooling. Locally elected officials should have more and better information about the needs of their communities and, thus, should be in a better position to shape services in ways that better match those needs. And citizens are more likely to be able to hold them accountable through both electoral and other accountability mechanisms, including tribal or kinship relationships. The dreadful experience of China with SARS (severe acute respiratory syndrome) in its early stages highlights the significance and necessity of bringing decisionmaking authority and accountability down to the local level (box 3.12).

Communities are better organized and prepared to take on responsibilities for the management of some services. In the small village of Ait Iktel in the High Atlas Mountains of Morocco, a community-based organization was established to promote the development needs of the village. Over the span of a few years, the villagers built a water well, constructed a school and literacy center, bought an ambulance, and installed electricity. Villagers contribute to the projects financially and in kind, creating a "village work" bank for every family to contribute five labor days a year. The Community-Managed School Program (EDUCO) in El Salvador is a good example of parent participation in managing primary school programs (box 3.13).

Some local governments have taken the involvement of citizen–clients further, by involving them directly in the process of setting budgetary priorities and of preparing and implementing programs funded through the local budget. Among the best known are the participatory budgeting processes developed over the past decade in Latin America, especially in Pôrto Alegre, Brazil (box 3.14).

The Link Between Citizens and Politicians

The link between citizens and politicians is fundamentally an issue of public participation to ensure external accountability in the governance process. Participation in this context consists of the range of activities through which citizens seek to influence government actions, either directly by affecting the formulation and implementation of public policy, or indirectly by affecting the selection of public officials (McClosky 1968, p. 252; Burns, Schlozman, and Verba 2001).

BOX 3.12

China and SARS—the Need for External Accountability for Complex Public Services

In the first half of 2003, China's terrible experience with the epidemic spread of SARS (severe acute respiratory syndrome) reinforced the movement there for political change.

Against the backdrop of more than 5,000 people infected with SARS, indications were that, for the first time, there would be political competition for local legislatures, with more than one candidate being allowed to compete. Meanwhile, the head of the emergency ward of a major hospital in Qingshu, 270 miles southwest of Beijing, was told by reporters that the cabinet had issued regulations mandating the treatment of all SARS patients. His reaction was that the hospital already had set procedures for when and how to prescribe medicine.

The link? The internal accountability mechanisms in China were insufficient, in the initial months, to arrest the spread of SARS. In a country with little external accountability and client feedback, officials had little information about the disease and how to control it.

For example, the propaganda ministry issued circulars that banned the circulation of reports about how to handle the disease because the reports were perceived as being "sensitive." And mid-level officials responded to the crisis by providing only the sort of information that they felt their superiors wanted to hear.

There is some hope that the government will establish a better-developed system of external accountability through directly elected officials, to improve the reliable transmission of information about complex and fast-changing situations. Giving the people the right to choose among local officials is also intended to improve officials' performance and responsiveness to the citizens they serve.

Sources: Adapted from Pomfret 2003a and 2003b.

Explaining the Link. An important dimension of such participation is political—reflecting the core definition of governance. Citizens have a choice in choosing their leaders and the policies they implement. Or viewed in the governance framework, they have a choice in forcing policymakers to compete for citizen approval. In democracies, the leverage from contestability relies on regular elections and thus from the threat of unseating incumbent presidents, parliamentarians, or council members who pay too little attention to the quality and reach of public services.

Elections may be the premier participation instrument for exacting accountability from the government. But they are also blunt accountability instruments, because they can be manipulated both legally and il-

---

BOX 3.13

Community Management of Schools—the EDUCO Program in El Salvador

During the decade-long civil war in El Salvador, many poor communities established informal community schools. With the termination of hostilities, the government decided to build a formal community primary school program for poorer municipalities. The program was dubbed EDUCO, which translates into "education through community participation."

Under this program, poor communities were required to establish an elected council of parents. This council, governed by an elected committee of five members, was given the responsibility for procuring classroom space, implementing the curriculum determined by the ministry of education, and maintaining schools and equipment, including hiring, firing, and monitoring teachers. The government provides regular budgetary support to councils, but, in exchange, parents are expected to contribute time, meals, and labor for school improvements.

The program increased coverage of education in rural areas. Before EDUCO, only 2 percent of rural children attended school. After its introduction, enrollment rose to 10 percent, with preschool enrollment (ages 4–6) up as much as 22 percent. According to test results for third graders, EDUCO students performed just as well as their counterparts in traditional schools. Because EDUCO caters to the poorer communities, the program has been considered a success because EDUCO students are greatly disadvantaged.

Source: Jimenez and Sawada 2000.

---

legally, as is often the case in both MENA countries and the rest of the world (Keefer 2003; Keefer and Khemani 2003). If elections are merely ceremonial or predetermined, they cannot hold leaders accountable. And public service issues are seldom central issues in political campaigns. In the Philippines, popularity, rather than bad roads, has become the driving force behind elections (De Dios and Hutchcroft 2002). Many members of parliament in Jordan are considered mainly as intermediaries to the government; they help constituents obtain jobs, contracts, development projects, and other resources (background, Khouri 2003, p. 6). Even good elections may not adequately reflect the public interest if there is insufficient or unreliable information on candidate views and actions. Effective competition depends on good information and, thus, on public transparency.

So the process of participating in governance—of holding politicians accountable—is much broader than elections. That process involves the many mechanisms, formal and otherwise, through which citizens put pressure on policymakers. Often, consultative mechanisms bring policy-

---

BOX 3.14

Participatory Budgeting in Pôrto Alegre, Brazil

In 1989, the citizens of the municipality of Pôrto Alegre, Brazil (population 1.2 million)—which was prosperous but had severe fiscal and governance problems—elected the populist workers party. The new government began to foster citizen groups to organize an annual process of participatory budgeting, which would deal with the harsh reality of a very limited budget and difficult choices available to improve the quality and coverage of services.

During the first year, participation was extremely low, and the few hundred citizens who took part in the process were skeptical. A decade later, nearly 100,000 citizens participated directly in the budgeting process through neighborhood and citywide meetings and forums.

One of the reasons for success is that the municipal government started a process of institutional learning, taking into account lessons from practice and comments from the public in redefining the participatory process. In addition, the municipality assisted the citizen movement in introducing technical viability to the participatory process—essentially a process of civic education in local governance.

Because the participatory budgeting approach of the Pôrto Allegre municipality is entirely outside the formal representative structures of government, it has created a citizen-led counterweight to formal structures of governance. Participatory budgeting made it possible for local governance to work.

Source: World Bank staff.

---

makers and citizens together: town hall meetings in the West Bank and Gaza are one example; congressional hearings in the United States are another. Citizen watchdog and advocacy groups, as well as independent analysts and journalists, intermediate between citizens and policymakers by feeding the public debate on the performance of policymakers. The surveys and advocacy by the Palestinian Center for Policy and Survey Research were widely disseminated to raise the awareness of Palestinian policymakers about the opinions of citizens on government performance. The tactic of "naming and shaming" public officials who betray public trust can be a powerful accountability tool.

Many of the mechanisms for strengthening the participation of citizens in holding service agencies accountable also strengthen citizens' ability to hold policymakers accountable. It is often at the micro level—at the interface of service agencies and clients—that issues coalesce and citizen groups gather strength, thereby forming the basis for dialogues with policymakers.

Participation has more than instrumental value. It is a right in itself. Even if internal accountability and effective interaction between clients and service agencies could ensure good service delivery, broad citizen participation in the political process of choosing leaders and defining policies would have merit. Why? Because only the right of open public participation by citizens can create and sustain an overall governance environment that enshrines inclusion and accountability, which are characterized by greater public transparency and competition in the political sphere. And only in such an environment will citizens be empowered to demand better services and will service agencies feel fully accountable for delivering them.

The importance of political participation rests on its role as an indispensable element of accountability. But its role in creating the climate of accountability may be even more compelling.

Examining the Link in MENA. In the MENA region, as demonstrated in chapter 1, public accountability mechanisms stand out for their weakness relative to the rest of the world. Competitive elections, when they occur, are rare and not usually meaningful, whether for national leaders or for legislatures. Lebanon and Algeria are the only two countries in the region that have seen a change in national leaders through competitive elections.

Citizens can also hold the executive accountable through elected parliamentary representatives. National parliaments exist in most MENA countries, with the authority to propose and enact legislation and to exercise fiscal oversight over the executive. But the concentrated power of the executive branch in MENA (described in chapter 1) constrains the ability of elected parliaments to exert accountability on behalf of citizens. Still, some parliaments in MENA have sought to raise citizens' awareness of the importance of enhancing transparency and of fighting corruption.

Irrespective of elections, the relative secrecy within administrations, the lack of information disclosure, and the restrictions on the media have limited an informed public debate about the role of government, accountability, and service delivery. However measured, the formal political channels for citizens to express preferences and to demand accountability for public services remain underdeveloped in all MENA countries.

Despite these constraints, there are some efforts by civil-society organizations in MENA to increase the information available to inform citizen opinion. In Lebanon, several civil-society groups are helping promote transparency by empowering citizens with information and booklets on administrative procedures for using services. In the Arab Republic of Egypt, civil-society organizations are helping women obtain birth certificates and identity cards by informing them of the numerous procedures involved in registration. In the Islamic Republic of Iran, where the interior ministry publishes detailed reports of election results, private and government research institutions routinely engage in postvote poll taking and in analysis of voters' preferences between the elections.

The same groups can also apply pressure on government and can influence decisionmakers. For example, Moroccan civil-society groups, particularly women's organizations, have advocated for years the need to reform the personal status code. Through their efforts, a royal commission was established in 2002 to review personal status laws. A concerted campaign by organizations in Morocco targeting parliamentarians brought about a new association law that was deemed more favorable, but not ideal, by civil society.

Despite restrictions on media freedom, the media in many MENA countries are monitoring the performance of politicians and informing citizens of corruption in the public sector. In the Islamic Republic of Iran, "newspapers and magazines ... have been instrumental in bringing into the open improprieties, ... and [revealing] information about the abuses of the system" (background, Farhi 2003, p. 27).

In addition, a variety of informal feedback mechanisms exist, including the tradition of consultation within some communities. Where the overall governance environment is good, those informal mechanisms are an important adjunct to formal mechanisms. And by providing detailed information to politicians and policymakers, they can reinforce messages delivered through elections.

But where the overall governance environment is weak, those informal channels are less likely to be a systematic and reliable means for transmitting information from the public to the politicians and service providers. And their effect is likely to be limited—such as lobbying by interest groups, tribal constituencies, or a civil-society organization (box 3.15). They may get particular service delivered adequately to some groups (for example, a clan or tribe) but poorly to the rest of the population, thus leaving service delivery as a whole mediocre. Although rarer, the occurrence of public demonstrations—which occasionally degenerate into violence, as in Algeria's Kabyle region in 2001—also provide feedback to the government about discontent with public services, and those demonstrations may sometimes lead to improvements (Layachi 2001).

Strengthening the Link. Improving participation and accountability in the political process requires action by both the government and the people. The government has to accept the right of the people to wider, deeper participation and has to help set up mechanisms for that to occur. Such mechanisms include electoral processes for representatives, as well as for expressing preferences for alternative public proposals. There must also be other channels of consultation and feedback, such as surveys. Those

---

BOX 3.15

Tribal Governance in Jordan—Then and Now

A rich historical legacy in Jordan is the wellspring of value systems that define most aspects of personal life and public decisionmaking—primarily collective or communal identities such as family, clan, and tribe; religious or ethnic groups; or common racial, cultural, or even geographic attributes. They are referred to broadly as "tribal" values, because the tribe is the most important, widest spread, and oldest of the various collective identities.

Such tribal identities met most people's real needs for security and well-being for generation after generation. They came to define how society worked, at both local and national levels. They were thus the governance system. They regulated the exercise of power. They ensured the rights of individuals. They defined relationships among different groups in society, simultaneously enforcing, in their own way, values now called participation, accountability, predictability, justice, the rule of law, and transparency.

Tribalism endures as the predominant Jordanian cultural value mainly because of its continuing efficacy. Tribal values, obligations, and relationships still provide Jordanians with a vital combination of practical and intangible elements that they cannot yet obtain elsewhere through any other single system.

The modern state, the monarchy, the private sector, religion, civil-society organizations, and other structures offer some of these elements. But none matches the capacity of tribalism to offer them all consistently, reliably, and generation after generation.

Linkages of blood, culture, ethnicity, religion, and neighborliness always come first, because they provide the security that has been the most basic need of human beings throughout time. These communal identities remain the primary driving forces of decisionmaking at the level of the individual, the community, and the state. The monarchy and reforms for modernity both operate on top of this foundation of communal and collective identity.

Source: Khouri 2003, background paper for this book.

---

mechanisms also include channels of direct participation, such as users' associations, parent councils, and citizen advisory or oversight committees. Many of these mechanisms have been discussed and illustrated in previous sections, and, as noted above, some countries in MENA have already begun to put some of them in place.

The responsibility of the people is to participate in such mechanisms or to demand that they be put in place where they do not yet exist. Citizen participation typically transits through, or depends on, civil-society organizations, which can help process information to inform citizens better.

Those organizations can aggregate and transmit citizen concerns to relevant government agencies. They also can both empower citizens and act on their behalf. A key step in strengthening the external accountability link is, thus, to create an environment that recognizes the value of civil-society organizations in the conduct of governance, that creates space for them to function, and that integrates them more readily into governing processes. Earlier sections have illustrated what role such organizations can play and how governments can work with them more effectively. Not illustrated, but highly important, are the actions that governments need to take to encourage the development of civil-society organizations.

The media are another vehicle for enhancing participation and accountability, which they do by distilling and digesting information from and on government, by offering a forum for more active public debate on policy, and by engaging in investigations to increase transparency and to demand accountability. Creating strong, responsible media is certainly a question of training and capacity. But of first-order importance is having a climate of media freedom and public expression, without which capacity has little value.

Challenges for the Future

Despite reasonably acceptable performance in some areas, public service delivery in MENA countries has generally been handicapped by poor accountability links. Global experience shows that better performance can be attained by strengthening internal accountability arrangements and by introducing a variety of stronger external accountability mechanisms—with action at both the micro and the macro levels.

Strengthening internal accountability arrangements within government means having procurement and contracting rules and systems that are transparent and that promote competition, predictable financial flows to service providers, stronger monitoring of actual agency performance, budget and personnel management policies that give more weight to performance, and independent audits of agency budgets, thereby imposing sanctions for wrongdoing. Progress in this process will require more attention to the ethic of integrity and service to the public within government, especially where services are delivered by public agencies.

Strengthening external accountability means having clients participate more directly in the delivery of public services—from providing feedback to policymakers, to actively participating in management of the delivery mechanism. The scope for innovation in the region is wide—regularly using client surveys, promoting competition among providers to give citizens a wider choice, enlisting or allowing clients to monitor actual performance, decentralizing to local governments, and trying other means to encourage users to participate in implementation.

The link between citizen–clients and politician–policymakers is perhaps the most difficult link to address in the MENA region. It touches directly on political accountability. It inevitably involves greater competition for politicians through greater transparency in government, through more (and more unfettered) public dialogue and debate, and through regular elections that are openly competitive.

Notes

1. In addition, Algeria and Tunisia had by then begun opening the market to competition.

2. In many countries, this investment targets basic education. In Jordan, for instance, 80 percent of total education spending goes toward basic education (World Bank 1999b).

3. One measure of the performance of a country's health system, an outcome, is the disability-adjusted life expectancy. When this rate is compared to a country's total spending on health, it is possible to estimate a (relative) efficiency index, which measures the extent to which spending has achieved its potential maximum. See WHO 2000.

4. This framework is adapted from that in World Bank 2003h.

5. This link is also associated with income levels; richer countries tend to have both better governance and better performance indicators for service delivery. Causality in a strict sense is difficult to determine. In fact, governance, income, and service performance are all interlinked, but good governance is one powerful intermediation channel: good governance helps translate the potential from higher income into better service performance, and good governance helps ensure that the results of good service performance are translated into higher growth.

6. For a description of the IQA, see chapter 1.

7. Note that in the case of regulation or any service involving the compliance of citizens, such as tax collection, the customer need not always be right, because in such cases the incentive of an individual is not to comply.

8. This point is made strongly in UNDP 2002a.

9. For example, Bangladesh, Bolivia, Cambodia, Ghana, India (Karnataka, Andhra Pradesh), and Latvia.

10. These surveys were supported by the World Bank in cooperation with the European Bank for Reconstruction and Development. See World Bank 2002g.

CHAPTER 4

Pathways to Better Governance

For the MENA region to gain from globalization and to keep up with strong demographic pressures, its public administration needs to create the best possible environment for investment and growth and to deliver the best possible public services—on par with the better-performing countries in the world. What those countries have done to strengthen their business and growth environments and their public service delivery should point the way to reforms for countries in the MENA region, as some have already recognized.

The Urgency for Action—Development and Governance Gaps

Population growth in MENA countries creates two pressures for social services. First, for any service, such growth will increase the number of places where the service needs to be provided—that is, the number of delivery nodes. Second, to the extent that it induces migration to the cities (as in other countries), such growth will likely increase the heterogeneity of the client base. Both will increase the complexity of public service delivery and will stretch the already thin monitoring and accountability systems. So, the governance of public service delivery will become more demanding and more difficult—and thus more complex.

But the gap is not just about growth and social services. Because of the gap in economic opportunities, there is also an aspirations gap, which reflects burgeoning young populations in the MENA region and the inevitable comparisons with other countries, comparisons made possible by the global revolution in information flows. The governance gap, both in the quality of public administration and in public accountabilities, has weakened the environment for efficient, productive private investment. And government-led growth efforts have been unable to compensate—as is the case worldwide. Just as the governance gap has weakened the provision of public services that private entrepreneurs need, so has the growth gap reduced the capacity of MENA governments to provide the public services that people expect.

People in the region are demanding more from their governments in terms of economic opportunities and the jobs they create; in quality of public services; and more broadly in equality, freedom, and participation. People are, in short, demanding development. Their demand for faster growth and more jobs, for better services (both social and regulatory), and for better governance will undoubtedly rise as the pace of globalization picks up.

The thesis of this book is that these gaps in economic and social development and in aspirations are—to a substantial degree—the unfortunate manifestations of an enduring gap in the quality of governance between the countries in this region and the better-performing countries elsewhere in the world. Weak governance only perpetuates the development gap.

The economic and social challenges that the region faces can be viewed, then, as largely a governance challenge—even if better governance is not the only change needed to improve economic and social performance in the MENA region. The governance challenge is to strengthen the incentives, mechanisms, and capacities for more accountable and inclusive public institutions and to expand the notions of equality and participation throughout society. Those good governance mechanisms, which are recognized worldwide, are first steps in a process of improving economic policies that themselves are instruments for improving the climate and incentives for efficient growth (Rodrick 1999; World Bank 1997, 2002i). And they are the foundation of human rights and dignity—the goal of human development.

So, the governance challenge is not one of prescribing economic or social policies, important as they are. Instead, it is to ensure that the process for conceiving, debating, designing, adopting, and implementing such policies is one in which all the people—as both citizens and clients—have an opportunity to express their preferences, to participate in the dialogue, to choose their representatives to act on their behalf, and to hold the government accountable for acting in their best interest. Good governance cannot itself guarantee a particular set of "good" policies and leaders. But it is a sine qua non for minimizing the persistence of disappointing outcomes and ineffective policies and leaders—and for moving toward better ones.

Overcoming the Governance Gap

Riches from hydrocarbons, instabilities caused by conflict or the threat of it, and interference stemming from geopolitical interests have handicapped the emergence of institutions of good governance in the MENA region. Worse, they have reinforced behaviors and governing arrangements that defy accountability and that put people at the mercy of government. Rising to the challenge of good governance will mean turning those handicaps into opportunities, as well as acting through a wide array of entry points that can eventually lead to better governance and, with it, better economic, social, and human performance.

Rising to the challenge of better governance is not solely, or even mainly, the responsibility of governments—because many in government (as well as many outside government) may resist the move to be more inclusive and more accountable. Although it inevitably requires actions by governments, better governance necessarily also requires more proactive participation by the people. The governance challenge is, thus, a challenge for everyone in the region.

Governments and organizations outside the region also have a role in helping the MENA countries meet their governance challenge. Many of those external partners are themselves vigorous proponents of governance reforms, but they may not always align their actions with the objective of strengthening governance in the region. Sometimes, they choose the maintenance of "stability" (in the guise of supporting a given regime) over the promotion of better governance.

If they are to create the right environment for progress on governance reforms, the region's external partners will need to commit themselves to act in specific ways. They should avoid countenancing bad governance institutions and behaviors—tolerance that may, for example, be manifested in self-interested aid or may result from particular alliances. They also need to continue to work for a peaceful and equitable settlement to the Arab–Israeli conflict, which has diverted the attention and resources of the region from building better governance.

In some cases, the prospects of a deeper voluntary economic association with some industrial countries and organizations, such as the European Union, may reinforce a dynamic within a MENA country to improve governance. Such agreements themselves can provide a lock-in device to help shore up the credibility of new governance institutions. And outside partners can reinforce efforts to enhance human and institutional capacity within the region—both to monitor and to debate governance issues and to build staff capability in institutions that underpin good governance (such as supreme audit organizations, which are within governments, and the media and citizen watchdog groups, which are outside governments).

Meeting the challenge is no simple matter, either technically or institutionally. Poor governance reflects the failure of institutions; yet the creation of better institutions itself requires the development of other institutions. One of the most important institutions is that of "tolerance—the willingness of individuals to accept disparate political views and social attitudes; sometimes to accept the profoundly important idea that there is no right answer," as well as an "attachment to the institutions which constitute civil society" (Norton 1993, p. 211, and Shils 1991, p. 4, as cited in Kazemi 2002).

To illustrate the conundrums in the transition, many of the institutions designed to ensure better representation of the people—in the face of tradition and other institutions that limit inclusion—themselves contain the seeds of poor governance. For example, representation of Copts in the parliament of the Arab Republic of Egypt is ensured in part by nomination and in part by election. In Morocco, a set number of parliamentary seats is reserved for women. In Bahrain, when none of the women candidates won seats in parliament, the emir created additional seats and appointed women to them. None of those actions is the hallmark of contestable accountability to the people, but all help achieve it.

Nurturing an attachment to the participatory institutions that constitute good governance requires time and tolerance. Time is needed to accumulate experience demonstrating that such institutions can function credibly and fairly. And the constant danger exists that the inability of fledgling participatory institutions to represent the people effectively against existing authoritarian institutions—that "the very public confrontation between democratically elected institutions and nonelective ones, duly reported by the fledgling and yet still vibrant print media"— will "highlight how and by whom democratic processes are being thwarted. The subsequent inability of democratically elected institutions to overcome the opposition [to them] and the ineffectiveness of democratic institutions in challenging those [constitutional] improprieties [of nonelected officials, risks] furthering the cynicism of the majority of the populace who voted the reformists into office" (background paper, Farhi 2003, p. 19). Cynicism itself is an enemy of effective participatory governance. These tensions reflect the fact that building governance is a two-way street: opening the governance arena without already having capable institutions can lead to chaos; capable institutions themselves need such an opening—as well as stability—to emerge and to thrive.

But what should MENA countries do while those institutions of participation gain capacity and respect? Among other things, countries (their people and their governments) need to tolerate and promote continual open dialogue (which will encourage and protect the emerging participatory institutions) and to avoid scrapping the institutions if they yield outcomes that some people do not like. This tolerance may mean accepting second-best solutions, such as an agreement of major groups to share power in order to minimize risks of instability or even civil strife, as in Lebanon with its consociational democracy (Salem 2003). The transition is, by its nature, uncharted. And it will vary by country. But a clear vision of what good governance means can be a powerful navigational tool.

As an example of governance reform, Latin America illustrates the varied paths to increasing participation through decentralization. In Argentina, Brazil, Ecuador, Peru, and the República Bolivariana de Venezuela, political decentralization, together with the transfer of resources or fiscal autonomy, preceded the strengthening of local responsibilities. This sequence of events led to economic and political crises in some of them. Chile, by contrast, focused on administrative delegation (or deconcentration) first, perhaps putting the country in a better position to achieve successful political devolution (World Bank 2003h, box 10.4).

The analytical and empirical backbone supporting the discussion of governance in this book helps define pathways for improving the process of governance. These pathways can be defined in terms of those that promote inclusiveness in governance and those that promote stronger accountability. The latter can be further grouped into internal accountability mechanisms—roughly parallel to the index of the quality of administration in the public sector—and external accountability mechanisms—roughly parallel to the index of public accountability (figure 4.1). The first is the initiative of governments, with impetus and pressure from the people; the second is the initiative of the people, with acceptance and accommodation by governments.

FIGURE 4.1

Multiple Channels of Accountability

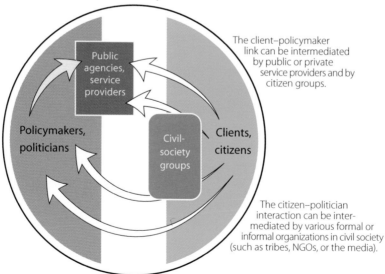

The arrows show accountability relationships: policymakers hold service providers internally accountable (upper left-hand arrow); and citizens, and clients, exert external accountabilities on both service providers and politicians, either directly or intermediated by civil society organizations (the other arrows).

A program to enhance governance must contain actionable measures aimed at improving the overall environment and dealing with specific constraints on greater inclusiveness and accountability. The measures would target existing restrictions and rules that limit inclusiveness and accountability, such as controls on the formation of citizen associations, the high-level approval of candidate lists, or the restricted access to government information on, say, government spending. And they would set up more active mechanisms to improve governance, such as legislating against discriminatory practices in the public sector and setting up a transparent—and preferably independent—monitoring (and recourse) system to assess adherence to the new laws.

The form of these measures, as well as the balance between removing restrictions and actively encouraging better governance, will depend on the governance problems in each country and on the constellation of political and social forces that shape the governance structure. For example, the explicit power-sharing arrangements among confessional groups in Lebanon may not be needed in more homogeneous countries, where other problems, such as promoting more public dialogue, might be more urgent.

Enhancing Inclusiveness

Inclusiveness, as noted earlier, is both a value in its own right—because equality of participation and of treatment by government is a touchstone of development—and an indispensable ingredient of better accountability, especially external accountability. The first, fundamental step in doing so is to adopt laws and regulations that widen and secure access to widely accepted basic rights and freedoms (including the right to be represented in and consulted by governments) and to ensure more equitable eligibility and treatment for public goods and services.

Many types of measures aim to secure equality in participation and treatment: universal suffrage; broader public consultation on proposed laws and regulations; fewer restrictions on the advocacy and community empowerment roles of civil-society organizations (even creating partnerships with them); abolition of discriminatory laws and regulations; and establishment of rules, mechanisms, and monitoring to ensure equal treatment in the delivery of public services such as health and education, as well as business registration and regulation. Often laws ensuring freedoms or opposing discrimination already exist but may be little more than a declaration of intentions.

So, the second fundamental step is to establish mechanisms that can ensure that such laws and regulations are respected—mechanisms of both internal and external accountability. For example, there needs to be explicit monitoring of whether public agencies treat all citizens equitably. In some cases, where necessary and possible, it may be desirable to redress past exclusionary action (for example, by using explicit quotas). An ombudsman can give citizens recourse against discriminatory treatment, even when access to the legal system remains insufficient or when the legal system itself is discriminatory. Acceptance, even encouragement, of citizen watchdog groups can pinpoint and spotlight lapses in inclusiveness.

Inclusiveness is also a state of mind—reflecting an ethic of tolerance and of acting in the public interest—both by bureaucrats in government and by citizens. For example, civil servants need to view their role as one of serving the people and serving as stewards of public trust and resources. Citizens need to conduct public discourse with honesty and tolerance—and with vigor. Instilling within both citizens and bureaucrats a sense of civic responsibility, as well as fostering an ethic of action in the public interest, is never easy. And it is more difficult in polarized societies or those in which some groups have been consistently denied voice and power. But the process of formulating, implementing, and monitoring a national program to enhance governance can itself mirror the ethic of inclusiveness, tolerance, and public interest. Irrespective of the form, the effort requires strong commitment from leaders in government and among the citizenry.

Gaining Stronger Accountability

Internal and external accountability are not substitutes. They are reinforcing mechanisms. Stronger external accountability systems will reveal weaknesses in internal accountability mechanisms, thus requiring action by governments to be able to respond more effectively to external demands. Stronger mechanisms and capacity for internal accountability are needed to generate the information about what government is doing, information on which external accountability depends.

For example, allowing more public debate on the public budget (external accountability) will inevitably lead governments to pay more attention to monitoring and evaluating the spending performance (internal accountability)—a phenomenon beginning to happen in the Islamic Republic of Iran and in Bahrain, for instance. Publication of reports by effective government audit agencies (internal accountability) can fuel public debate on corruption (external accountability). Popular election of parliaments (external accountability) can strengthen the power of parliaments to provide checks and balances on the executive (internal accountability). So, any action plan needs to include measures on both fronts.

Within each accountability arrangement, it is possible to distinguish broadly between macro- and microgovernance actions. The macro governance issues typically focus on nationwide accountability arrangements—

both internal and external—that define the overall governance environment, including the sharing of power (structure of government), the flow of public information and scope for public debate, and the functioning of various external contestability mechanisms (including but not limited to competitive elections). Microgovernance focuses more on the specific arrangements that affect the incentives and performance of individuals, agencies, and groups in the governance process. Those arrangements include administrative measures to improve the internal budget and personnel management systems, such as controls and reporting, as well as the local, community arrangements to involve citizens in local government and service delivery. Many governance measures, such as elections, consultations, and citizen advocacy, apply equally at both national and local levels.

In a discussion of mechanisms to enhance accountabilities, it is useful to recall the two main components of accountability in the governance framework: transparency and contestability. Better governance is impossible without greater public sector transparency; everyone needs to know what government is doing, who in government is responsible, and how citizens are expected to interact with government. And better governance is impossible without greater contestability in the choice of public officials and policies; citizens need regular opportunities and well-established channels to select, renew, and replace public officials and to confirm or reject public policies. Thus, any efforts to improve governance must favor greater transparency and contestability.

Improving External Accountability—National Actions

Improving external accountability in MENA must be the foundation of any program to enhance governance. Why? Because external accountability is a fundamental right (deriving from the precept that authority to govern is granted by the people), and because it is critical in providing incentives for governments to strengthen their structures of internal accountability. External accountability is the linchpin for improved governance, and it is the especially weak external accountability to the public that actually opens the governance gap between MENA and the rest of the world. Actions on this level will determine whether a country's overall institutional environment supports good governance or not. The actions will determine how quickly the MENA region can close its governance gap.

Greater Public Disclosure, Freedom of Information, and Public Debate. Accountability rests on transparency, and information is the currency of transparency. Therefore, countries need to minimize government secrecy and to mandate the disclosure of what government is doing. Enshrining in laws the public's right to know is an important step, but is one that has to be complemented by mechanisms that permit citizens to exercise that right—including legal proceedings. Governments can choose to become active in disclosing and communicating with the public. Many governments in MENA have recognized the value of e-government, even if their programs are still below their potential, compared with the rest of the world (box 4.1).

Providing access to information is only the first half of transparency. Citizens need to have the liberty to discuss and to conduct uncensored (but responsible) public debate in the media and academic institutions—debate on the performance of government officials and agencies and on

---

BOX 4.1

The Move to E-government in MENA Countries

E-government applies information and communication technologies to the delivery of government services for citizens–clients, the private sector, and other government agencies. It provides greater access to government information that can support citizen oversight and external accountability. Almost all governments, including most in MENA, have launched e-government efforts.

E-government can be a powerful tool for better governance, but it takes more than simply requiring computers or setting up Web sites. Improving the efficiency and cost-effectiveness of public services, as well as increasing the transparency and accountability of government agencies, requires planning, sustained effort, and clear political support from the executive.

In an attempt to measure progress with e-government, the United Nations has created an index that includes measures of technological infrastructure and its use by the population, plus measures of overall economic and social development, transparency, and urbanization. The index does not measure the effectiveness of e-government as much as its potential. On this broad index, the MENA region scores slightly above the global median—not surprising, because government subsidies related to the Internet are the highest in the world. Indeed, Bahrain, Kuwait, Lebanon, and the United Arab Emirates rank with Europe. But this potential is not being translated into better public service delivery or broader access to information. Compared with countries in other regions, those in MENA have the lowest scores on the transparency component of the index (consistent with the region's gap on the index of public accountability, as shown in chapter 1). They also have the lowest percentage of Internet sites focused on citizen service delivery and have among the lowest per capita ratios of Internet hosts.

Sources: InfoDev and the Center for Democracy and Technology 2002; United Nations Division for Public Economics and Public Administration and American Society for Public Administration 2002.

the merits of policies, even if the content is critical. Citizens also need the freedom to collect additional information through, for example, independent research and public opinion polls. This ability is more likely to exist where the press is free and the government actually solicits public debate. It is unlikely where pollsters are systematically prohibited from posing sensitive questions or where journalists are periodically, if not systematically, harassed or jailed by governments. A few MENA countries currently allow relatively unfettered debate on public affairs and officials, notably Lebanon and Algeria. Others, such as Morocco, are moving haltingly in the same direction.

Open, Fair, Regular Elections. Regular, competitive elections are typically one of the most formal mechanisms of participation—a mechanism that is underdeveloped in the region. Regular, open, and fairly conducted elections are the ultimate competitive mechanism for executive leaders and parliamentary representatives. They are the pinnacle of citizen participation. But as experience in the region and elsewhere attests, holding elections is no guarantee of effective participation. Achieving electoral processes that efficiently and fairly reflect voter interests requires attention to additional governance issues, including the vetting of candidate slates, the inclusiveness of voting rules, the role and financing of political parties, and the independence of election monitors. So, even if elections are widely accepted as an accountability mechanism, countries need to invest substantially in techniques to enhance their credibility. A place to start is with more, and more credible, local elections—as experience in the Islamic Republic of Iran and Lebanon show.

Even well-designed electoral processes provide only periodic participation; they must be supplemented with a variety of other forms of participation, such as broad official consultations and hearings on government policies, including citizen surveys and electronic feedback. Those alternative participatory mechanisms lack the element of contestability. And they typically leave the initiative for consulting, as well as for acting on advice received, in the hands of the government and not the citizen (although the publication of the consultations may force politicians to accept what citizens say). These mechanisms are no substitute for elections, but as governments around the world have found, they are an indispensable supplemental channel for participation. They are channels that all levels of government can use more effectively.

Within the MENA region, the traditional consultative institutions, such as the Shura councils in the Gulf states, offer one basis for building more accessible consultation. Other governments have sought to create new mechanisms for enhancing consultation, especially at a high level with the executive, mechanisms such as the National Social and Economic Council in Algeria (box 4.2). The executive branches in Lebanon, Morocco, and Tunisia have similar arrangements. Likewise, the active involvement of citizens in local government decisions, as in Aden in the Republic of Yemen and Alexandria and Qena in the Arab Republic of Egypt, provide yet another model. One step, widely used in countries with good governance, is for government to mandate that all public agencies solicit, disclose, and respond to public reactions on all proposed regulations before they are finalized.

Civil-Society Advocacy and Participation. With or without elections, civil-society advocacy organizations are key intermediaries in ensuring ac-countability in the citizen–politician link. Such organizations cannot be

---

BOX 4.2

Expanding Consultative Organisms—Algeria's National Social and Economic Council

Algeria has many national advisory organisms that monitor the government in a variety of domains. One of them, the National Social and Economic Council, deserves particu-lar attention. It allows the various economic, social, and cultural segments of Algerian so-ciety to be represented, parallel to their representation through elected political bodies. The council's members are designated by the government, sometimes at the suggestion of interest groups (unions, associations, public enterprises, and universities).

The council's mission is to debate government policy and to give its opinion on the situation of the country and on particular projects as the council puts special emphasis on the social and economic effect on the citizenry. Because of its composition, which de-pends on government authorities and favors the public sector, the expectation was that the council would serve as a merely consultative organism, putting its seal of approval on governmental action. But its dedication and the quality of its reports (the annual status report in particular) have enabled it to do much in analyzing the social and economic sit-uation of the country.

The council's independence has at times led to tensions or conflicting relations with government authorities, who seldom appreciate the critical assessments and concerns ex-pressed, especially when the Algerian press—one of the freest in the Arab world—makes them available to the public. In its last status report in December 2002, the council fo-cused on the gap between the discourse of the government and the implementation of policy reforms, on the lack of willingness to advance reforms, and on the absence of any strategy or vision for the role of the state.

Source: Adapted from Mahiou 2003, background paper for this book.

mandated, but their emergence does require an enabling legal environment in which they can work openly to mobilize citizens and to push governments to perform effectively and without discrimination. It is standard worldwide to require registration and approval of civil-society organizations that seek fiscal exemptions allowed by law. But few MENA countries, if any, openly welcome civil-society organizations as indispensable participants in good governance. Still, the existence of thousands of such organizations is testament to their growing importance in the region—and to governments' need to accept them.

Better Monitoring and Data on the Quality of Governance. What stands out in any analysis of governance in the MENA region is the relative paucity of data, compared with other regions. Sources are limited, typically only from external rating agencies, and both country and indicator coverage is partial at best. The lack of data, especially from within the region, is itself symptomatic of weak transparency and public debate in almost all MENA countries. This lack of data hampers objective assessments and the design of sensible action plans. A key step in fostering a dialogue on improving governance is for governments to encourage the collection, analysis, and publication of better governance data through surveys, interviews, and studies. The experience of other countries described in chapter 3 offers some guidance.

Independent, Responsible Media. The media play a key role in transparency, both by demanding more and better information on government performance (as in the Islamic Republic of Iran) and by helping to digest the data and to shape them into issues for public debate. Plus, the media offer a forum for citizen expression. They also play a role in contestability as they help highlight and debate the strengths and weaknesses of government officials and policies. For the media to be effective, they need to be independent from government control and influence so the media can have more freedom to debate and to criticize government officials and policies. People also need access to a wide array of competing media organizations, which will ensure pluralism and avoid control by a few private, vested-interest groups. At the same time, the media need to respect standards of integrity and professionalism when reporting and analyzing governance issues.

Improving External Accountability—Local Actions

The macro environment supports accountability actions at the micro, or local, level—actions that typically rest on greater citizen participation (the citizen–service provider accountability link). As elsewhere, many local actions depend on the willingness of governments to accommodate them by establishing participatory mechanisms, publishing information, and abiding by the outcomes. Still, evidence worldwide shows that an active, informed civil society can claim greater participation, especially at the local level, as is illustrated by the example of women demanding identity cards in Egypt. The objective is to put the initiative for participation in the hands of the citizens and to have government respond—which for all governments in MENA would be a reversal of roles. But micro-level accountability is not necessarily in opposition to government. It can be an ally of governments seeking to improve their internal accountabilities, because it provides better monitoring of public agencies than internal accountability mechanisms alone (such as administrative reporting requirements and inspectorate investigations).

More Reliable Information on Public Service Performance. To be responsive, government agencies need to know what citizens want and how citizens evaluate the quality of public services provided. Thus, they need transparency. User surveys can be a powerful feedback tool, and they can be implemented in a variety of ways (for example, by involving citizens and businesses through e-government sites that are focused on specific issues such as investment programming or customs clearance). In all cases, their effectiveness increases when high-level policymakers are strongly committed to listening to and using the results—and when the results are widely published and debated. Client feedback surveys, as used in the West Bank and Gaza (box 4.3) and in Jordan, are a powerful tool for improving the quality of governance data. E-government is yet another mechanism (box 4.1).

Increased Competition among Public Service Agencies. Allowing citizens to choose among alternative public service providers minimizes the need for centralized monitoring to ensure quality. Increasing competition requires creativity. For social services, where government financing remains significant, voucher schemes widen the choice of citizens among eligible providers while still allowing government to finance the services. For infrastructure services, increasing competition typically requires carefully designed regulatory arrangements for providers who offer services at market cost. The MENA region lags behind the rest of the world in creating competitive mechanisms, although telecommunications regulation in Morocco is one of the more successful mechanisms in the region of this sort (see box 3.3). Foundations—such as the Imam Khomeini's Emdad Committee in the Islamic Republic of Iran, which provides the same social services as the government's State Welfare Organization—can also be a source of competition (Esfahani 2003).

BOX 4.3

Service Delivery Surveys in the West Bank and Gaza

A 1998 service delivery survey in the West Bank and Gaza asked a representative sample of beneficiaries about the provision of health and education services by the NGOs, the private sector, and the Palestinian Authority. To evaluate the quality of the equipment and service, specialists also carried out institutional reviews of education and health facilities. The findings show that beneficiaries often select a particular provider because of easy access to the service or because of the provider's quality—areas where NGOs and private providers ranked higher than the government. The findings were presented at dissemination workshops that were attended by ministers, senior civil servants, and senior representatives from NGOs and private organizations. How did the ministers of health and education react? They used the findings to improve the quality of health and education services across the board and to foster a better division of labor among the government, the NGOs, and the private sector.

Source: World Bank 1999c, p. 38.

Stronger Local Governments. Devolving responsibility (and resources) to local or municipal governments can improve accountability relationships by putting leaders closer to the people, thus increasing the likelihood that the people's voices are heard. But devolution also brings risks. And whether such devolution enhances governance depends on how local governments are structured, how reliable local elections are, how much power local governments actually have, and how great their administrative capacities are. Nonetheless, local governments are a powerful channel for increasing accountability, and there are examples of how some have substantially improved the participation of citizens and citizen groups (for example, in setting budget priorities). The recent effort in the Republic of Yemen to devolve more authority to local governments is illustrated by advances in Aden, where efforts to enhance local administrative capacity were intertwined with greater citizen involvement (box 4.4).

More Active Role for Community Empowerment Associations. Local external accountability mechanisms are poorly developed in MENA, especially in comparison with the innovative efforts worldwide (illustrated in chapter 3). All require stronger, community-level, civil-society organizations. The macro environment sets the overall parameters for the emergence and the functioning of such associations. But it is the micro, or local, environment that draws them actively into the governance process, notably

BOX 4.4

Decentralizing Political Power—Local Economic Development in Aden

In 2000, the parliament of the Republic of Yemen approved an ambitious Local Authorities Law that provides unprecedented powers to local governments over administrative and fiscal authority and functions. The law gives further support to a decentralization process that began on a pilot basis in 1995 in the Ibb governorate, grounding it institutionally in the legal framework and building on the strong historical tradition of local self-governance in the country. It also paved the way for the first local elections in 2001.

But implementation of the law—particularly in transferring responsibilities to local authorities—has been a slow-moving process, largely because of limited local capacity. To overcome this constraint, Aden, the country's commercial capital, established a local economic development department in 2002, with funding from the Cities Alliance and the World Bank. It works at the local government level, with a city development strategy team comprising representatives from the city's private sector, universities, women's organizations, and other civic groups in a broad-based city-visioning exercise, and it is carrying out complementary city revitalization investments.

Initial plans include revitalizing a pier and fish market that have tourism potential, plus upgrading an industrial area to provide small businesses with needed infrastructure services that will better enable them to respond to a growing demand for diversified services at the port and free-zone facilities. Physical infrastructure in the city is being improved to strengthen linkages among its key economic clusters.

In addition to improving the competitiveness of the city, local authorities in Aden are implementing a wide range of local reforms and capacity-building initiatives—thus streamlining local business regulatory processes, strengthening physical and investment planning, and improving municipal asset management. In an effort to strengthen the relationship between the newly elected local council and its constituents, a workshop was organized in mid-2002 with local officials and city residents to encourage participatory planning. This workshop improved the local planning process and strengthened accountability between local government and its constituents.

The process of political decentralization (through local elections) fosters ownership of development efforts at the local level, helps mobilize local talent, and improves the design and implementation of measures tailored to local needs. In addition, Aden's local reform task force serves as an important voice in pressing for national reforms—including proposed improvements in customs administration, land registration, and investment promotion, all vital to Aden's economic competitiveness regionally and globally.

Source: World Bank staff.

in the oversight of the performance of public agencies in general and of public service delivery agencies in particular—especially where each transaction has to be tailored to the client. The challenge for governments is both to empower such organizations and to devise mechanisms that capitalize on their capacity to contribute. This process is not absent in the MENA region, as shown by recent efforts in Morocco to formalize cooperation between the government and civil society (box 4.5).

Improving Internal Accountability—National Checks and Balances

Improving internal accountability at the macro level is also about establishing an environment of accountability within government by increasing the transparency and contestability within government, as well as by fostering an ethic of and commitment to service in the public interest.

Strengthening national-level internal accountability is primarily, but not only, a question of modifying the structure and organization of government to increase separation of powers. Governments in the MENA region, al-

---

BOX 4.5

Cooperating with Civil Society

Morocco's latest five-year development plan (2000–04) attempts to engage civil-society organizations as a main actor in the development process: "Civil society has to be given the opportunity to participate in the process of economic, social, and cultural development. In fact, these groups are not just a venue to articulate the moral interest; they seek to undertake initiatives, mobilize existing resources, and be actors in the field of development."

The plan highlights the need to improve the poverty focus of public policies and expenditures to achieve equity and inclusion, including through the creation of a social fund that works directly with civil-society organizations. It also stresses social development and poverty eradication—thereby improving access to basic services, combating illiteracy, integrating women and youth in the development process, and improving health care. On decentralization, the plan calls for a clarification of roles at all levels of intervention, as well as for the adoption of formal contracts between local government and civil-society organizations to define the rights and duties of contracting parties. The plan also calls for integrated and participatory rural development programs targeted at the poorest rural areas.

Sources: Morocco 2000; World Bank 2002c.

most without exception, concentrate authority in an executive branch (as shown in chapter 1). Parliaments exist, but they seldom provide an independent check on the executive; more often, they merely legitimize executive decisions. And when they do act independently, the parliaments can be suspended to allow the executive greater latitude, as in Jordan in 2001. Even if the judiciary fairly upholds the rule of law for citizens, in every country in MENA, the judiciary has weak oversight over other branches of government and lacks the prerogative to question the executive.

So a key governance-enhancing step is to ensure contestability in the exercise of state authority, typically through a constitutional separation of powers among the branches of government. A step that is especially important is to make it difficult for a powerful executive to sidestep accountability obligations. Of course, nearly all constitutions in the region have enshrined the classic separation of powers of government, but they have been unable to ensure that separation in practice. Constitutions can be changed or their provisions ignored, as experience in the region demonstrates. Still, strong provisions to empower the three branches of government signal to those inside and outside the region that a country is serious about governance structures. And when coupled with contestability mechanisms that make it harder to change constitutions and that give stronger voice to citizens about such changes, constitutional guarantees of separation of powers gain credibility. Even with constitutional guarantees, implementation remains the key. And good technical design of the structure of government can facilitate, or complicate, effective implementation.

Stronger Parliaments. Stronger parliaments depend on constitutional safeguards, on popular support, and on their technical capacities. Legal safeguards should protect parliaments from executive predation. For example, executives should not have unchecked power to suspend parliaments. Parliaments should have the power to initiate legislation or to amend or reject what executives propose. Parliaments should have full oversight over government spending and cabinets. When parliaments are elected through fair and regular elections, executives that try to weaken parliaments may face stronger resistance from both elected representatives and the electorate.

Efforts to strengthen the capacity of parliamentarians to act independently (such as the Parliamentary Research Center in the Islamic Republic of Iran) will enhance their ability to offer effective checks and balances. Even though dominant executive authority remains the norm in MENA, some countries have begun to redress the balance of power. The recent creation of a parliament in Bahrain propelled the executive to begin to consider new mechanisms to enhance the quality of its expenditure management. Morocco adopted reforms in the 1990s to strengthen the power and authority of its bicameral parliament (background paper, Filali-Ansari 2003). Since the victory of reform-minded candidates in the 2000 parliamentary elections in the Islamic Republic of Iran, parliamentarians have used their voice in an attempt to balance the power of the supreme leader, with some, if halting, success (background paper, Farhi 2003).

A More Independent Judiciary. In a region with strong respect for the rule of law, as in MENA, the judiciary should be able to play a powerful role in maintaining an appropriate balance of power. But in the MENA region, the judiciary is systematically shackled by executive dominance, is ignored, or, worse, becomes an agency of the executive itself. To counteract executive pressures, the country needs a minimum standard of guarantees for judges' positions (such as their irremovability and security of employment). At least half of the organism in charge of appointing and supervising judges (such as the Higher Judiciary Council in Tunisia) should be elected (by any of various mechanisms) (background paper, Charfi 2003). There are some recent examples of judicial power, such as the overturning of Egypt's law limiting the freedom of citizens to form associations.

Empowerment of Other Independent Oversight Agencies. Within the government broadly, other agencies may also provide checks and balances. Key among them is an independent audit organization that is responsible for examining the financial probity of executive spending. Some countries (such as Algeria in box 4.6 and Tunisia in box 1.8) have also experimented with an ombudsman as an alternative channel of recourse against abuse of power, usually but not always by the executive.

Improving Internal Accountability—Administrative Measures

Even without constitutional reform to establish checks and balances, even without elections and decentralized political power, and even without freer press and public information, multiple administrative actions can strengthen the accountability—within government—of agencies that provide public services. Among the most powerful mechanisms developed elsewhere are those that focus on the management of public sector performance.

Public Expenditure Management. The budget is the operational tool of governments. So, the actions that link the process of budget formulation and execution to tangible measures of performance—including value for money as well as actual results—underpin accountability. A focus on budget performance demands a definition and publication of tangible

---

BOX 4.6

Toward External Accountability in Algeria: The National Ombudsman

Inspired by foreign experiences, Algeria recently attempted to add a new form of external accountability to its existing institutions: the National Ombudsman (*Médiateur de la République*). A presidential decree on March 23, 1996, instituted an ombudsman who reports to the president and has the mission of promoting human rights and ensuring the regular functioning of the public administration as the ombudsman pays special attention to the quality of the relationship between the administration and the citizens.

A subsequent decree on August 26, 1996, identified the prerogatives of the ombudsman, as well as the staff assisting him, at both the national and the local levels. The initiative bolstered the channels offered to citizens to defend themselves against the perpetrations of the administration, thereby strengthening the rule of law.

Before the effectiveness of the ombudsman's mission could be assessed, the institution was abolished on August 2, 1999. According to the press, an annual average of some 38,000 complaints had been brought to the ombudsman and his local deputies, underscoring its usefulness.

Government authorities reversed their position on March 25, 2001, putting in place a National Commission for the Promotion and Protection of Human Rights to "undertake mediation activities in the context of its mandate to improve the relationship between the administration and the citizens." The commission's mandate assumes, however, that it will have the judicial, human, and material means to implement such a complex mission, which does not seem to be the case so far.

Source: Mahiou 2003, background paper for this book.

---

performance targets for government agencies, a more rigorous examination of spending decisions (for example, through cost-benefit analyses), a workable information system for monitoring and evaluating agency performance, and a system of rewards and sanctions for managers who are in charge.

Instituting public expenditure management is a complex and long-term process, as shown by experience in many industrial countries (such as Sweden and the United States) and in some developing countries (such as Malaysia in box 3.5). And governments typically adhere to the process only in the face of strong public or external demand. But even initial steps in this direction can foster a climate of greater internal accountability. The Islamic Republic of Iran and Bahrain have perhaps shown the greatest interest in adopting modern techniques of performance-oriented budget management, and both remain at the very initial stages. There is beginning to be some limited discussion of performance-oriented budget management in some other countries, such as Egypt, Jordan, and the Republic of Yemen.

These efforts must be complemented by actions to improve the flow of information and the quality of debate and dialogue within the administration. The need for better information and debate underlines the importance of having an overall governance environment that is supportive of transparency and contestability. A strong parliament (or the prospect of one), as well as a powerful independent audit organization, can encourage executive agencies to pay more attention to performance.

Finally, a stronger focus on government performance may depend as much on instituting and adhering to an ethic of service to the public and of stewardship of public resources as it depends on demanding accountability through various technical or political measures.

Civil Service Reform. Irrespective of government policy and financing, the civil service sits at the interface of citizens and government. The challenge is to make the civil service more accountable for emphasizing results over bureaucratic action, for ensuring faithful implementation of policies, and for treating all citizens fairly and competently. Human resource management practices that enshrine transparency and contestability are steps in this direction: more transparent hiring of civil servants (as Jordan is attempting through electronic posting of openings and candidates), competitive entry exams, and meritocratic promotion provide incentives for better performance. The Republic of Yemen has a major civil service reform program under way, and Morocco has been engaged in similar efforts for the past decade.

There are other ways to improve civil service performance besides reform of internal management. For example, instauration of a code of integrity, coupled with such concrete measures as declarations of assets and similar fiduciary requirements, creates a climate inimical to corruption. Instituting these measures is difficult in any civil service. It is more difficult when recruitment into the civil service is used to combat unemployment, as is the case in many MENA countries.

Alternatively, policymakers can strengthen internal accountability by reducing the discretionary power of bureaucrats. When Algeria established its Agency to Promote and to Monitor Investments (*Agence de Promotion et de Suivi des Investissements*) in 1994, it stipulated that investors had the right to a response within two months and that the failure of the administration to honor that deadline automatically conferred approval (background paper, Mahiou 2003).

Finally, although it is an internal affair, civil service management can be strengthened by enlisting external accountability mechanisms—such as direct citizen feedback (for example, through surveys) and administrative recourse mechanisms (for example, ombudsmen).

Deconcentration. Some governance problems in central governments can be alleviated, in part, through greater deconcentration, which is an alternative (or first step) in the decentralization and devolution of political authority. The power of deconcentrating many functions of government is that it brings central government agencies closer to users, who have both a direct stake in performance (unlike a supervisory bureaucrat at the center) and the information needed to assess agency performance. Deconcentrating can also help strengthen internal oversight by creating, in effect, a further separation of powers. The Moroccan government has committed itself to greater deconcentration, (for example, by empowering centrally appointed leaders at the regional level—the king selects the governors, or *walis*—who have authority over ministerial officials in the regions and who have been delegated decisions on behalf of their central ministries).

Regulatory Independence. A key public service is proper regulation of private activities that have important externalities or where there are market failures. Such regulation fails its purpose when it is captured by either private vested interests or officials within government who have a political agenda. The challenge is to design such regulatory agencies to preserve their independence, while holding them accountable for effective regulation. Some MENA governments have begun to establish such agencies; the nascent experience with telecommunications regulation in the region both shows the difficulties and points to lessons. Worldwide, there is a rich experience to draw on.

An Ethic of Public Service. The sanctions that are part of contestability mechanisms are powerful accountability incentives, but they depend on effective enforcement, which itself requires strong administrative capacity. The need for such enforcement is lowered when there is an ethic of service to the public and of stewardship of public resources, which are hallmarks of truly effective organizations of public service delivery. The value system itself becomes self-enforcing because civil servants will tend to judge the performance and reputation of themselves—and of others—in terms of this ethic, thus lowering the costs of formal monitoring and sanctions. Creating such an ethic requires vision and leadership from the top; it also requires collaborative arrangements between citizens and staff of public agencies to build trust and mutual recognition (Tendler 1999). Many civil-society organizations, in MENA as elsewhere, that deliver social services often rely on the commitment of their staff to such ideals; in certain cases, these civil-society organizations may be able to help governments develop such values for their own agencies.

Moving the Governance Agenda Forward

One lesson of governance reform worldwide is that increasing inclusion and accountability and broadening participation will take time, because the process inevitably entails changing traditions and confronting privileged interests. Universal suffrage was not common in industrial countries until the mid-20th century—nearly 200 years after being enshrined as a concept in the American and French revolutions (table 4.1). Performance-oriented budgeting was initiated as a way to increase the accountability of the government in the United States in the 1960s, and it is still not universally adhered to. In the MENA region, external factors that have handicapped the emergence of institutions for good governance are unlikely to disappear. Their persistence makes the challenge in MENA countries perhaps even greater than elsewhere, given the starting point.

Still, there are reasons for optimism. Governments in MENA remain, by and large, strongly committed to providing citizens with good public services. The debate on governance in the region, hampered though it may be by government censure and limited information, is under way. There is evidence of some progress on many fronts, however limited or timid.

Even the exogenous factors described in chapter 1—oil, conflict, geopolitics—can be engines for change. Oil revenue provides the financial wherewithal to prepare and introduce governance reforms while being a highly visible symbol of why better governance is needed. The threat of conflict, notably internal strife, can be (but seldom is) viewed in part as a manifestation of weak governance. The enduring solution is not military—it is greater political accountability and stronger government performance.

Global forces do not necessarily have to weaken governance in MENA countries. Indeed, trade and other economic agreements—when they reflect a genuine social consensus and are entered into voluntarily—

TABLE 4.1

Modern Governance Institutions Took a Long Time to Develop

Institution/reform	First	Majority (of industrial countries)	Last	United Kingdom	United States[a]
Universal male suffrage	1848 (France)	1907	1925 (Japan)	1918	1870/1965
Universal suffrage	1907 (New Zealand)	1946	1971 (Switzerland)	1928	1920/1965

a. The 1965 date reflects legislation to eliminate racial discrimination in voting.
Source: Chang 2002.

offer opportunities that can be used to strengthen the movement for reforms in governance. They can also provide a brake on efforts to reverse them, as in several Eastern European countries. And external partners can play other positive roles in a country's quest for better governance.

What are the grounds for optimism that a transition to better governance and to better growth and development is feasible? Look at the experience of other countries that have gradually strengthened governance mechanisms without instability and with the reward of better economic performance. The governance reforms in Eastern Europe were generally better than those in the countries from the former Soviet Union because of their more contestable political systems that favored the power and growth of a wide array of citizen associations that voice support for reforms (box 4.7). Similarly, in Mexico, significant governance reforms that expanded participation and increased external accountabilities were accompanied by a strong economy recovery (box 4.8).

BOX 4.7

Good Governance Can Improve Economic Policies—Lessons from the Europe and Central Asia Transition

In the 10 years following the dissolution of the Soviet Union, countries in Eastern Europe typically managed the economic transition from command to market economy better than countries emerging from the breakup of the Soviet Union. The first group tended to have governments that "emerged from roundtable negotiations among broadly representative popular fronts and a wide range of other organized interests." The more concentrated political regimes in the second group sought to preserve the narrow vested interests they represented.

The "competitive democracies" in Central Europe focused more on promoting new constituencies of winners from better policies—in part by welcoming the emergence of entrepreneurial and other citizen associations that gave voice to citizens other than the oligarchs. Amplifying the economic effect of reforms were generally strong public administrations that improved the overall business environment, as well as the pull of accession to the European Union.

One conclusion is that a very strong executive generally fails to stand up to entrenched, concentrated, vested interests. Another is that mobilizing a broader array of constituent groups through greater political inclusion strengthens the hand of economic reformers facing entrenched interests. The emergence and mobilization of this broad range of constituent groups are more likely in "competitive democracies" than in concentrated political regimes.

Source: World Bank 2002h.

BOX 4.8

Political Pluralism and Economic Recovery in Mexico

Like many MENA countries, Mexico is an oil-rich economy traditionally governed by a dominant political party that allowed little open competition. Governance reforms began as early as the 1980s, because the share of votes won by the dominant political party had gradually fallen from more than 90 percent to about 50 percent. But it was only in 1997 that political competition was significantly enhanced by having a parliament controlled by opposition parties, substantially greater decentralization of governing authority to local constituencies, and efforts to enhance internal oversight. For example, the government's internal audit agency's installation of a telephone complaint system in 1997 tripled registered complaints from citizens.

Many factors other than political governance affect growth, including a free trade agreement with the United States, which is itself a spur to governance reforms. But the Mexican economy not only weathered the political opening but also flourished, despite potentially destabilizing governance reforms.

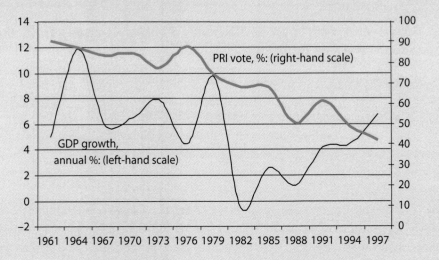

Note: PRI is the Institutional Revolutionary Party (*Partido Revolucionario Institucional*).

Sources: Giugale, Lafourcade, and Nguyen 2001; Diaz-Cayeros and Magaloni 2000; World Bank data.

It would be difficult, even ill-advised, to draft a single blueprint laying out a sequence of specific actions to improve governance. But some broad principles—as laid out in this book—should inform the choice and design of actions. Inclusiveness and accountability are the portals through which any program of enhancing governance must emerge. For inclusiveness, the ensurance of basic rights—including the right to participate fully in the governance process, the right to equality before the law, and the right to equal treatment by government agencies—needs to be guaranteed in every element of the program. For accountability—both internal and external—transparency and contestability should guide the process of designing the program and deciding its content.

A panoply of important and feasible actions span the spectrum of government activity and citizen involvement with government, all of which help countries move in the direction of better governance. Any good action program needs to address all fronts, even if there is a wide menu of appropriate measures for each. The elements of each national program and the specific mechanisms for implementing the programs will be matters for individual societies to decide consensually through consultation and debate. The immediate challenge that countries in the MENA region face is to forge a credible and solid commitment to raising the quality of governance to levels commensurate with their levels of development and with the aspirations of their people.

The need to improve governance is urgent, pushed by the exigencies of global pressures and opportunities and by a burgeoning, youthful population whose aspirations fuel both despair and hope. The process is continuous and long. But one lesson is certain—without action today, governance will not improve tomorrow.

A Commitment for Action …

The first action today would be clear commitment of governments to strengthen governance generally, coupled with an invitation to all members of civil society to join this process. That action would be a public commitment to improve the inclusiveness and accountability of government, which will increase transparency and contestability in the conduct of public affairs. This commitment should be a joint commitment—of government (in all branches) and of the people (individually and through their civil-society advocacy and community empowerment organizations).

There are signs of such commitment in the region—of various strength and breadth. The movement in Bahrain over the past half decade to establish a parliament with some voice over the conduct of government is evidence of evolution. Efforts in Morocco over the past decade to establish and empower a parliament and to strengthen local governments reflect an effort to introduce greater participation of citizens in government (box 4.9). The Republic of Yemen has launched an ambitious decentralization process that would make local, especially municipal, governments more accountable to local communities and less to the central government. Presidential and parliamentary elections in the Islamic Republic of Iran have established a strong, popularly elected voice alongside the powerful clergy, showing that some democratic prin-

---

BOX 4.9

Toward Governance Reforms in Morocco

The Kingdom of Morocco adopted several institutional reforms in the 1990s. Among the most significant were the following five:

- The Advisory Council of Human Rights on April 20, 1990

- Administrative Courts on September 10, 1993

- The Ministry in Charge of Human Rights, in 1993

- The Constitutional Council on February 25, 1994

- The Advisory Council for the Follow-Up of Social Dialogue on November 24, 1994.

In addition, the new Moroccan constitution contained several innovative governance features, thus instituting a bicameral parliament with stronger oversight authority, institutionalizing the Economic and Social Council, and enshrining decentralization (currently interpreted mainly as deconcentration). The unwritten rule obliging the king to appoint the prime minister from the majority party or coalition in parliament was not, however, respected after the most recent elections.

Moreover, the preamble stipulates that "the Kingdom of Morocco is aware of the necessity to inscribe its action in the context of international organisms, of which he is an active and dynamic member; the Kingdom subscribes to the principles, rights, and obligations stemming from the charts of the aforementioned organisms and reaffirms its attachment to human rights as they are recognized internationally."

Sources: Filali-Ansari 2003, background paper for this book, with citation from Tozy 1999. See also Morocco 1996.

---

ciples can be integrated with an Islamic theocratic government. The lesson from the region: some ruling elites can commit themselves to improving governance, and such commitments can be sustained despite backtracking and setbacks.

Formal declarations by governments to broaden participation in the governance process are too often empty efforts to appease some local and foreign constituencies. But the declarations serve notice of new directions in a visible—and, therefore, monitorable—way. Such declarations gain credibility when they are formulated in a participatory process that gives voice to citizen concerns, that models inclusiveness and transparency, and that helps build a social consensus in which everyone has a stake.

… And Formulation of a Program to Enhance Governance

The second action today would be engagement in a process to formulate a program to enhance governance; the aim is to reach a consensus on a set of key directions for enhancing governance, on a series of actions to enhance inclusiveness and accountability across a wide array of governance issues and institutions, and on a definition of indicators that could be used to chart progress and to progressively adapt the program. This process itself should set high standards by including all segments of society in the consultation and debate, by making all deliberations public, by inviting debate within the media to ensure maximum transparency, and by proceeding with strong civic buy-in and commitment. Responsibilities for realizing the program, as well as for monitoring progress, could then be shared widely among both government and civil-society organizations.

The program to enhance governance could be elaborated along five pathways to good governance (figure 4.2):

- Enhanced inclusiveness.

- National actions to strengthen external accountabilities.

- National checks and balances to strengthen internal accountabilities.

- Local actions to strengthen external accountability.

- Administrative, internal accountability measures.

Although this book suggests actions that would lead to better governance along each pathway, these examples of possible actions are neither exhaustive nor limiting. The suggested actions are intended to nourish the work by people and governments in formulating a national program to enhance governance. Most of the measures focus on strengthening the triad of accountability channels. But good governance also requires an overarching commitment and an effort to ensure inclusiveness, both for its own sake and because accountability mechanisms must themselves be inclusive to be effective. Better accountability mechanisms are also one element in ensuring enhanced inclusiveness. The priorities attached to each, their phasing, and the details of their implementation would constitute the core elements of a program that would enhance governance and would be formulated by those MENA countries seeking to take their place among the best-governed and most-developed countries of the world.

FIGURE 4.2

A Program to Enhance Governance

Inclusiveness

Enhancement measures

- Mandate universal suffrage for all elected posts.
- Reduce discrimination in laws and regulations.
- Broaden government consultative mechanisms.
- Encourage broad-based civil-society organizations.
- Monitor whether public service agency staff treat citizens equitably.
- Redress past exclusions.

Program to enhance governance

Internal accountability

National checks and balances

- Increase oversight authority and capability of parliaments over the executive.
- Ensure greater independence of the judiciary.
- Improve professional capacity of parliaments and the judiciary.
- Empower other independent oversight agencies, and mandate reviews by them.

Administrative measures

- Improve performance orientation, including monitoring of government budgets.
- Reform the civil service to enhance its service orientation and professional competence.
- Strengthen the resources and capacity of local agencies to design, adapt, and deliver public services.
- Ensure independence of regulatory agencies.
- Foster an ethic of service to the public in the civil service.

External accountability

National actions

- Mandate greater freedom of information and public disclosure of government operations.
- Invite external oversight to ensure open, fair, regular elections.
- Invite public debate on policies by representative civil-society groups.
- Generate, monitor, and disseminate data on governance quality.
- Encourage independent and responsible media.

Local actions

- Introduce feedback mechanisms, from clients to providers, and publish results.
- Increase competition among public service agencies—and with private providers.
- Move toward increased devolution to elected local authorities.
- Create opportunities for involvement of community empowerment associations.

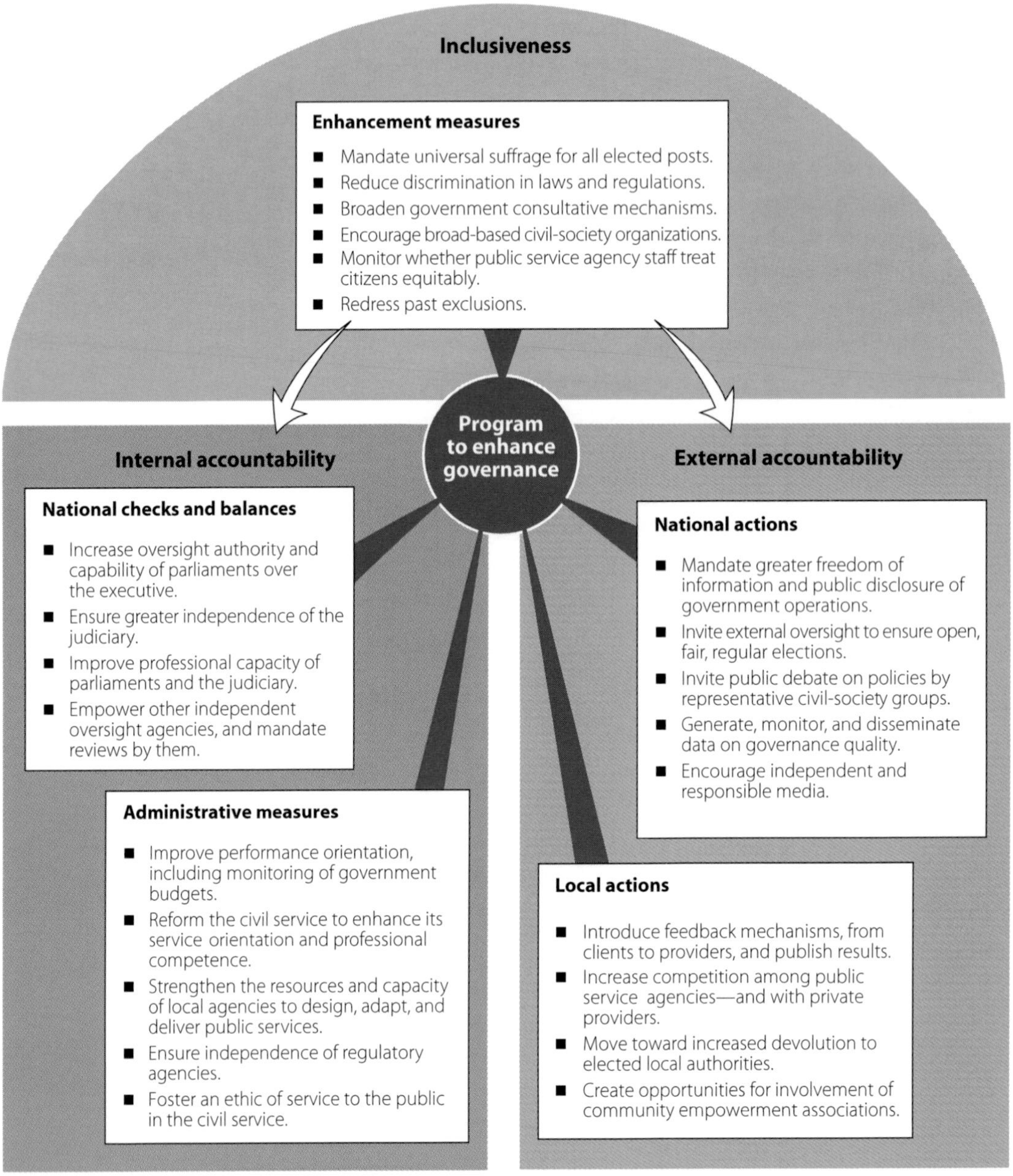

APPENDIX A

Construction of Governance Indexes

Principal component analysis[1] (PCA) is performed on 22 indicators of governance to derive three broad indexes:

1. index of public accountability (IPA), which aggregates 12 indicators from the dataset

2. index of quality of administration (IQA), which aggregates 10 indicators from the dataset

3. index of governance quality (IGQ), which aggregates all 22 indicators.

The indexes are constructed using a sample of 173 countries from all regions and all income levels. They are then linearly rescaled from –2 to +2, with –2 reflecting the lowest score and +2 the highest. (In some parts of the book, the scaling used is 0–100, with 100 being the highest score.)

Index of Public Accountability

The IPA assesses four areas. First, the level of openness of political institutions in a country. Second, the extent to which free, fair, and competitive political participation is exercised; civil liberties are assumed and respected; and the press and voice are free from control, violation, harassment, and censorship. Third, the degree of transparency and responsiveness of the government to its people. And fourth, the degree of political accountability in the public sphere.

Twelve indicators are used: from Freedom House (FRH) 2002a and 2002b (political rights, civil liberties, and freedom of the press); Center for International Development and Conflict Management (CIDCM) 2000 (polity score, regulation of executive recruitment, competitiveness of executive recruitment, openness of executive recruitment, regulation of participation, competitiveness of participation, and executive constraints); Political Risk Services (PRS) 2001 (democratic accountability); and the World Bank Country Policy and Institutional Assessment (CPIA) 2001a (transparency and accountability).

FRH—Political Rights

This item addresses the following questions:

- Is the head of state, head of government, or other chief authority elected through free and fair elections?

- Are the legislative representatives elected through free and fair elections?

- Are there fair electoral laws?

- Are the voters able to endow their freely elected representatives with real power?

- Do the people have the right to freely organize in different political parties or other competitive political groupings of their choice, and is the system open to the rise and fall of those competing parties or groupings?

- Are there a significant opposition vote, a de facto opposition power, and a realistic possibility for the opposition to increase its support or gain power through elections?

- Are the people free from domination by the military, foreign powers, totalitarian parties, religious hierarchies, economic oligarchies, or any other powerful groups?

- Do cultural, ethnic, religious, and other minority groups have reasonable self-determination, self-government, autonomy, or participation through informal consensus in the decisionmaking process?

- For traditional monarchies that have no parties or electoral process, does the system provide for consultation with the people, encourage discussion of policy, and allow the right to petition the ruler?

FRH—Civil Liberties

This item addresses the following questions, among others:

- Are there free and independent media, literature, and other forms of cultural expressions?

- Is there open public discussion and free private discussion?

- Is there freedom of assembly and demonstration?

- Is there freedom of political or quasi-political organization?

- Are citizens equal under the law; do they have access to an independent, nondiscriminatory judiciary; and are they respected by the security forces?

- Is there protection from unjustified imprisonment, exile, or torture, whether by groups that support or oppose the system? Is there freedom from war or insurgency situations?

- Are there free trade unions and peasant organizations or equivalents, and is there effective collective bargaining?

- Are there free professional and other private organizations?

- Are there free businesses or cooperatives?

- Are there free religious institutions, and free private and public religious expressions?

- Are there personal social freedoms, which include aspects such as gender equality, property rights, freedom of movement, choice of residence, and choice of marriage and size of family?

- Is there equality of opportunity—which includes freedom from exploitation by or dependency on landlords, employers, union leaders, bureaucrats, or any other type of denigrating obstacle—to a share of legitimate economic gains?

- Is there freedom from extreme government indifference and corruption?

FRH—Freedom of the Press

This item addresses the following questions, among others:

- What is the structure of the news delivery system; what influence do the laws and administrative decisions have on the content of the news media?

- What is the degree of political influence or control over the content of the news systems?

- What economic influences are exerted on news content by either the government or private entrepreneurs?

- What are the actual violations against the media, including murder, physical attack, harassment, and censorship?

CIDCM—Combined Polity Score

This item addresses the general openness of political institutions.

CIDCM—Regulation of Executive Recruitment

This item addresses the extent to which a polity has institutionalized procedures for transferring executive power.

CIDCM—Competitiveness of Executive Recruitment

This item addresses the extent to which executives are chosen through competitive elections.

CIDCM—Openness of Executive Recruitment

This item addresses whether recruitment of the chief executive is "open," to the extent that all the politically active population has an opportunity, in principle, to attain the position through a regularized process.

CIDCM—Executive Constraints

This item refers to the extent of institutionalized constraints on the decisionmaking powers of chief executives, whether individuals or collectivities. Such limitations may be imposed by any "accountability groups."

CIDCM—Regulation of Participation

This item addresses whether participation is regulated to the extent that there are binding rules on when, whether, and how political preferences are expressed. A higher score means relatively stable and enduring political groups regularly compete for political influence and positions with little use of coercion. No significant groups, issues, or types of conventional political action are regularly excluded from the political process.

CIDCM—Competitiveness of Participation

This item addresses the extent to which nonelites are able to access institutional structures for political expression, or the extent to which alternative preferences for policy and leadership can be pursued in the political arena.

PRS—Democratic Accountability

This item quantifies how responsive government is to its people, on the basis that the less response there is, the more likely it is that the government will fall, peacefully or violently. It includes not only whether free and fair elections are in place, but also how likely the government is to remain in power or remain popular.

CPIA—Transparency and Accountability

This item assesses the extent to which (1) the executive can be held accountable for its use of funds and the results of its actions by the electorate and by the legislature and judiciary, and (2) the public employees within the executive are required to account for their use of resources, administrative decisions, and results obtained. Both levels of accountability are enhanced by transparency in decisionmaking, public audit institutions, access to relevant and timely information, and public and media scrutiny. A high degree of accountability and transparency discourages corruption (the abuse of public office for private gain). National and subnational governments should be appropriately weighted.

Index of Quality of Administration

The IQA assesses the risk and level of corruption and black market activity, the degree and extent to which certain rules and rights are protected and enforced (such as property rights or business regulations and procedures), the quality of the budgetary processes and public management, the efficiency of revenue mobilization, the overall quality of the bureaucracy, and the independence of civil service from political pressure.

Ten indicators are used: from Political Risk Services (PRS) 2001 (corruption, bureaucratic quality); the World Bank Country Policy and Institutional Assessment (CPIA) 2001a (property rights and rule-based governance, quality of budgetary and financial management, efficiency of revenue mobilization, quality of public administration); the Heritage Foundation/*Wall Street Journal* (HWJ) 2002 (property rights, regulation, black market); and an additional variable from Djankov and others 2000 (number of procedures).

PRS—Corruption

This item is concerned with actual or potential corruption in the form of excessive patronage, nepotism, job reservations, "favor-for-favors," secret party funding, and suspiciously close ties between politics and business. These insidious sorts of corruption potentially are thought to be of much greater risk to foreign business in that they can lead to popular discontent, give rise to unrealistic and inefficient controls on the state economy, and encourage the development of the black market.

PRS—Bureaucratic Quality

This factor measures the institutional strength and quality of the civil service, thereby assessing how much strength and expertise the bureaucrats have and how able they are to manage political alternations without drastic interruptions in government services or without policy changes. Good performers have somewhat autonomous bureaucracies, which are free from political pressures, plus an established mechanism for recruitment and training.

HWJ—Property Rights

This factor scores the degree to which private property rights are protected and the degree to which the government enforces laws that protect private property. It also accounts for the possibility that private property will be expropriated. In addition, it analyzes the independence of the judiciary, the existence of corruption within the judiciary, and the ability of individuals and businesses to enforce contracts.

HWJ—Regulation

This factor measures how easy or difficult it is to open and operate a business. The more regulations that are imposed on a business, the harder it is to establish one. The factor also examines the degree of corruption in government and whether regulations are applied uniformly to all businesses.

HWJ—Black Market

This factor measures the extent to which black market activities occur in a country. The larger the black market in a particular country, the lower the level of economic freedom and the more prevalent black market activities (smuggling, piracy of intellectual property, and agricultural production, manufacturing, services, transportation, and labor supplied on the black market).

CPIA—Property Rights and Rule-Based Governance

This item assesses the extent to which private economic activity is facilitated by an effective legal system and a rule-based governance structure in which property and contract rights are reliably respected and enforced.

CPIA—Quality of Budgetary and Financial Management

This item assesses the extent to which there are (1) a comprehensive and credible budget, linked to policy priorities, which in turn are linked to a poverty reduction strategy; (2) effective financial management systems to ensure that incurred expenditures are consistent with the approved budget, that budgeted revenues are achieved, and that aggregate fiscal control is maintained; (3) timely and accurate fiscal reporting, including timely and audited public accounts and effective arrangements for followup; and (4) clear and balanced assignment of expenditures and revenues to each level of government.

CPIA—Efficiency of Revenue Mobilization

This item evaluates the overall pattern of revenue mobilization—not only the tax structure as it exists on paper, but also the revenues from all sources as they are actually collected.

CPIA—Quality of Public Administration

This item assesses the extent to which civilian central government staffs (including teachers, health workers, and police) are structured to design and implement government policy and to deliver services effectively. Civilian central government staffs include the central executive, together with all other ministries and administrative departments, including autonomous agencies. It excludes the armed forces, state-owned enterprises, and subnational government.

Djankov and Others (2000)—Number of Procedures

This item indicates the number of all procedures that are required by law to start a business. A separate step in the start-up process is a "procedure" only if it requires that the entrepreneur interact with outside entities: state and local government offices, lawyers, auditors, notaries, company seal manufacturers, and so forth. Each office that the entrepreneur visits counts as a separate procedure.

Index of Governance Quality

The IGQ is a composite index, constructed using all the indicators for the IPA and the IQA together. It thus assesses the overall quality of governance, giving equivalent weight to public accountability and to the quality of administration in the public sector.

Note

1. PCA is a widely used aggregation technique, designed to *linearly* transform a set of *interrelated* variables into a new set of *uncorrelated* components, which account for *all* of the variance in the original variables. Usually only the first or the first two components are retained, because they explain most of the variance in the dataset. For the purpose of this exercise, all components are retained, and the governance indexes are constructed as the weighted average of components, where weights are variances of successive principal components.

Governance and Income Correlations

The empirical exercise tries to derive a fitted equation line that best portrays the relationship between governance quality, as measured by three constructed indexes—index of governance quality (IGQ), index of public accountability (IPA), and index of quality of administration (IQA)—and the income levels, as measured by GDP per capita (in PPP terms, 2000).

Thus, through the use of simple ordinary least squares (OLS), each of the three governance indexes is regressed against the logarithm of per capita income, in three separate equations:

(1)   IGQ = constant + A_1 × log of per capita income + error

(2)   IPA = constant + A_2 × log of per capita income + error

(3)   IQA = constant + A_3 × log of per capita income + error.

The equations are regressed on a cross-country sample of 154 countries.

The R^2 of the regressions is, respectively, 66 percent, 43 percent, and 69 percent.

All estimated A coefficients are positive and statistically significant.

A MENA dummy (a variable that takes a value of 1 if the country belongs to the MENA region,[1] and 0 otherwise) is added to each of the three regressions. The MENA dummy captures the average variation between MENA countries' estimated governance levels and that of the rest of the world:

(4)   IGQ = constant + A_1 × log of per capita income + B_1 × MENA dummy + error

(5)   IPA = constant + A_2 × log of per capita income + B_2 × MENA dummy + error

(6) $IQA = \text{constant} + A_3 \times \log \text{ of per capita income} + B_3 \times \text{MENA}$ dummy + error.

The R^2 of the regressions is, respectively, 72 percent, 57 percent, and 70 percent.

All estimated A coefficients are positive and statistically significant.

All estimated B coefficients are negative and significant. These coefficients show the extent to which MENA countries are clustered away from the rest of the world.

The results of the six regressions are presented in table B.1 below.

Thus, two fitted lines are derived: a fitted line for the rest of the world, when the MENA dummy is set to be equal to 0, and a MENA dummy line, when the MENA dummy is set to be equal to 1. On an *x-y* scatter (*x* measuring income levels and *y* measuring governance levels), the two lines have

TABLE B.1

Governance and Per Capita Incomes: Estimated Coefficients and *t* Values

Index of governance quality (IGQ)	Equation (1), $n = 154, R^2 = 0.66$	Equation (4), $n = 154, R^2 = 0.72$
Log of per capita income	0.70 (16.34)***	0.72 (18.7)***
Constant	−6.0 (−16.17)***	−6.08 (−17.7)***
MENA dummy		−0.80 (−5.64)***
Index of political accountability (IPA)	**Equation (2),** $n = 154, R^2 = 0.43$	**Equation (5),** $n = 154, R^2 = 0.57$
Log of per capita income	0.63 (10.84)***	0.67 (13.56)***
Constant	−5.06 (−10.06)***	−5.20 (−11.73)***
MENA dummy		−1.43 (−7.72)***
Index of quality of administration (IQA)	**Equation (3),** $n = 154, R^2 = 0.69$	**Equation (6),** $n = 154, R^2 = 0.70$
Log of per capita income	0.65 (17.37)***	0.65 (18.1)***
Constant	−5.55 (−17.08)***	−5.58 (−17.54)***
MENA dummy		−0.35 (−2.7)***

*** Significant at 99 percent.
Note: Numbers in parentheses are *t*-statistics.
Source: Authors' calculations.

the same slope, estimated A, but different intercepts, the difference being estimated B. (Since the estimated B is negative, the MENA dummy line is located below the fitted line for the rest of the world).

The average MENA gap in governance is then measured as the vertical distance between the two lines. It indicates the difference between the average governance index as determined by the fitted line for the rest of the world and the average governance index as determined by the MENA dummy line, given the same per capita income level (figure B.1). (The same scatters are derived for the two other governance indexes.)

Next, the same original regressions are run only for the sample of MENA countries, and a fitted line is derived for each, thus portraying the relationship between governance and incomes across MENA countries.

The adjusted R^2 of the regressions is, respectively, 34 percent, 0.7 percent, and 39 percent.

All estimated A coefficients are positive, with only A_1 and A_3 being significant (table B.2).

Keeping the same average MENA gap previously derived, the scatter diagram is now illustrated in figure B.2. (The same scatters are derived for the two other governance indexes.)

FIGURE B.1

Governance and Per Capita Incomes: Estimating the Average MENA Effect

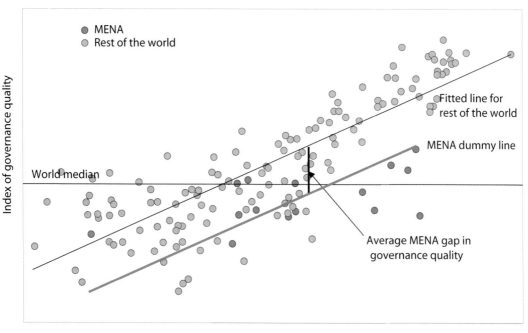

Log of per capita GDP

TABLE B.2

MENA's Governance Gap: Estimated Coefficients and *t* Values

Index of governance quality (IGQ)	Equation (1.1), $n = 15$, $R^2 = 0.34$
Log of per capita income	0.27
	$(2.69)^{**}$
Constant	−2.9
	$(−3.37)^{***}$
Index of political accountability (IPA)	Equation (2.1), $n = 15$, $R^2 = 0.007$
Log of per capita income	0.035
	(0.29)
Constant	−1.03
	(0.92)
Index of quality of administration (IQA)	Equation (3.1), $n = 15$, $R^2 = 0.39$
Log of per capita income	0.36
	$(2.94)^{**}$
Constant	−3.3
	$(−3.13)^{***}$

** Significant at 95 percent.
*** Significant at 99 percent.
Note: Numbers in parentheses are *t*-statistics.
Source: Authors' calculations.

FIGURE B.2

MENA's Governance Gap Compared with the Rest of the World

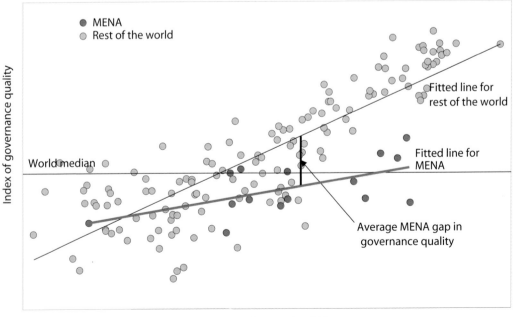

Log of per capita GDP

Although the regressions performed above show simply that better governance is associated with higher income levels, they do not address the issue of causality. Because governance is not exogenously determined, a simple OLS estimating the effect of governance on incomes would lead to inconsistent estimators. An instrumental variable with a two-stage least-squares approach is thus used to correct for the endogeneity problem. The issue, however, becomes the choice of the appropriate instrument for the model, a variable that is highly correlated with governance but that has no direct effect on income levels.

Three main instruments were considered. The first instrument was the settler mortality index, developed by Acemoglu, Johnson, and Robinson (2001). The authors used settler mortality in the 18th and 19th centuries as instruments; they argued that colonial powers had weak incentives to establish the institutions of good governance in colonies where a permanent European presence was unlikely to take root. One caveat regarding this index pertains to its limited coverage (68 countries).

The second instrument that has been used in the governance literature is the percentage of a country's population who speak one of the five main Western languages (English, German, French, Portuguese, and Spanish) as their mother tongue, developed by Hall and Jones (1999). The authors argue that Western European influence brought about stronger institutions in some countries.

Not only do the two indexes suffer from an ethnocentric bias, but also their relevancy to MENA—a region where the colonial legacies led to checkered state-building trajectories—is problematic.

The third instrument is the "index of political particularism," developed by Wallack and others (2002), which is designed to measure the incentives that electoral laws create for politicians to adhere to party platforms or build personal support bases. Panizza (2001) empirically explores the links between this index and institutional quality, and finds that intermediate levels of the index of political particularism are strongly associated with higher institutional quality.

The major caveat is that being an electoral phenomenon, political particularism—and thus its link to institutional quality—may not be well defined or valid in a nondemocratic system. In particular, Panizza (2001) finds that the correlation between government effectiveness (one of the measures of governance used by Kaufmann, Kraay, and Zoido-Lobaton 2002) and political particularism completely disappears when nondemocratic countries are dropped from the sample.

Given these caveats, it becomes difficult to find convincing examples of instrumental variables. The difficulty of finding appropriate instruments has not allowed the authors of this book to address empirically the causal relationship between governance and income.

Note

1. Four countries—Djibouti, Iraq, Libya and the West Bank and Gaza—are excluded from the analysis because of lack of reliable data.

Estimating the Effect of Governance on Growth

The literature on the determinants of growth presents a wide array of models, including Sachs and Warner (1997); Barro (1991); King and Levine (1993); Mankiw, Romer, and Weil (1992); and De Long and Summers (1991).

The estimations of the effects of governance on growth draw heavily on those models and on a dataset compiled and used by Sachs and Warner (1997).

Model 1: Based on Sachs and Warner (1997)

The growth rate of GDP is a function of domestic investment, degree of openness, resource endowments, initial income levels, terms of trade (TOT) growth, and a measure of institutional quality.

> Growth = constant + A × investment + B × openness + C × resource endowments + D × income + E × TOT growth + F × institutional quality + error

- The growth rate of GDP is measured as the average annual rate of growth of real GDP divided by the economically active population between the years 1970 and 1990.

- Domestic investment is measured as the natural log of the ratio of real gross domestic investment (public and private) to real GDP, averaged over the period 1970–89.

- The degree of openness is the fraction of years during the period 1970–90 in which the country is rated as an open economy according to the criteria in Sachs and Warner (1995b).

- The degree of resource endowments is measured as the share of exports of primary products in the GNP in 1970. Primary products or natural resource exports are exports of "fuels" and "nonfuel primary products."

- Initial income is measured as the natural log of real GDP divided by the economically active population in 1970.

- The terms of trade growth is measured as the average annual growth in the log of the external terms of trade between 1970 and 1990. The external terms of trade is the ratio of an export price index to an import price index.

- Institutional quality is measured as a weighted average[1] of three indexes: rule of law, bureaucratic quality, and corruption. The rule of law index reflects "the degree to which the citizens of a country are willing to accept the established institutions to make and implement laws and adjudicate disputes." Bureaucratic quality and corruption indexes are explained in detail in appendix A. The three indexes originate from the *International Country Risk Guide* and are measured as of 1982.

It is important to note that the original model used by the authors (Sachs and Warner 1997) included the rule of law index only as a measure of institutional quality. For this exercise—and to make it more compatible with the governance indexes constructed in the book, one should add the two other measures of bureaucratic quality and corruption. The optimal situation would be to add all remaining indicators that form the IQA (index of quality of administration); however, those data are not made available. Thus, the analysis below reflects very roughly the measure of the quality of administration adopted in the book.

The equation is regressed on a cross-country sample of 74 countries.

The estimated coefficient of institutional quality is positive and statistically significant.

The R^2 of the regression is on the order of 76 percent. It is important to note that without the institutional quality variable, the R^2 is on the order of 66 percent.

Moreover, when the variable is included in the regression, the coefficient of investment loses some explanatory power (becomes less significant), hinting at the possibility of investment as one channel through which governance (as proxied by institutional quality here) affects growth.

Model 2: Based on Barro (1991)

The growth rate of GDP is a function of domestic investment, enrollment in secondary education, enrollment in primary education, government spending, revolutions and coups, assassinations, price distortions, initial income levels, and the measure of institutional quality.

Growth = constant + $A \times$ investment + $B \times$ secondary + $C \times$ primary +
$D \times$ government spending + $E \times$ revolutions and coups +
$F \times$ assassinations + $G \times$ price distortions + $H \times$ income +
$I \times$ institutional quality + error

- The growth rate of GDP is measured as the average annual rate of growth of real GDP divided by the economically active population between the years 1970 and 1990.

- Domestic investment is measured as the natural log of the ratio of real gross domestic investment (public and private) to real GDP, averaged over the period 1970–89.

- The primary and secondary school enrollment rates data are those reported in Barro and Lee (1994).

- Government spending is measured as the ratio of real government "consumption" spending, which is the net of spending on the military and education, to real GDP (Barro and Lee 1994).

- Revolutions and coups refer to the number of revolutions and coups per year, averaged over the period 1970–85.

- Assassinations refer to the number of assassinations per million population per year, averaged over the period 1970–85.

- Price distortions are measured as the deviation of the log of the price level of investment relative to the United States from the cross-country sample mean in 1970.

- Initial income is measured as the natural log of real GDP divided by the economically active population in 1970.

- Institutional quality is measured as explained above.

The equation is regressed on a cross-country sample of 67 countries. Adding the institutional quality variable to the regression increases R^2 from 33 percent to 53 percent. The corresponding estimated coefficient is positive and statistically significant.

Model 3: Based on King and Levine (1993)

The growth rate of GDP is a function of secondary education attainment, financial depth, initial income levels, and the measure of institutional quality.

Growth = constant + $A \times$ secondary attainment + $B \times$ financial
depth + $C \times$ income + $D \times$ institutional quality + error

- The growth rate of GDP is measured as the average annual rate of growth of real GDP divided by the economically active population between the years 1970 and 1990.

- Secondary education attainment is measured as the log of years of secondary education in the population averaged over the period 1970–89.

- Financial depth is measured as the ratio of the liabilities of financial intermediaries, plus currency in circulation, to GDP in 1970.

- Initial income is measured as the natural log of real GDP divided by the economically active population in 1970.

- Institutional quality is measured as explained above.

The equation is regressed on a cross-country sample of 61 countries. Adding the institutional quality variable to the regression increases R^2 from 18 percent to 43 percent. The corresponding estimated coefficient is positive and statistically significant.

Model 4: Based on Mankiw, Romer, and Weil (1992)

The growth rate of GDP is a function of domestic investment, population growth, initial income levels, and the measure of institutional quality.

$$\text{Growth} = \text{constant} + A \times \text{investment} + B \times \text{population growth} + C \times \text{income} + D \times \text{institutional quality} + \text{error}$$

- The growth rate of GDP is measured as the average annual rate of growth of real GDP divided by the economically active population between the years 1970 and 1990.

- Domestic investment is measured as the natural log of the ratio of real gross domestic investment (public and private) to real GDP, averaged over the period 1970–89.

- Population growth is measured per year during the period 1970–90.

- Initial income is measured as the natural log of real GDP divided by the economically active population in 1970.

- Institutional quality is measured as explained above.

The equation is regressed on a cross-country sample of 75 countries. Adding the institutional quality variable to the regression increases R^2 from 32 percent to 45 percent. The corresponding estimated coefficient is positive and statistically significant.

Model 5: Based on De Long and Summers (1991)

The growth rate of GDP is a function of labor force growth, equipment investment, nonequipment investment, initial income levels, and the measure of institutional quality.

> Growth = constant + $A \times$ labor force growth + $B \times$ equipment
> investment + $C \times$ nonequipment investment + $D \times$
> income + $E \times$ institutional quality + error

- The growth rate of GDP is measured as the average annual rate of growth of real GDP divided by the economically active population between the years 1970 and 1990.

- Labor force growth is taken from De Long and Summers (1991).

- Investment spending on equipment is measured as a fraction of GDP, averaged over the period 1970–85.

- Investment spending on structures and goods other than equipment is measured as a fraction of GDP, averaged over the period 1970–85.

- Initial income is measured as the natural log of real GDP divided by the economically active population in 1970.

- Institutional quality is measured as explained above.

The equation is regressed on a cross-country sample of 52 countries.

Adding the institutional quality variable to the regression increases R^2 from 22 percent to 34 percent. The corresponding estimated coefficient is positive and statistically significant.

Governance and Growth in MENA

The analysis of the effects of governance on growth for the MENA region relies on the first model (Sachs and Warner 1997), basically because it captures the effect of resource endowments relevant to the region and because the MENA sample included in the analysis is the most comprehensive. It includes Algeria, the Arab Republic of Egypt, the Islamic Republic of Iran, Jordan, Morocco, the Syrian Arab Republic, and Tunisia. The rest of the countries were excluded mainly because of lack of data (table C.1).

The estimated growth rate of the MENA region is on the order of 1.11 percent.

As one studies the effect of an improvement in the governance levels on growth in the MENA region, the institutional quality level of MENA

TABLE C.1

Estimating Growth

Estimated coefficients and *t* values

Real GDP growth rate	$n = 74, R^2 = 0.76$
Log of real GDP per economically active population	−1.82
	(−7.09)***
Primary exports as share of GNP	−8.00
	(−6.16)***
Openness index	1.45
	(4.15)***
Log of domestic investment to real GDP	0.73
	(2.5)**
Terms of trade growth	0.13
	(2.45)**
Institutional quality index	0.57
	(3.87)***
Constant	15.02
	(6.86)***

** Significant at 95 percent.
*** Significant at 99 percent.
Note: Numbers in parentheses are *t*-statistics.
Source: Authors' calculations based on data set compiled by Sachs and Warner (1997).

as an average is assigned the same average level of a sample of six Latin American (LA6) countries (Argentina, Brazil, Chile, Mexico, República Bolivariana de Venezuela, and Uruguay).

If one uses the same original coefficients from the regression equation and holds all other variables constant, the calculated estimated growth rate of the MENA region increases to 1.98 percent, an increase of 0.87 percentage points.

This new estimated increase of the annual growth rate is what MENA would have gained if only institutional quality were improved (to the level of LA6).

The same exercise is repeated, this time assigning the same average level of a sample of five East Asian (EA5) countries (Indonesia, Malaysia, the Philippines, Singapore, and Thailand).

In this case, the calculated estimated growth rate of the MENA region increases to 1.94 percent, an increase of 0.83 percentage point. This new estimated increase of the annual growth rate is what MENA would have gained if only institutional quality were improved (to the level of EA5).

Note

1. For consistency, principal component analysis is used as the aggregation method.

Literature Review: Examining Factors that Help Explain the Governance Gap in MENA

Mineral Wealth and Governance

The effect of mineral wealth and external rents on governance and institutional development has been widely researched over the past two decades. Two main strands of the literature can be identified.

The Resource Curse School

The "resource curse" literature, led mainly by econometric research, has traditionally focused on the effect of resource wealth on economic development.[1] There are two main findings.

First, resource-abundant states tend to grow more slowly than their resource-poor counterparts. The argument is that resource wealth is associated with economic hardships known as the Dutch Disease effects that deter growth.[2] Despite its statistical validity, this argument remains insufficient—because it does not explain why some governments are able to offset the economic hardships associated with the Dutch Disease and others are not.

Second, resource-rich countries are more likely to suffer from conflicts and civil wars.[3] Mineral wealth is often geographically concentrated. If that wealth happens to be concentrated in a region populated by an ethnic or religious minority, the oil-as-spoils thesis maintains that conflicts are likely to arise through two main channels: by presenting an attractive set of spoils to potential rebels or state-breakers and by creating resentment over unequal distribution of oil rents. But the claim does not explain why some ethnically diverse resource-rich countries, such as Botswana, have managed to avoid conflict.

More recent empirical studies take an interesting twist on the resource curse argument, thus showing that differences in governance (measured by institutional quality) explain why some resource-rich countries have managed to grow while others have not.[4] The corollary is that sustained improvements in governance quality can offset the economic and sociopolitical hardships associated with resource abundance and can allow them to achieve faster and equitable growth.

The Rentier State School

The rentier state literature—led mostly by political scientists—presents a second claim: oil-reliant states tend to be more authoritarian.[5] This claim will be explored in more detail, because it is one of the common explanations for the governance gap in the MENA region.

Central to this discussion is the concept of "exogenous rents," which are revenues that a regime derives from sources external to society. The rents can take the form of oil and gas paid directly to the government by foreign companies or of economic aid that goes directly to the state budget. Area specialists often describe most countries in the MENA region as rentier states, because governments derive a large fraction of their revenues from external rents, mostly from the sale of oil and gas.[6] Although external rents apply specifically to oil-reliant states in the region, they also accrue to some nonoil states.[7]

What are the main causal mechanisms that help explain how exogenous rents that are derived from natural resource wealth make some MENA governments, but not others, more authoritarian? Two main explanations are advanced in the literature: the "rentier state" effect (through rent-led patronage) and the "repression" thesis (through rent-financed coercive institutions).[8]

The Rentier State Thesis. This thesis argues that governments use oil revenues to relieve social pressures that might otherwise lead to demands for greater accountability. This relief of pressure can happen through three main channels.

The first channel is the "taxation effect." When governments derive sufficient revenues from the sale of oil, they are likely to tax their populations less heavily. In turn, citizens will be less likely to demand accountability—and representation—from their government. But Waterbury (1994) provides evidence that the MENA region has not been "undertaxed" as is often claimed, when compared with other developing regions.[9] According to the author, the crux of the argument of "no taxation, no representation" and its link to the weak accountability in MENA is not so much the tax burden as the nature of the taxes. Waterbury (1994) notes that in oil-rich MENA countries, governments rely more on oil rents than on direct tax revenues, and the reliance on rents means that governments are not obliged to develop organic links to their citizens. The greatest source of tax revenue is indirect (tariffs, excise and sales taxes). Not only are direct taxes typically low, but also corporate profit taxes—often generated by publicly owned enterprises such as petroleum companies—tend to outweigh income taxes by a considerable margin.

It is also argued that taxation encourages institutional development to be able to respond to demand representation (Herb 2003). Historical evidence suggests that, in MENA, this institutional development did not occur.[10] It seems plausible to contend that in MENA, rentier states, ruling elites, and their supporters had little incentive to specify property rights, to improve the legal and regulatory framework, or to enhance state capacity to run their economies.

The second channel is through rent-led patronage (what Ross 2001 calls the "spending effect"). The argument here is that oil wealth may lead to greater spending on patronage that minimizes pressure for reforms. Civil servants and citizens alike turn into a rentier class so they can capture gains from rents without the need for strong institutions. In MENA, there is enough evidence to suggest that in most oil-reliant countries, state institutions became channels for distributive purposes, while their already weak institutional frameworks remained underdeveloped.[11]

The third channel is what Ross terms the "group formation" effect. Here the contention is that when oil rents provide the government with enough revenues, the government will use its largesse to prevent the formation of social groups that are independent from the state. Yet, whether these group formations are deliberate actions initiated by the governments or are simply byproducts of the rentier economies is a matter of some disagreement, and the evidence in MENA countries is not conclusive (Chaudry 1997; Vandewalle 1998; Bellin 1994).

The Repression Thesis. It is also argued that oil wealth and authoritarianism are linked by "repression" (Ross 2001). Governments of oil-rich countries may spend more on internal security and may have large military apparatuses. In MENA, the rise of the military and national security forces (*mukhabarat*) was consolidated by the prevalence of conflicts within and between states. Oil wealth and authoritarianism in MENA could be linked by the narrow coalitions that had emerged since independence and that relied on highly coercive institutions.

Empirically, however, such links are found to be weak. In a recent study, Ross (2001) finds an uncertain relationship between the presence of oil wealth and an increase in military spending. Furthermore, no empirical connection between military expenditure and repression has been established, which raises the question of whether many oil states might invest in their militaries simply to protect themselves from perceived or real external threats (as argued earlier).

Taking up the question of the "repressive argument," Bellin (2001) provides a compelling argument for the "robustness" of authoritarianism in MENA. Despite growing fiscal challenges, the capacity of oil-rich authoritarian regimes to survive is linked to a combination of factors—such as the sufficient access to revenues, the low levels of popular mobilization, and the strategic value of oil for international powers. Those factors were made manifest in the past through international support of internal coercive institutions or through smaller external pressures to reform. Yet, the prospects for the end of authoritarianism in the region are less gloomy when one looks at the declining oil reserves, the commitment by multilateral organizations to support moves toward better governance in the region, and the increasing levels of popular demand for greater accountability and participation in most MENA countries.

Other Factors—Development, Culture, Religion, Regimes

The Economic Explanation: The Modernization Theory

Proponents of the modernization school argue that economic development automatically propels societies toward more open and participatory forms of governance (Lipset 1959; Inglehart 1997). Good governance is a luxury good that automatically accrues as economies become richer. Economic development brings about social and cultural changes that, in turn, lead to more open and participatory forms of governance. Rising education and communications levels produce a more articulate public that is better equipped to organize and mobilize. And rising occupational specialization produces a more autonomous work force with specialized skills that enhance the public's bargaining power with ruling elites.

In MENA, good records in certain socioeconomic indicators appear to correlate with varying degrees of political opening in a few countries (such as Jordan, Kuwait, and Lebanon, where literacy rates are more than 75 percent and Internet use rates are relatively high). But evidence in other countries points out that access to the Internet has not led to governance changes. In Syria, for example, it is illegal to use the Internet except through government-controlled servers, which will block a wide assortment of Web sites. Country evidence worldwide suggests that lower levels of both literacy and Internet use have not blocked transitions toward more participatory forms of governance in regions such as Africa and South Asia. Overall, empirical studies on the validity of the modernization theory are inconclusive.

The Cultural Explanation: "Neopatrimonialism" and "Neoorientalism"

The first strand of thought is represented by the advocates of the role of "patrimonialism and patriarchy" as the genesis of MENA political authoritarianism (Sharabi 1988; Hammoudi 1997). Proponents contend that the origins of authoritarianism are to be found in microstructures endogenous to the MENA world—the tribe, the clan, and the patriarchal family, all of which provide the models of submission at the national level. Yet, apart from the methodological weakness of the argument, evidence outside the MENA region does not support this thesis. Norms of hierarchical authority are also found in the Confucian and Roman Catholic traditions. And some countries where these traditions predominate (Portugal, the Republic of Korea, and Spain and some countries in Latin America) have open and participatory political systems.

An alternative explanation for the persistence of the authoritarianism in MENA is offered by the advocates of the "orientalist" argument. According to them, Islam is ill-suited for ensuring participatory forms of governance (Huntington 1993, pp. 22–49; Hudson 1995). Thus, Islam's failure to distinguish the realms of Caesar and God; its insistence that sovereignty rests with God and that the essence of the law is divinely revealed and, therefore, beyond human emendation; and its religiously enshrined discriminatory treatment of women and non-Muslim minorities—all appear quite inconsistent with inclusive and accountable participatory forms of governance.

But the explanation is problematic in several respects. First, the approach assumes that there is a single, monolithic interpretation of Islam. Yet, various strains exist, and within them are strong debates over the role of political participation. Second, Islam, like all other great religions, embodies elements that can be used instrumentally for both authoritarian and participatory forms of governance. As Esposito and Voll (1996) posit, the Islamic heritage contains broad concepts and traditions that provide the foundation for the modern concepts of governance. The broader sense of limited sovereignty of the ruler and the effective separation of powers within the state are already part of the repertoire of political concepts that are available to those participating in the political processes in contemporary Islamic societies.[12] The real question becomes how and under what circumstances the elements in Islam that are favorable to participatory and accountable forms of governance can be applied in the political realm.

Political Quietism in Islam. Other analysts have argued that Islamic political culture promotes political quietism—citing a famous Islamic admonition: "Better one hundred years of the Sultan's tyranny than one year of people's tyranny over each other" (Lewis 1993). As a result, the political experience of the Middle East is one of unrelieved autocracy, in which obedience to the sovereign was a religious as well as a political obligation, and in which disobedience was a sin as well as a crime (Lewis 1964). A related claim argues that the level of religiosity among the Muslim population in the region has negatively affected attitudes toward political openness and participation. But recent empirical evidence reveals that individuals' support for political aspects of Islam and their levels of mosque involvement have little influence on their attitudes toward political participation (Tessler 2002).[13]

Political Radicalism in Islam. When the rise of religious fundamentalist movements throughout the Islamic world during the late 1970s and 1980s appeared to belie the claim that Islam promoted political quietism, a second argument gained currency. That argument contended that Islam inhibits the emergence of participatory modes of governance by encouraging resistance to political authority (Crone 2002). But the argument is questionable that the presence of radical Islamic groups helps explain the authoritarianism of political regimes by providing governments with a pretext to rule with "an iron fist." Variation in the political and military strength of Islamist groups—both between and within countries over time—does not appear to correlate closely with the level of political and civil liberties permitted by MENA governments.

The Social Explanation: The Fluidity of Class Structure

Some analysts argue that weak associational life or civil society in MENA accounts for the governance "deficit" in the region. They draw from the work of Toqueville—and more recently Robert Putnam—that independent, nongovernmental associations would help foster participatory forms of governance. The lack of horizontal voluntary associations and the persistence of strong clan, tribal, and kinship ties could help explain the persistence of authoritarianism in the region. This argument suffers from weaknesses similar to the cultural arguments delineated above. Moreover, many scholars have documented the level and vitality of civil society in MENA countries and have shown that it is not a new phenomenon in the region (Norton and Kazemi 1996).[14]

The Political Explanation: The Type of Political Regime

It has also been argued that some political regimes are more prone to engage in more open and participatory forms of governance than others (Kamrava 1998, pp. 63–85; Anderson 1991c, pp. 53–77). Yet, reforms toward more participatory forms of governance in MENA have stalled irrespective of the type of government regime—monarchy or sultanates (Jordan, Morocco, Oman, Saudi Arabia), socialist (Syria, Iraq), Islamic (the Islamic Republic of Iran), secular or nationalist (Algeria, Tunisia)—and irrespective of whether they are single or multiparty systems (Vandewalle 1998; Lust-Okar and Jamal 2002).

Notes

1. See Sachs and Warner 1995a; Leite and Weidmann 1999; Ross 1999; Auty 2001.

2. In the early 1980s, the Dutch Disease looked like a promising explanation for the ailments of resource-abundant states. It describes the combined influence of two effects that commonly follow resource booms. The first is the appreciation of a state's real exchange rate caused by the sharp rise in exports. The second is the tendency of a booming resource sector to draw capital and labor away from a country's manufacturing and agricultural sectors, raising their production costs. Together, those effects can lead to a decline in the export of agricultural and manufactured goods and can inflate the costs of goods and services that cannot be imported (the nontradable sector).

3. See Collier and Hoeffler 1998; deSoysa 2000.

4. These authors (Mehlum, Moene, and Torvik 2002; Herb 2002) argue that the positive effects of rent wealth are canceled out by the negative effects of "rentierism" in MENA and elsewhere.

5. This claim has been empirically validated by Ross (2001). It has also been made by most Middle East scholars, as they explain the prevalence of authoritarianism in MENA (Mahdavy 1970, p. 428; Luciani 1987). See also Crystal 1994; Vandewalle 1998; Bellin 1994; Chaudry 1997; Skocpol 1985; Gausse 1996.

6. Beblawi (1987) defines "rentier state" as one where the rents are paid by foreign actors, where they accrue directly to the state, and where "only a few are engaged in the generation of this rent (wealth), the majority being only involved in the distribution or utilization of it."

7. The governments of the Arab Republic of Egypt, Jordan, and the Syrian Arab Republic, earn large locational rents from payments for pipeline crossings, transit fees, and passage through the Suez Canal. Foreign aid flows may also be considered as a type of economic rent. Worker remittances are external rents, but those go (at least initially) to private actors, not the state.

8. For a detailed account of the arguments presented by the rentier literature scholars, see Ross (2001).

9. According to Waterbury (1994), "over the period 1975 to 1985, tax revenues as a proportion of GNP averaged 25 percent for Middle Eastern countries while Latin America averaged about 12 percent.... On average, 19 percent of total tax revenues in the Middle East came from corporate profit tax, while the corresponding figure for Africa was 20 percent, for Asia 19 percent, and for Latin America 10 percent" (p. 29).

10. See Luciani 1984. Crystal (1995) found that the discovery of oil made the governments of Kuwait and Qatar less accountable to the traditional merchant class. Brand (1992) found that a drop in foreign aid in the 1980s led to greater pressures for political representation in Jordan. More recently, Ross (2003) tested whether the claim "taxation leads to representation" was linked to a higher absolute tax burden or was a higher tax burden relative to the services that the government provides. Only the latter passes the empirical test.

11. Entelis (1976) argues that the Saudi Arabian government used its oil wealth for populist spending programs that reduced pressures for reforms. Vandewalle (1998) makes a similar argument about the Libyan government.

12. For a review of the concept of accountability in Islam, see Anderson (1991c).

13. See also Inglehart and Norris 2002; Moaddel 2002; Pettersson 2003.

14. See the original argument in Crystal (1994, pp. 26–89).

Governance and Growth: Reviewing the Evidence

A growing body of evidence points to governance failures as a root cause of slow and unsustainable growth. The governance literature is largely empirical. The successes and failures on the empirical side of the literature, however, are related to the clarity and precision of its theoretical underpinnings. Clarity is inherently difficult to achieve with a concept as heterogeneous as governance. It helps to consider two sets of governance concepts separately: those related to government performance of its core functions (quality of public institutions) and those related to the incentives of government officials to act on behalf of the public interest (public accountability).

Quality of Public Institutions and Growth

Evidence from cross-country statistical research amply supports the importance of secure property rights, the rule of law, or the credibility of government for growth (Knack and Keefer 1995; Acemoglu, Johnson, and Robinson 2001; Rodrik, Subramanian, and Trebbi 2002) or per capita incomes (Hall and Jones 1999). However, as Weyland (2003) argues, there are large potential econometric problems that emerge in this literature. For example, the empirical governance measures are usually subjective, introducing noise and, possibly, bias into the resulting estimates. Nevertheless, they represent a quantum leap in the ability to bring statistical analysis to bear on topics that were previously investigated only in theory or case studies, a leap that can be measured in terms of the sharp increase in research on governance-related topics that followed the introduction of these measures into the literature. Some of this literature is reviewed here.

The text of this appendix was adapted from Keefer 2003.

Rule of Law

With respect to the issue of property rights or the rule of law, fairly exhaustive attempts have been made to control for empirical difficulties ranging from endogeneity to measurement error. Results documenting the importance of secure property rights for growth have been robust to causality testing (Calderón and Chong 2000), to ingenious instruments and historical investigation (Acemoglu, Johnson, and Robinson 2001), and to the substitution of income for growth as the dependent variable (Hall and Jones 1999). Although there is still room for skepticism, it is, nevertheless, true that the influence of secure property rights has withstood an unusually large amount of scrutiny. The security of property rights has also been linked to development phenomena other than economic growth. Dollar and Kraay (2002) consider the effect of secure property rights on inequality. They find that the security of property rights raises the incomes of the rich and poor equally.

In a much different application, Deacon (1999) has found that the security of property rights is negatively related to rates of deforestation. The hypothesis that secure property rights accelerate economic development is supported by quantitative approaches other than those using cross-country data. Natural experiments involving property rights include work by Feder (1993) on the consequences of land titling for farmers in Thailand; by Jimenez (1984) on the effects of titling on investment in and prices of homes in Manila; by Alston, Libecap, and Mueller (1999) on the effects of property rights security on farm productivity and deforestation in the Brazilian Amazon; and by O'Rourke (1999) on the effects of land tenure insecurity on the adoption of efficient butter production methods in Ireland when contrasted with Denmark.

Corruption and Bureaucratic Quality

The conclusions from the empirical work on corruption and bureaucratic quality are broadly similar to the work on property rights. In the first and prototypical empirical contribution, Mauro (1995) shows that corruption reduces growth, though Li, Xu, and Xou (2000) show that taking inequality into account reduces the estimated effect of corruption. Gupta, Davoodi, and Alonso-Terme (2002) present evidence that corruption exacerbates income inequality and poverty. Mo (2001) documents a causal chain linking higher corruption to lower growth through reduced investment in human and private capital. Evans and Rauch (2000) present quantitative evidence that supports the "embedded autonomy" hypothesis of Evans and that controls for income, education, and ethnic and linguistic diversity. They find that some characteristics of an "autonomous" bureaucracy (especially meritocratic recruitment) predict the assessments of property rights security and bureaucratic quality used elsewhere in the literature.

It is, however, more difficult to draw firm conclusions about the effect of corruption and bureaucratic quality on economic development. On the one hand, in the cross-country work exemplified by Mauro (1995), the corruption variables exhibit considerable overlap with the measures used in the property rights literature. On the other hand, the more fundamental difficulty in drawing inferences about the effect of corruption and bureaucratic quality on development is the greater vulnerability of these two variables to causality problems. Both are sensitive to the political leadership's incentives, which are typically not controlled for in, for example, corruption work and are sure to have a significant independent effect on government performance and economic development.

Governments often put into place distortionary policies that directly slow economic development while giving rise to corruption. Broadman and Recanatini (2002) use evidence from surveys of business people in transition countries regarding corruption and the effects of regulation to show that high regulatory barriers to entry and soft budget constraints on firms are both conducive to corruption. More optimistically, Cheng, Haggard, and Kang (1998) argue that well-functioning bureaucracies in the Republic of Korea and in Taiwan, China, were the result of conscious decisions by political actors who, in turn, were motivated by a desire to avert past crises or to deter the aggression of large neighbors.

Public Accountability and Growth

There are no agreed indicators of the concepts of "voice" and "accountability," either in theory or in the empirical literature. The literature uses proxies ranging from Freedom House indicators of political freedoms and civil liberties (found by Scully 1988 to be predictors of growth), to structural indicators of democracy (whether there are competitive elections and whether the executive is constrained by a legislature). With respect to the Freedom House indicators, the empirical record is reasonably convincing that these variables are important for development. Like governance itself, these variables are themselves multidimensional. Their multidimensionality makes it difficult to determine which of the concrete and objectively observable characteristics can be traced specifically to notions of voice and accountability, and which characteristics are specifically responsible for observed changes in development outcomes.

The democracy literature, relying on more structural and objective characteristics of polities, yields much more ambiguous results. One source of confusion is that democratic countries are both richer and better performing. This observation naturally gives rise to the difficult question: are countries better performing because they are rich or because they are democratic? For example, as we would expect, corruption and rent seeking are higher in countries that lack fully competitive elections, as are the risks of expropriation. However, countries with competitive elections are also substantially richer than other countries, even excluding the richest 20 democracies from the comparison. In part because of this, a large literature that always controls for per capita incomes at the beginning of the period finds only an ambiguous relationship between democracy and growth. Many of the income gains that democracy generates may already be embedded in the higher initial per capita incomes of democratic countries.

A number of investigations use more global indicators to test broader notions of "governance" or "institutions" on economic development. As they also engage the debate on the role of institutions versus geography in economic development, Easterly and Levine (2002) use the global governance index of Kaufmann, Kraay, and Zoido-Lobaton (2002) rather than more narrow property rights and rule of law indicators. The broad governance index has the advantage of including more dimensions of a country's institutions. However, the aggregate measure exacerbates the problem of interpretation. Provided the coefficient estimates are significant, one can say only that some factors related to governance are positively associated with growth. One cannot say, however, which factors those are, nor even be sure that some other factors do not also have a negative effect on growth.

Regardless of the endogeneity and causality issues that are preoccupations of the governance literature, the determinants of good governance—of secure property rights, voice and accountability, or honest and efficient bureaucratic behavior—are key issues in their own right. Intellectually, those issues are some of the most challenging in the social sciences.

Country Tables

Data Notes

Data in the country tables may differ from other data found in World Bank publications because of differences in computation methodologies. Information from non–World Bank sources, without either endorsement or verification, is reported in the interest of providing a consolidated data set of governance indicators that are widely used in global discussions of governance.

Data Sources

- Sources include World Bank Data 1996–2002, Encyclopaedia Britannica 2003, Central Intelligence Agency 2002, Freedom House 2002a and 2002b, Political Risk Services 2001, Center for International Development and Conflict Management 2000, Heritage Foundation/*Wall Street Journal* 2002, Djankov and others 2000, and Inter-Parliamentary Union 2003.

- The index of public accountability is an aggregated index of 12 subjective/perception measures: political rights, civil liberties, freedom of the press (Freedom House), polity score, regulation of executive recruitment, competitiveness of executive recruitment, openness of executive recruitment, regulation of participation, competitiveness of participation, executive constraints (CIDCM), democratic accountability (*International Country Risk Guide*), and transparency and accountability (World Bank data).

- The index of the quality of administration is an aggregated index of 10 subjective/perception measures: corruption, bureaucratic quality (*International Country Risk Guide*), property rights and rule-based governance, quality of budgetary and financial management, efficiency of revenue mobilization, quality of public administration (World Bank data), property rights, regulation, black market (Heritage Foundation), and number of procedures (Djankov and others 2000).

- The index of governance quality is an aggregated index of all 22 subjective/perception measures in the index of public accountability and the index of the quality of administration.

- The method of aggregation used is principal component analysis. (Refer to appendix A on the construction of the indexes and a detailed description for each indicator used.)

- For illustrative purposes, the income index in the "governance and development diamond" is calculated by dividing per capita gross national income (GNI) by 100. The infant survival index is calculated by subtracting the infant mortality (per 1,000 live births) from 100, so that the higher the infant survival index, the better.

- On the variable "measure of judicial efficiency," the "number of procedures" covers all independent procedural actions that are mandated by law or court regulation, and that demand interaction between the parties or between them and the judge or court officer.

- LIC: low-income countries (GNI per capita, Atlas method, US$755 or less)
  LMIC: lower-middle-income countries (GNI per capita, Atlas method, US$756–2,995)
  UMIC: upper-middle-income countries (GNI per capita, Atlas method, US$2,996–9,265)
  HIC: high-income countries (GNI per capita, Atlas method, US$9,266 or more)
  GNI: gross national income
  GDP: gross domestic product

- MENA15 includes Algeria, the Arab Republic of Egypt, Bahrain, the Islamic Republic of Iran, Jordan, Kuwait, Lebanon, Morocco, Oman, Qatar, the Republic of Yemen, Saudi Arabia, the Syrian Arab Republic, Tunisia, and the United Arab Emirates.

- MENA13 includes Algeria, Bahrain, Egypt, the Islamic Republic of Iran, Jordan, Kuwait, Lebanon, Morocco, Oman, the Republic of Yemen, Saudi Arabia, Syria, and Tunisia.

- MENA average in government expenditure (percent of GDP, 1999) excludes Egypt and Saudi Arabia.

- MENA average in judicial efficiency (contract enforcement) excludes Bahrain, Kuwait, and Oman.

- MENA average in public spending on education (percent of GDP, 1998) excludes Algeria, Egypt, Kuwait, and the Republic of Yemen.

- MENA average in ratio of girls to boys in primary and secondary education includes 1998 values for Jordan, Kuwait, Morocco, and the Republic of Yemen.

- MENA average in access to improved water (percent of population) and access to improved sanitation (percent of population) excludes Bahrain and Kuwait.

- MENA average in roads, paved (percent of total roads, 1999) excludes the Islamic Republic of Iran, Saudi Arabia, and Syria.

ALGERIA

Key socioeconomic indicators (2000 or most recent)

	Algeria	MENA13	LMIC
Population, mid-year (millions, aggregate)	30.4	265	2,140
Population under 15 years (%)	36	36	27
Life expectancy at birth (years)	70	70	69
Urban population (%)	57	72	45
Population growth (average annual, 1995–2001,%)	1.6	2.0	1.0
GNI per capita (PPP, US$)	5,840	5,198	4,500
GNI (PPP, US$ billions, aggregate)	177	1,380	9,640
GDP per capita growth (average annual, 1995–2001,%)	2	2.5	..
Exports of goods and services (% GDP)	42.5	38	34
Net petroleum exports (% GDP)	33	24.5	5
Government expenditure (% GDP, 1999)	30	21	20.6
Military expenditures (% GDP)	3.5	6	2.6

Governance and Development Diamond

Income index

Quality of administration index

Public accountability index

Infant survival index

——— Algeria
•••••• Lower-middle income

Key sociopolitical indicators

Political structure	Republic
Legal system	Socialist, based on French and Islamic law
Structure of government	
Executive branch	*Chief of state:* President (elected by popular vote, most recent 1999)
	Head of government: Prime minister (appointed by president, most recent appointment 2003)
	Cabinet: Appointed by president
	Elections: Universal suffrage, minimum voting age 18
Legislative branch	*Upper chamber:* National People's Assembly, or *Al-Majliss Ech-Chaabi Al-Watani* (389 seats; elected by popular vote, most recent 2002)
	Lower chamber: Council of Nations (144 seats; one-third appointed by the president, two-thirds elected by communal councils)
Judicial branch	Supreme Court
Administrative divisions	48 provinces
Most recent local elections held	2002
Political parties *(seats in parliament)*	Multiseat constituencies by proportional representation
Year women received right to vote	1962
Women in parliament (%)	6
Women at ministerial level (%)	0
Independence	July 5, 1962, from France
Constitution	November 19, 1976, most recent revision 1996
Ethnic groups	Arab (80%), Kabyle (13%), other (7%)
Religious groups	Sunni Muslim (99%), other (1%)
Circulation of daily newspapers, 1996 (copies printed per 1,000 people)	27
Internet users (%)	0.16

Measures of public sector performance (2000 or most recent)

	Algeria	MENA13	LMIC
Number of procedures to start business	..	..	13
Judicial efficiency (contract enforcement)			
Number of procedures	20	23	25
Number of days	387	284	311
Government expenditure (% GDP, 1999)	30	31	20.6
Public spending on education (% GDP, 1998)	..	6.7	4.1
Public spending on health (% GDP, 1998)	3.5	2.9	2.6
Infant mortality (per 1,000 live births)	40	31	34
Maternal mortality (per 100,000 live births, 1995)	150	180	..
Illiteracy (% population age 15+)	33	28	15
Female illiteracy (% female population age 15+)	43	38	20.5
Ratio of girls to boys in primary and secondary education	98	93	..
Access to improved water (% population)	89	83	80
Access to improved sanitation (% population)	92	85	55
Roads, paved (% total roads, 1999)	69	65	53
Telephone mainlines (per 1,000 people)	58	123	120

Measures of governance quality

(0–100, higher is better)	Algeria	MENA15	LMIC
Index of public accountability (IPA)	31.3	32	54
Index of quality of administration (IQA)	41	47	41
Index of governance quality (IGQ)	32	37	41.3

Governance quality

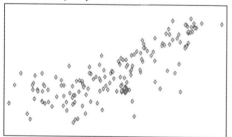

Per capita income

Quality of administration

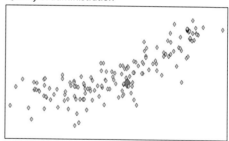

Per capita income

Public accountability

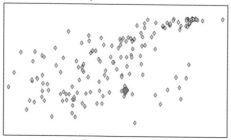

Per capita income

BAHRAIN

Key socioeconomic indicators (2000 or most recent)

	Bahrain	MENA13	UMIC
Population, mid-year			
(millions, aggregate)	0.6	265	497
Population under 15 years (%)	29	36	29
Life expectancy at birth (years)	73	70	71
Urban population (%)	92	72	72
Population growth (average			
annual, 1995–2001,%)	2.4	2.0	1.3
GNI per capita (PPP, US$)	15,370	5,198	8,500
GNI (PPP, US$ billions,			
aggregate)	9.97	1,380	4,230
GDP per capita growth			
(average annual, 1995–2001,%)	3.0	2.5	2.7
Exports of goods and			
services (% GDP)	82	38	26
Net petroleum exports			
(% GDP)	13	24.5	4.5
Government expenditure			
(% GDP, 1999)	28	21	..
Military expenditures (% GDP)	4	6	2.1

Governance and Development Diamond

Income index — Public accountability index — Infant survival index — Quality of administration index

— Bahrain
······ Upper-middle income

Key sociopolitical indicators

Political structure	Constitutional hereditary monarchy
Legal system	Based on English common law and Islamic law
Structure of government	
Executive branch	*Chief of state*: King, or monarch
	Head of government: Prime minister, appointed by monarch (most recent appointment 1971)
	Cabinet: Appointed by monarch
	Elections: None; monarchy is hereditary
Legislative branch	Unicameral National Assembly dissolved in August 1975
	Appointed Advisory Council established in December 1992
	Bicameral legislature created in December 2000, approved by referendum in February 2001
Judicial branch	High Civil Appeals Court
Administrative divisions	12 municipalities
Most recent local elections held	2002
Political parties (seats in parliament)	None
Year women received right to vote	1973
Women in parliament (% total)	6.25
Women at ministerial level (% total)	..
Independence	August 15, 1971, from the United Kingdom
Constitutiona	Late December 2000
Ethnic groups	Arab (64%), Asian (30%), other (6%)
Religious groups	Shii Muslim (61%), Sunni Muslim (20%), other (19%)
Circulation of daily newspapers, 1996 (copies printed per 1,000 people)	112
Internet users (%)	6.1

a. Bahraini voters approved on February 13–14, 2001, a referendum on legislative changes (revised constitution calls for a partially elected legislature, a constitutional monarchy, and an independent judiciary) (Source: Central Intelligence Agency 2002).

Measures of public sector performance (2000 or most recent)

	Bahrain	MENA13	UMIC
Number of procedures to start business	..	..	11
Judicial efficiency (contract enforcement)			
Number of procedures	..	23	27
Number of days	..	284	351
Government expenditure (% GDP, 1999)	28	31	..
Public spending on education (% GDP, 1998)	3.7	6.7	4.2
Public spending on health (% GDP, 1998)	3.5	2.9	3.5
Infant mortality (per 1,000 live births)	13	31	24
Maternal mortality (per 100,000 live births, 1995)	38	180	112
Illiteracy (% population age 15+)	12.5	28	9
Female illiteracy (% female population age 15+)	17.5	38	10
Ratio of girls to boys in primary and secondary education	103	93	101
Access to improved water (% population)	..	83	88
Access to improved sanitation (% population)	..	85	79
Roads, paved (% total roads, 1999)	77	65	51
Telephone mainlines (per 1,000 people)	250	123	192

Measures of governance quality

(0–100, higher is better)	Bahrain	MENA15	UMIC
Index of public accountability (IPA)	31.5	32.	65
Index of quality of administration (IQA)	66	47	56
Index of governance quality (IGQ)	50	37	56

Governance quality

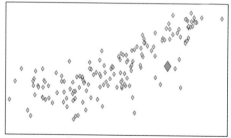

Per capita income

Quality of administration

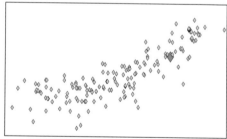

Per capita income

Public accountability

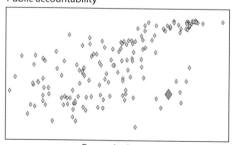

Per capita income

ARAB REPUBLIC OF EGYPT

Key socioeconomic indicators (2000 ορ μοστ ρεχεντ)

	Egypt	MENA13	LMIC
Population, mid-year (millions, aggregate)	64	265	2,140
Population under 15 years (%)	35	36	27
Life expectancy at birth (years)	68	70	69
Urban population (%)	43	72	45
Population growth (average annual, 1995–2001,%)	1.9	2.0	1.0
GNI per capita (PPP, US$)	3,510	5,198	4,500
GNI (PPP, US$ billions, aggregate)	224	1,380	9,640
GDP per capita growth (average annual, 1995–2001,%)	3.8	2.5	..
Exports of goods and services (% GDP)	16	38	34
Net petroleum exports (% GDP)	2	24.5	5
Government expenditure (% GDP, 1999)	..	21	20.6
Military expenditures (% GDP)	2.5	6	2.6

Governance and Development Diamond

Income index — Egypt ----- Lower-middle income

Quality of administration index — Public accountability index — Infant survival index

---

Key sociopolitical indicators

Political structure	Republic
Legal system	English common law, Islamic law, and Napoleonic codes
Structure of government	
Executive branch	*Chief of state*: President of the Republic (nominated by the People's Assembly, 1981/1999)
	Head of government: Prime minister (appointed by president, most recent appointment 1999)
	Cabinet: Appointed by president
Legislative branch	*Upper chamber*: People's Assembly, or *Majliss al-Sha'b* (454 seats; 444 elected by popular vote, 10 appointed by the president, most recent 2000)
	Lower chamber: Advisory Council, or *Majliss As Shura* (264 seats; 176 elected by popular vote, 88 appointed by the president, most recent 1995)
	Elections: Universal and compulsory suffrage, minimum voting age 18
Judicial branch	Supreme Constitutional Court
Administrative divisions	26 governorates
Most recent local elections held	2002
Political parties (seats in parliament)	National Democratic Party (88%), Independents (8%), Opposition (4%)
Year women received right to vote	1956
Women in parliament (%)	2.4
Women at ministerial level (%)	6.1
Independence	February 28, 1922, from the United Kingdom
Constitution	September 11, 1971
Ethnic groups	Arab (90%), Copts (10%)
Religious groups	Sunni Muslim (89%), Coptic Orthodox (10%), Protestant (1%)
Circulation of daily newspapers, 1996 (copies printed per 1,000 people)	31
Internet users (%)	0.7

Measures of public sector performance (2000 or most recent)

	Egypt	MENA13	LMIC
Number of procedures to start business	15	..	13
Judicial efficiency (contract enforcement)			
Number of procedures	19	23	25
Number of days	202	284	311
Government expenditure (% GDP, 1999)	..	31	20.6
Public spending on education (% GDP, 1998)	..	6.7	4.1
Public spending on health (% GDP, 1998)	1.8	2.9	2.6
Infant mortality (per 1,000 live births)	37	31	34
Maternal mortality (per 100,000 live births, 1995)	170	180	..
Illiteracy (% population age 15+)	45	28	15
Female illiteracy (% female population age 15+)	56	38	20.5
Ratio of girls to boys in primary and secondary education	94	93	..
Access to improved water (% population)	97	83	80
Access to improved sanitation (% population)	98	85	55
Roads, paved (% total roads, 1999)	78	65	53
Telephone mainlines (per 1,000 people)	86	123	120

Measures of governance quality

(0–100, higher is better)	Egypt	MENA15	LMIC
Index of public accountability (IPA)	30	32	54
Index of quality of administration (IQA)	38	47	41
Index of governance quality (IGQ)	30	37	41.3

Governance quality

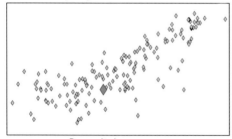

Per capita income

Quality of administration

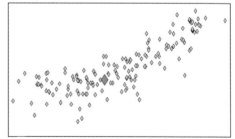

Per capita income

Public accountability

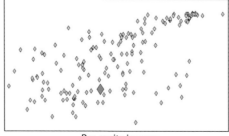

Per capita income

ISLAMIC REPUBLIC OF IRAN

Key socioeconomic indicators (2000 ορ μοστ ρεχεντ)

	Iran, Islamic Rep. of	MENA13	LMIC
Population, mid-year (millions, aggregate)	63.7	265	2,140
Population under 15 years (%)	34	36	27
Life expectancy at birth (years)	69	70	69
Urban population (%)	64	72	45
Population growth (average annual, 1995–2001,%)	1.5	2.0	1.0
GNI per capita (PPP, US$)	5,710	5,198	4,500
GNI (PPP, US$ billions, aggregate)	364	1,380	9,640
GDP per capita growth (average annual, 1995–2001,%)	3.6	2.5	..
Exports of goods and services (% GDP)	25	38	34
Net petroleum exports (% GDP)	21	24.5	5
Government expenditure (% GDP, 1999)	25.6	21	20.6
Military expenditures (% GDP)	4	6	2.6

Governance and Development Diamond

Key sociopolitical indicators

Political structure	Theocratic republic
Legal system	Islamic principles of government
Structure of government	
Executive branch	*Chief of state*: Leader of Islamic Revolution (since 1989, appointed for life by Assembly of Experts)
	Head of government: President (elected by popular vote, 1997/2001)
	Cabinet: Selected by president, with legislative approval
	Elections: Universal suffrage, minimum voting age 15
Legislative branch	Unicameral Islamic Consultative Assembly, or *Majliss-e-Shura-ye-Eslami* (290 seats; elected by popular vote, most recent 2000)
Judicial branch	Supreme Court
Administrative divisions	28 provinces
Most recent local elections held	2003
Political parties (seats in parliament)	Reformists (189), Conservatives (54), Independent (42) (last elections)
Year women received right to vote	1963
Women in parliament (%)	4.1
Women at ministerial level (%)	9.4
Independence	April 1, 1979, Islamic Republic of Iran proclaimed
Constitution	December 2–3, 1979, revised 1989
Ethnic groups	Persian (51%), Azeri (24%), other (25%)
Religious groups	Shii Muslim (94%), Sunni Muslim (6%)
Circulation of daily newspapers, 1996 (copies printed per 1,000 people)	27
Internet users (%)	1

Measures of public sector performance (2000 or most recent)

	Iran, Islamic Rep. of	MENA13	LMIC
Number of procedures to start business	..	..	13
Judicial efficiency (contract enforcement)			
Number of procedures	23	23	25
Number of days	150	284	311
Government expenditure (% GDP, 1999)	25.6	31	20.6
Public spending on education (% GDP, 1998)	4.5	6.7	4.1
Public spending on health (% GDP, 1998)	1.8	2.9	2.6
Infant mortality (per 1,000 live births)	36	31	34
Maternal mortality (per 100,000 live births, 1995)	130	180	..
Illiteracy (% population age 15+)	24	28	15
Female illiteracy (% female population age 15+)	31	38	20.5
Ratio of girls to boys in primary and secondary education	95	93	..
Access to improved water (% population)	92	83	80
Access to improved sanitation (% population)	83	85	55
Roads, paved (% total roads, 1999)	..	65	53
Telephone mainlines (per 1,000 people)	149	123	120

Measures of governance quality

(0–100, higher is better)	Iran, Islamic Rep. of	MENA15	LMIC
Index of public accountability (IPA)	44	32	54
Index of quality of administration (IQA)	29.7	47	41
Index of governance quality (IGQ)	30	37	41.3

Governance quality

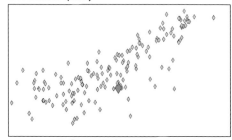

Per capita income

Quality of administration

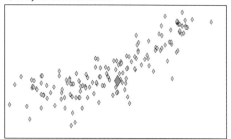

Per capita income

Public accountability

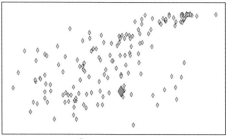

Per capita income

JORDAN

Key socioeconomic indicators (2000 or most recent)

	Jordan	MENA13	LMIC
Population, mid-year			
(millions, aggregate)	4.9	265	2,140
Population under 15 years (%)	38	36	27
Life expectancy at birth (years)	71	70	69
Urban population (%)	79	72	45
Population growth (average			
annual, 1995–2001,%)	3.1	2.0	1.0
GNI per capita (PPP, US$)	3,810	5,198	4,500
GNI (PPP, US$ billions,			
aggregate)	18.6	1,380	9,640
GDP per capita growth			
(average annual, 1995–2001,%)	0.4	2.5	..
Exports of goods and			
services (% GDP)	42	38	34
Net petroleum exports			
(% GDP)	0	24.5	5
Government expenditure			
(% GDP, 1999)	31	21	20.6
Military expenditures (% GDP)	9	6	2.6

Governance and Development Diamond

Income index

—— Jordan
·····Lower-middle income

Quality of administration index

Public accountability index

Infant survival index

Key sociopolitical indicators

Political structure	Constitutional monarchy
Legal system	Islamic law and French codes
Structure of government	
Executive branch	*Chief of state*: King, or monarch (since 1999)
	Head of government: Prime minister (appointed by monarch, most recent appointment 2000)
	Cabinet: Appointed by the prime minister in consultation with the monarch
Legislative branch	*Upper chamber*: Senate, or *Majliss al-Aayan* (40 seats; appointed by the monarch)
	Lower chamber: House of Representatives, or *Majliss al-Nuwaab* (80 seats; elected by popular vote, most recent 1997)
	Elections: Universal suffrage, minimum voting age 20
Judicial branch	Court of Cassation; Supreme Court
Administrative divisions	12 governorates
Most recent local elections held	2003
Political parties (seats in parliament)	National Constitutional Party (3), Ba'th Party (1), Independents (76)
Year women received right to vote	1974
Women in parliament (%)	3.3
Women at ministerial level (%)	0
Independence	May 25, 1946, from British Mandate
Constitution	January 8, 1952
Ethnic groups	Arab (98%), other (2%)
Religious groups	Sunni Muslim (96%), Christian (4%)
Circulation of daily newspapers, 1996 (copies printed per 1,000 people)	75
Internet users (%)	2.6

Measures of public sector performance (2000 or most recent)

	Jordan	MENA13	LMIC
Number of procedures to start business	13	..	13
Judicial efficiency (contract enforcement)			
Number of procedures	32	23	25
Number of days	147	284	311
Government expenditure (% GDP, 1999)	31	31	20.6
Public spending on education (% GDP, 1998)	6.0	6.7	4.1
Public spending on health (% GDP, 1998)	5.0	2.9	2.6
Infant mortality (per 1,000 live births)	28	31	34
Maternal mortality (per 100,000 live births, 1995)	41	180	..
Illiteracy (% population age 15+)	10	28	15
Female illiteracy (% female population age 15+)	16	38	20.5
Ratio of girls to boys in primary and secondary education	101	93	..
Access to improved water (% population)	96	83	80
Access to improved sanitation (% population)	99	85	55
Roads, paved (% total roads, 1999)	100	65	53
Telephone mainlines (per 1,000 people)	123	123	120

Measures of governance quality

(0–100, higher is better)	Jordan	MENA15	LMIC
Index of public accountability (IPA)	45	32	54
Index of quality of administration (IQA)	50.7	47	41
Index of governance quality (IGQ)	44	37	41.3

Governance quality

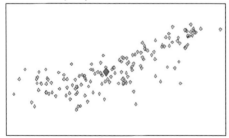

Per capita income

Quality of administration

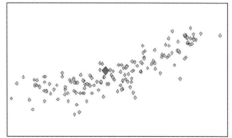

Per capita income

Public accountability

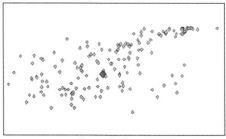

Per capita income

KUWAIT

Key socioeconomic indicators (2000 or most recent)

	Kuwait	MENA13	Non-OECD HIC
Population, mid-year			
(millions, aggregate)	1.9	265	50.3
Population under 15 years (%)	33	36	23
Life expectancy at birth (years)	76	70	76
Urban population (%)	96	72	50
Population growth (average			
annual, 1995–2001,%)	4.6	2.0	4.0
GNI per capita (PPP, US$)	22,290	5,198	..
GNI (PPP, US$ billions,			
aggregate)	44.2	1,380	..
GDP per capita growth			
(average annual, 1995–2001,%)	–2.2	2.5	..
Exports of goods and			
services (% GDP)	59	38	90
Net petroleum exports			
(% GDP)	50	24.5	10.2
Government expenditure			
(% GDP, 1999)	44	21	..
Military expenditures (% GDP)	8	6	4.2

Governance and Development Diamond

Key sociopolitical indicators

Political structure	Nominal constitutional monarchy
Legal system	Civil law system, Islamic law for personal matters
Structure of government	
Executive branch	*Chief of state*: Emir, or monarch
	Head of government: Prime minister and crown prince
	Cabinet: Appointed by prime minister
Legislative branch	Unicameral National Assembly, or *Majliss al-Umma* (50 seats; members elected by popular vote, most recent 1999)
	Elections: Limited suffrage (adult males who have been naturalized for 30 years or more or who have resided in Kuwait since before 1920 and their male descendants at age 21)
Judicial branch	High Court of Appeal
Administrative divisions	5 governorates
Most recent local elections held	1999
Political parties (seats in parliament)	None
Year women received right to vote	Not recognized
Women in parliament (%)	0
Women at ministerial level (%)	0
Independence	June 19, 1961, from the United Kingdom
Constitution	November 11, 1962
Ethnic groups	Kuwaiti (45%), other Arab (35%), other (20%)
Religious groups	Sunni Muslim (45%), Shii Muslim (30%), other (25%)
Circulation of daily newspapers, 1996	374
(copies printed per 1,000 people)	
Internet users (%)	7.6

Measures of public sector performance (2000 or most recent)

	Kuwait	MENA13	HIC
Number of procedures to start business	..	..	7
Judicial efficiency (contract enforcement)			
Number of procedures	..	23	21
Number of days	..	284	276
Government expenditure (% GDP, 1999)	44	31	..
Public spending on education (% GDP, 1998)	..	6.7	..
Public spending on health (% GDP, 1998)	3.4	2.9	..
Infant mortality (per 1,000 live births)	9	31	6.3
Maternal mortality (per 100,000 live births, 1995)	25	180	..
Illiteracy (% population age 15+)	18	28	..
Female illiteracy (% female population age 15+)	20	38	..
Ratio of girls to boys in primary and secondary education	101	93	..
Access to improved water (% population)	..	83	..
Access to improved sanitation (% population)	..	85	..
Roads, paved (% total roads, 1999)	81	65	100
Telephone mainlines (per 1,000 people)	244	123	506

Measures of governance quality

(0–100, higher is better)	Kuwait	MENA15	HIC
Index of public accountability (IPA)	44	32	74
Index of quality of administration (IQA)	56.6	47	65
Index of governance quality (IGQ)	48.5	37	68.5

Governance quality

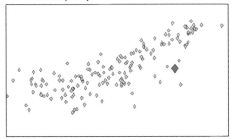

Per capita income

Quality of administration

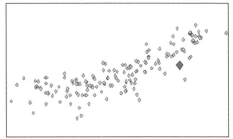

Per capita income

Public accountability

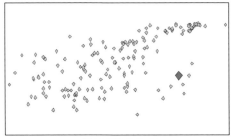

Per capita income

LEBANON

Key socioeconomic indicators (2000 or most recent)

	Lebanon	MENA13	UMIC
Population, mid-year			
(millions, aggregate)	4.3	265	497
Population under 15 years (%)	32	36	29
Life expectancy at birth (years)	70	70	71
Urban population (%)	90	57	72
Population growth (average			
annual, 1995–2001,%)	1.6	2.0	1.3
GNI per capita (PPP, US$)	4,380	5,198	8,500
GNI (PPP, US$ billions,			
aggregate)	19	1,380	4,230
GDP per capita growth			
(average annual, 1995–2001,%)	1.5	2.5	2.7
Exports of goods and			
services (% GDP)	13	38	26
Net petroleum exports			
(% GDP)	–4.2	24.5	4.5
Government expenditure			
(% GDP, 1999)	35.7	21	..
Military expenditures (% GDP)	5.4	6	2.1

Governance and Development Diamond

Income index

— Lebanon
····· Upper-middle income

Quality of administration index

Public accountability index

Infant survival index

Key sociopolitical indicators

Political structure	Republic
Legal system	Mixture of Ottoman law, canon law, Napoleonic code, and civil law
Structure of government	
Executive branch	*Chief of state*: President of the Republic (elected by parliament, most recent 1998)
	Head of government: Prime minister (appointed by president, most recent appointment 2000)
	Cabinet: Chosen by prime minister
Legislative branch	Unicameral National Assembly (128 seats; elected by popular vote, most recent 2000)
	Elections: Universal suffrage, minimum voting age 21
Judicial branch	5-person Court of Justice, 4 Courts of Appeal, Constitutional Council (half selected by executive, half by parliament), Supreme Council; executive controls judges' appointment
Administrative divisions	5 governorates, 26 districts
Most recent local elections held	1998
Political parties (seats in parliament)	Pre-established allotment of seats among religious groups
Year women received right to vote	1952
Women in parliament (%)	2.3
Women at ministerial level (%)	0
Independence	November 22, 1943, from French Mandate
Constitution	May 23, 1926, Taif Accord 1989
Ethnic groups	Arab (93%), Armenian (6%), Kurdish (1%)
Religious groups	Shii Muslim (34%), Sunni Muslim (21%), Catholic (19%), Druze (7%), Greek Orthodox (6%), other (13%)
Circulation of daily newspapers, 1996	107
(copies printed per 1,000 people)	
Internet users (%)	7.0

Measures of public sector performance (2000 or most recent)

	Lebanon	MENA13	UMIC
Number of procedures to start business	8	..	11
Judicial efficiency (contract enforcement)			
Number of procedures	27	23	27
Number of days	721	284	351
Government expenditure (% GDP, 1999)	35.7	31	..
Public spending on education (% GDP, 1998)	2.1	6.7	4.2
Public spending on health (% GDP, 1998)	2.5	2.9	3.5
Infant mortality (per 1,000 live births)	28	31	24
Maternal mortality (per 100,000 live births, 1995)	130	180	112
Illiteracy (% population age 15+)	14	28	9
Female illiteracy (% female population age 15+)	20	38	10
Ratio of girls to boys in primary and secondary education	102	93	101
Access to improved water (% population)	100	83	88
Access to improved sanitation (% population)	99	85	79
Roads, paved (% total roads, 1999)	85	65	51
Telephone mainlines (per 1,000 people)	195	123	192

Measures of governance quality

(0–100, higher is better)	Lebanon	MENA15	UMIC
Index of public accountability (IPA)	42	32	65
Index of quality of administration (IQA)	35	47	56
Index of governance quality (IGQ)	32	37	56

Governance quality

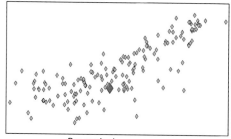

Per capita income

Quality of administration

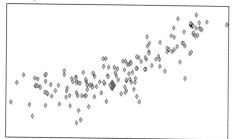

Per capita income

Public accountability

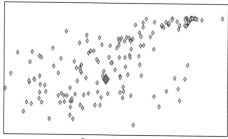

Per capita income

MOROCCO

Key socioeconomic indicators (2000 or most recent)

	Morocco	MENA13	LMIC
Population, mid-year			
(millions, aggregate)	28.7	265	2,140
Population under 15 years (%)	35	36	27
Life expectancy at birth (years)	67	70	69
Urban population (% total)	55	72	45
Population growth (average			
annual, 1995–2001,%)	1.7	2.0	1.0
GNI per capita (PPP, US$)	3,320	5,198	4,500
GNI (PPP, US$ billions,			
aggregate)	95.4	1,380	9,640
GDP per capita growth			
(average annual, 1995–2001,%)	3.2	2.5	..
Exports of goods and			
services (% GDP)	31	38	34
Net petroleum exports			
(% GDP)	–0.6	24.5	5
Government expenditure			
(% GDP, 1999)	32.5	21	20.6
Military expenditures (% GDP)	4	6	2.6

Governance and Development Diamond

Key sociopolitical indicators

Political structure	Constitutional monarchy
Legal system	Islamic law and French and Spanish civil law system
Structure of government	
Executive branch	*Chief of state*: King, or monarch (since 1999)
	Head of government: Prime minister (appointed by monarch, most recent appointment 2002)
	Cabinet: Appointed by monarch
Legislative branch	*Upper chamber*: Chamber of Counselors (270 seats; indirect vote)
	Lower Chamber: Chamber of Representatives (325 seats; elected by popular vote, most recent 2002)
	Elections: Universal suffrage, minimum voting age 21
Judicial branch	Supreme Court
Administrative divisions	37 provinces and 2 *wilayas*
Most recent local elections held	1997
Political parties (seats in parliament)	Multiple parties
Year women received right to vote	1963
Women in parliament (%)	6
Women at ministerial level (%)	4.9
Independence	March 2, 1956, from France
Constitution	March 10, 1972, amended 1996
Ethnic groups	Arab (60%), Berbers (40%)
Religious groups	Sunni Muslim (99%), other (1%)
Circulation of daily newspapers, 1996	28
(copies printed per 1,000 people)	
Internet users (%)	0.7

Measures of public sector performance (2000 or most recent)

	Morocco	MENA13	LMIC
Number of procedures to start business	..	..	13
Judicial efficiency (contract enforcement)			
Number of procedures	17	23	25
Number of days	192	284	311
Government expenditure (% GDP, 1999)	32	31	20.6
Public spending on education (% GDP, 1998)	6.0	6.7	4.1
Public spending on health (% GDP, 1998)	1.4	2.9	2.6
Infant mortality (per 1,000 live births)	41	31	34
Maternal mortality (per 100,000 live births, 1995)	390	180	..
Illiteracy (% population age 15+)	51	28	15
Female illiteracy (% female population age 15+)	64	38	20.5
Ratio of girls to boys in primary and secondary education	81	93	..
Access to improved water (% population)	80	83	80
Access to improved sanitation (% population)	68	85	55
Roads, paved (% total roads, 1999)	56	65	53
Telephone mainlines (per 1,000 people)	50	123	120

Measures of governance quality

(0–100, higher is better)	Morocco	MENA15	LMIC
Index of public accountability (IPA)	39	32	54
Index of quality of administration (IQA)	51.6	47	41
Index of governance quality (IGQ)	42.7	37	41.3

Governance quality

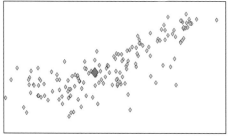

Per capita income

Quality of administration

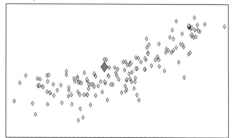

Per capita income

Public accountability

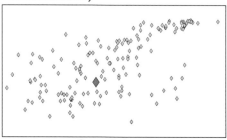

Per capita income

OMAN

Key socioeconomic indicators (2000 or most recent)

	Oman	MENA13	UMIC
Population, mid-year			
(millions, aggregate)	2.4	265	497
Population under 15 years (%)	44	36	29
Life expectancy at birth (years)	73	70	71
Urban population (%)	76	72	72
Population growth (average			
annual, 1995–2001,%)	2.5	2.0	1.3
GNI per capita (PPP, US$)	10,720	5,198	8,500
GNI (PPP, US$ billions,			
aggregate)	25.8	1,380	4,230
GDP per capita growth			
(average annual, 1995–2001,%)	..	2.5	2.7
Exports of goods and			
services (% GDP)	58	38	26
Net petroleum exports			
(% GDP)	47	24.5	4.5
Government expenditure			
(% GDP, 1999)	31	21	..
Military expenditures (% GDP)	10.6	6	2.1

Governance and Development Diamond

Key sociopolitical indicators

Political structure	Monarchy
Legal system	Based on English common law and Islamic law; ultimate appeal to the monarch
Structure of government	
Executive branch	*Chief of state*: Sultan, or monarch, and prime minister
	Head of government: Monarch, same as head of state
	Cabinet: Appointed by monarch
	Elections: None; monarchy is hereditary
Legislative branch	*Upper chamber*: Majliss al-Dawla (48 seats; appointed by monarch)
	Lower chamber: Consultative Council, or Majliss As Shura (83 seats; elected by limited suffrage for 3 years, most recent 2000)
Judicial branch	Supreme Court
Administrative divisions	6 regions and 2 governorates
Most recent local elections held	..
Political parties (seats in parliament)	None
Year women received right to vote	Not recognized
Women in parliament (%)	..
Women at ministerial level (%)	..
Independence	1650
Constitution a	None
Ethnic groups	Arab (74%), Indian (13%), other (13%)
Religious groups	Ibadiyah Muslim (74%), Sunni Muslim (14%), Hindu (7%), other (5%)
Circulation of daily newspapers, 1996	29
(copies printed per 1,000 people)	
Internet users (%)	4.0

a. In 1996, the monarch or sultan issued a royal decree promulgating a new basic law that, among other things, clarifies the royal succession, provides for a prime minister, bars ministers from holding interests in companies doing business with the government, establishes a bicameral legislature, and guarantees basic civil liberties for Omani citizens (Source: Central Intelligence Agency 2002).

Measures of public sector performance (2000 or most recent)

	Oman	MENA13	UMIC
Number of procedures to start business	..	..	11
Judicial efficiency (contract enforcement)			
Number of procedures	..	23	27
Number of days	..	284	351
Government expenditure (% GDP, 1999)	31	31	..
Public spending on education (% GDP, 1998)	4	6.7	4.2
Public spending on health (% GDP, 1998)	2.4	2.9	3..5
Infant mortality (per 1,000 live births)	12	31	24
Maternal mortality (per 100,000 live births, 1995)	120	180	112
Illiteracy (% population age 15+)	28	28	9
Female illiteracy (% female population age 15+)	38	38	10
Ratio of girls to boys in primary and secondary education	97	93	101
Access to improved water (% population)	39	83	88
Access to improved sanitation (% population)	90	85	79
Roads, paved (% total roads, 1999)	30	65	51
Telephone mainlines (per 1,000 people)	89	123	192

Measures of governance quality

(0–100, higher is better)	Oman	MENA15	UMIC
Index of public accountability (IPA)	26.6	32	65
Index of quality of administration (IQA)	53	47	56
Index of governance quality (IGQ)	39	37	56

Governance quality

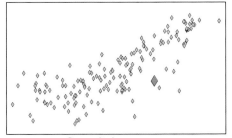

Per capita income

Quality of administration

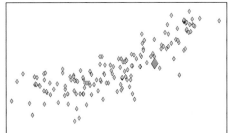

Per capita income

Public accountability

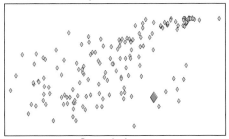

Per capita income

QATAR

Key socioeconomic indicators (2000 or most recent)

	Qatar	MENA13	Non-OECD HIC
Population, mid-year			
(millions, aggregate)	0.58	265	50.3
Population under 15 years (%)	26.5	36	23
Life expectancy at birth (years)	75	70	76
Urban population (% total)	93	72	50
Population growth (average			
annual, 1995–2001,%)	3	2.0	4.0
GNI per capita (PPP, US$)	..	5,198	..
GNI (PPP, US$ billions,			
aggregate)	..	1,380	..
GDP per capita growth			
(average annual, 1995–2001,%)	..	2.5	..
Exports of goods and			
services (% GDP)	68	38	90
Net petroleum exports			
(% GDP)	72	24.5	10.2
Government expenditure			
(% GDP, 1999)	..	21	..
Military expenditures (% GDP)	..	6	4.2

Governance and Development Diamond

Key sociopolitical indicators

Political structure	Traditional monarchy
Legal system	Discretionary system of law controlled by the emir; Islamic law dominates family and per-
Structure of government	sonal matters
Executive branch	Chief of state: Emir, or monarch
	Head of government: Prime minister (brother of monarch)
	Cabinet: Appointed by monarch
	Elections: None; monarchy is hereditary
Legislative branch	Unicameral Advisory Council, or Majliss As Shura (appointed by monarch)[a]
Judicial branch	Court of Appeal
Administrative divisions	9 municipalities
Most recent local elections held	2003
Political parties (seats in parliament)	None
Year women received right to vote	Not recognized
Women in parliament (%)	..
Women at ministerial level (%)	0
Independence	September 3, 1971, from the United Kingdom
Constitution	Provisional constitution enacted April 19, 1972[b]
Ethnic groups	Arab (40%), Pakistani (18%), Indian (18%), Iranian (10%), other (14%)
Religious groups	Sunni Muslim (95%), other (5%)
Circulation of daily newspapers, 1996	175
(copies printed per 1,000 people)	
Internet users (%)	5.1

a. The constitution calls for elections for part of this consultative body, but no elections have been held since 1970, when there were partial elections to the body; council members have had their terms extended every four years since (Source: Central Intelligence Agency 2002).
b. In July 1999, the emir issued a decree forming a committee to draft a permanent constitution (Source: Central Intelligence Agency 2002).

Measures of public sector performance (2000 or most recent)

	Qatar	MENA13	HIC
Number of procedures to start business	..	..	7
Judicial efficiency (contract enforcement)			
Number of procedures	..	23	21
Number of days	..	284	276
Government expenditure (% GDP, 1999)	..	31	..
Public spending on education (% GDP, 1998)	3.6	6.7	..
Public spending on health (% GDP, 1998)	3.4	2.9	..
Infant mortality (per 1,000 live births)	12	31	6.3
Maternal mortality (per 100,000 live births, 1995)	41	180	..
Illiteracy (% population age 15+)	19	28	..
Female illiteracy (% female population age 15+)	17	38	..
Ratio of girls to boys in primary and secondary education	102	93	..
Access to improved water (% population)	..	83	..
Access to improved sanitation (% population)	..	85	..
Roads, paved (% total roads, 1999)	90	65	100
Telephone mainlines (per 1,000 people)	268	123	506

Measures of governance quality

(0–100, higher is better)	Qatar	MENA15	HIC
Index of public accountability (IPA)	23	32	74
Index of quality of administration (IQA)	42	47	65
Index of governance quality (IGQ)	30	37	68.5

Governance quality

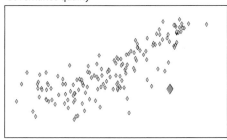

Per capita income

Quality of administration

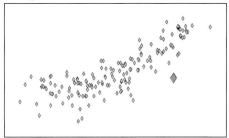

Per capita income

Public accountability

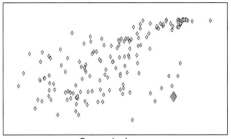

Per capita income

SAUDI ARABIA

Key socioeconomic indicators (2000 or most recent)

	Saudi Arabia	MENA13	UMIC
Population, mid-year (millions, aggregate)	20.7	265	497
Population under 15 years (%)	41	36	29
Life expectancy at birth (years)	72	70	71
Urban population (%)	86	72	72
Population growth (average annual, 1995–2001,%)	2.6	2.0	1.3
GNI per capita (PPP, US$)	13,490	5,198	8,500
GNI (PPP, US$ billions, aggregate)	280	1,380	4,230
GDP per capita growth (average annual, 1995–2001,%)	0.5	2.5	2.7
Exports of goods and services (% GDP)	44	38	26
Net petroleum exports (% GDP)	41	24.5	4.5
Government expenditure (% GDP, 1999)	..	21	..
Military expenditures (% GDP)	10.6	6	2.1

Governance and Development Diamond

Income index
Quality of administration index
Public accountability index
Infant survival index

— Saudi Arabia
····· Upper-middle income

Key sociopolitical indicators

Political structure	Monarchy
Legal system	Based on Islamic law; introduction of some secular codes
Structure of government	
Executive branch	*Chief of state*: King and prime minister; crown prince and first deputy prime minister (heir since 1982)
	Head of government: Monarch, same as head of state
	Elections: None; monarchy is hereditary
Legislative branch	Consultative Council, or *Majliss As Shura* (appointed by monarch)
Judicial branch	Supreme Council of Justice
Administrative divisions	13 provinces
Most recent local elections held	..
Political parties (seats in parliament)	None
Year women received right to vote	Not recognized
Women in parliament (%)	..
Women at ministerial level (%)	..
Independence	September 23, 1932, Unification of the Kingdom
Constitution	Shari'a (Islamic law); Basic Law 1993 (articulates government's rights and responsibilities)
Ethnic groups	Arab (90%), Afro-Asian (10%)
Religious groups	Sunni Muslim (93%), Shii Muslim (3%), other (4%)
Circulation of daily newspapers, 1996 (copies printed per 1,000 people)	326
Internet users (%)	1.0

Measures of public sector performance (2000 or most recent)

	Saudi Arabia	MENA13	UMIC
Number of procedures to start business	..	..	11
Judicial efficiency (contract enforcement)			
Number of procedures	19	23	27
Number of days	195	284	351
Government expenditure (% GDP, 1999)	..	31	..
Public spending on education (% GDP, 1998)	9.5	6.7	4.2
Public spending on health (% GDP, 1998)	4.5	2.9	3.5
Infant mortality (per 1,000 live births)	24	31	24
Maternal mortality (per 100,000 live births, 1995)	23	180	112
Illiteracy (% population age 15+)	24	28	9
Female illiteracy (% female population age 15+)	33	38	10
Ratio of girls to boys in primary and secondary education	94	93	101
Access to improved water (% population)	95	83	88
Access to improved sanitation (% population)	100	85	79
Roads, paved (% total roads, 1999)	..	65	51
Telephone mainlines (per 1,000 people)	137	123	192

Measures of governance quality

(0–100, higher is better)	Saudi Arabia	MENA15	UMIC
Index of public accountability (IPA)	17	32	65
Index of quality of administration (IQA)	48	47	56
Index of governance quality (IGQ)	32	37	56

Governance quality

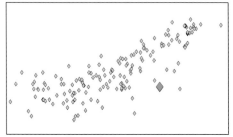

Per capita income

Quality of administration

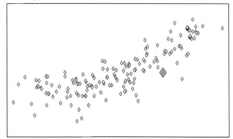

Per capita income

Public accountability

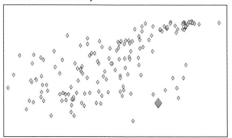

Per capita income

SYRIAN ARAB REPUBLIC

Key socioeconomic indicators (2000 or most recent)

	Syria	MENA13	LMIC
Population, mid-year			
(millions, aggregate)	16.2	265	2,140
Population under 15 years (%)	41	36	27
Life expectancy at birth (years)	70	70	69
Urban population (%)	51	72	45
Population growth (average			
annual, 1995–2001,%)	2.6	2.0	1.0
GNI per capita (PPP, US$)	3,130	5,198	4,500
GNI (PPP, US$ billions,			
aggregate)	50.7	1,380	9.640
GDP per capita growth			
(average annual, 1995–2001,%)	1.8	2.5	..
Exports of goods and			
services (% GDP)	38	38	34
Net petroleum exports			
(% GDP)	21	24.5	5
Government expenditure			
(% GDP, 1999)	23	21	20.6
Military expenditures (% GDP)	5.5	6	2.6

Governance and Development Diamond

Key sociopolitical indicators

Political structure	Republic
Legal system	Islamic law and civil law system, special religious courts
Structure of government	
Executive branch	Chief of state: President of the Republic (elected by popular vote, most recent 2000)
	Head of government: Prime minister (appointed by president, most recent appointment 2000)
	Cabinet: Appointed by president
	Elections: Universal suffrage, minimum voting age 18
Legislative branch	Unicameral People's Council, or Majliss al-shaab (250 seats; elected by popular vote, most recent 2003)
Judicial branch	Supreme Constitutional Court (justices appointed by the president); High Judicial Council; Court of Cassation; State Security Courts
Administrative divisions	14 provinces
Most recent local elections held	1999
Political parties (seats in parliament)	National Patriotic Front (includes Ba'th party) 67%, Independents 33%
Year women received right to vote	1949
Women in parliament (%)	12
Women at ministerial level (%)	11.1
Independence	April 17, 1946, from French Mandate
Constitution	March 13, 1973
Ethnic groups	Arab (90%), Kurds and other (10%)
Religious groups	Sunni Muslim (74%), Shii Muslim (12%), other (14%)
Circulation of daily newspapers, 1996 (copies printed per 1,000 people)	20
Internet users (%)	0.2

Measures of public sector performance (2000 or most recent)

	Syria	MENA13	LMIC
Number of procedures to start business	..	..	13
Judicial efficiency (contract enforcement)			
Number of procedures	36	23	25
Number of days	596	284	311
Government expenditure (% GDP, 1999)	23	31	20.6
Public spending on education (% GDP, 1998)	3.6	6.7	4.1
Public spending on health (% GDP, 1998)	1.5	2.9	2.6
Infant mortality (per 1,000 live births)	24	31	34
Maternal mortality (per 100,000 live births, 1995)	200	180	..
Illiteracy (% population age 15+)	25	28	15
Female illiteracy (% female population age 15+)	40	38	20.5
Ratio of girls to boys in primary and secondary education	92	93	..
Access to improved water (% population)	80	83	80
Access to improved sanitation (% population)	90	85	55
Roads, paved (% total roads, 1999)	..	65	53
Telephone mainlines (per 1,000 people)	103	123	120

Measures of governance quality

(0–100, higher is better)	Syria	MENA15	LMIC
Index of public accountability (IPA)	18	32	54
Index of quality of administration (IQA)	28	47	41
Index of governance quality (IGQ)	18.6	37	41.3

Governance quality

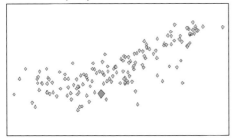

Per capita income

Quality of administration

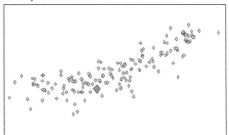

Per capita income

Public accountability

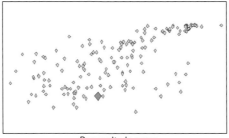

Per capita income

TUNISIA

Key socioeconomic indicators (2000 or most recent)

	Tunisia	MENA13	LMIC
Population, mid-year (millions, aggregate)	9.5	265	2,140
Population under 15 years (%)	30	36	27
Life expectancy at birth (years)	72	70	69
Urban population (%)	65	72	45
Population growth (average annual, 1995–2001,%)	1.3	2.0	1.0
GNI per capita (PPP, US$)	5,840	5,198	4,500
GNI (PPP, US$ billions, aggregate)	55.9	1,380	9,640
GDP per capita growth (average annual, 1995–2001,%)	5.2	2.5	..
Exports of goods and services (% GDP)	44	38	34
Net petroleum exports (% GDP)	0	24.5	5
Government expenditure (% GDP, 1999)	31.6	21	20.6
Military expenditures (% GDP)	1.7	6	2.6

Governance and Development Diamond

Key sociopolitical indicators

Political structure	Republic
Legal system	French civil law system and Islamic law
Structure of government	
Executive branch	*Chief of state*: President (elected by popular vote, 1987/1999)
	Head of government: Prime minister (appointed by president, most recent appointment 1999)
	Cabinet: Appointed by president
	Elections: Universal suffrage, minimum voting age 20
Legislative branch	Unicameral Chamber of Deputies, or *Majliss al-Nuwaab* (182 seats; elected by popular vote, most recent 1999)
Judicial branch	Court of Cassation
Administrative divisions	23 governorates
Most recent local elections held	2000
Political parties (seats in parliament)	Majority to Constitutional Democratic Rally Party (official ruling party)
Year women received right to vote	1957
Women in parliament (%)	11.5
Women at ministerial level (%)	10
Independence	March 20, 1956, from France
Constitution	June 1, 1959, amended 1988
Ethnic groups	Arab (98%), other (2%)
Religious groups	Sunni Muslim (99%), other (1%)
Circulation of daily newspapers, 1996 (copies printed per 1,000 people)	19
Internet users (%)	2.6

Measures of public sector performance (2000 or most recent)

	Tunisia	MENA13	LMIC
Number of procedures to start business	13	..	13
Judicial efficiency (contract enforcement)			
Number of procedures	14	23	25
Number of days	7	284	311
Government expenditure (% GDP, 1999)	31.6	31	20.6
Public spending on education (% GDP, 1998)	7.5	6.7	4.1
Public spending on health (% GDP, 1998)	2.8	2.9	2.6
Infant mortality (per 1,000 live births)	26	31	34
Maternal mortality (per 100,000 live births, 1995)	70	180	..
Illiteracy (% population age 15+)	29	28	15
Female illiteracy (% female population age 15+)	39	38	20.5
Ratio of girls to boys in primary and secondary education	100	93	..
Access to improved water (% population)	80	83	80
Access to improved sanitation (% population)	84	85	55
Roads, paved (% total roads, 1999)	64	65	53
Telephone mainlines (per 1,000 people)	99	123	120

Measures of governance quality

(0–100, higher is better)	Tunisia	MENA15	LMIC
Index of public accountability (IPA)	35	32	54
Index of quality of administration (IQA)	54	47	41
Index of governance quality (IGQ)	43	37	41.3

Governance quality

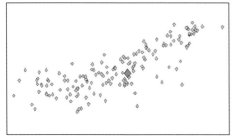

Per capita income

Quality of administration

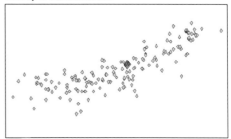

Per capita income

Public accountability

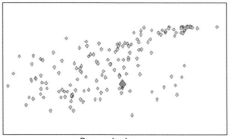

Per capita income

UNITED ARAB EMIRATES

Key socioeconomic indicators (2000 or most recent)

	United Arab Emirates	MENA13	Non-OECD HIC
Population, mid-year (millions, aggregate)	2.9	265	50.3
Population under 15 years (%)	27	36	23
Life expectancy at birth (years)	75	70	76
Urban population (%)	87	72	50
Population growth (average annual, 1995–2001,%)	4.4	2.0	4.0
GNI per capita (PPP, US$)	..	5,198	..
GNI (PPP, US$ billions, aggregate)	..	1,380	..
GDP per capita growth (average annual, 1995–2001,%)	..	2.5	..
Exports of goods and services (% GDP)	71	38	90
Net petroleum exports (% GDP)	38	24.5	10.2
Government expenditure (% GDP, 1999)	..	21	..
Military expenditures (% GDP)	2.5	6	4.2

Governance and Development Diamond

— United Arab Emirates
····· High income

Income index · Public accountability index · Infant survival index · Quality of administration index

---

Key sociopolitical indicators

Political structure	Federation
Legal system	Federal court system (1971), secular and Islamic law
Structure of government	
Executive branch	*Chief of state*: President (elected by FSC[a]), Ruler of Capital Emirate or Abu Dhabi
	Head of government: Prime minister (appointed by president, most recent appointment 1990), ruler of Dubai Emirate
	Cabinet: Appointed by president
	Elections: None
Legislative branch	Unicameral Federal National Council, or *Majliss al-Ittihad al-Watani* (40 seats; members appointed by rulers of Emirates)
Judicial branch	Union Supreme Court (judges appointed by the president)
Administrative divisions	7 emirates
Most recent local elections held	..
Political parties (seats in parliament)	None
Year women received right to vote	Not recognized
Women in parliament (%)	0
Women at ministerial level (%)	..
Independence	December 2, 1971, from the United Kingdom
Constitution	December 2, 1971
Ethnic groups	Asian (53%), Arab (25%), Iranian (17%), other (5%)
Religious groups	Sunni Muslim (80%), Shii Muslim (16%), other (4%)
Circulation of daily newspapers, 1996 (copies printed per 1,000 people)	156
Internet users (%)	26

a. The Federal Supreme Council (FSC) is composed of the seven emirate rulers. The FSC is the highest constitutional authority in the UAE; it establishes general policies and sanctions federal legislation. It meets four times a year (Source: Central Intelligence Agency 2002).

Measures of public sector performance (2000 or most recent)

	United Arab Emirates	MENA13	HIC
Number of procedures to start business	..	..	7
Judicial efficiency (contract enforcement)			
Number of procedures	27	23	21
Number of days	559	284	276
Government expenditure (% GDP, 1999)	..	31	..
Public spending on education (% GDP, 1998)	2	6.7	..
Public spending on health (% GDP, 1998)	3.2	2.9	..
Infant mortality (per 1,000 live births)	8	31	6.3
Maternal mortality (per 100,000 live births, 1995)	30	180	..
Illiteracy (% population age 15+)	24	28	..
Female illiteracy (% female population age 15+)	21	38	..
Ratio of girls to boys in primary and secondary education	105	93	..
Access to improved water (% population)	..	83	..
Access to improved sanitation (% population)	..	85	..
Roads, paved (% total roads, 1999)	100	65	100
Telephone mainlines (per 1,000 people)	347	123	506

Measures of governance quality

(0–100, higher is better)	United Arab Emirates	MENA15	HIC
Index of public accountability (IPA)	34	32	74
Index of quality of administration (IQA)	73.6	47	65
Index of governance quality (IGQ)	56.4	37	68.5

Governance quality

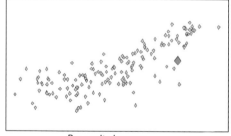

Per capita income

Quality of administration

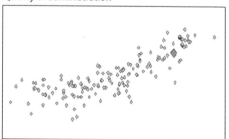

Per capita income

Public accountability

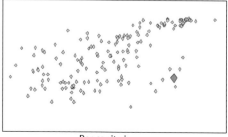

Per capita income

REPUBLIC OF YEMEN

Key socioeconomic indicators (2000 or most recent)

	Yemen	MENA13	LIC
Population, mid-year			
(millions, aggregate)	17.5	265	2,460
Population under 15 years (%)	46	36	37
Life expectancy at birth (years)	56	70	59
Urban population (%)	25	72	30
Population growth (average			
annual, 1995–2001,%)	2.9	2.0	1.9
GNI per capita (PPP, US$)	730	5,198	2,110
GNI (PPP, US$ billions,			
aggregate)	12.8	1,380	5,210
GDP per capita growth			
(average annual, 1995–2001,%)	2	2.5	..
Exports of goods and			
services (% GDP)	43.7	38	29
Net petroleum exports			
(% GDP)	33	24.5	4
Government expenditure			
(% GDP, 1999)	27	21	18
Military expenditures (% GDP)	5.4	6	2.2

Governance and Development Diamond

Income index — Yemen ••••• High income

Quality of administration index — Public accountability index

Infant survival index

Key sociopolitical indicators

Political structure	Republic
Legal system	Islamic law, Turkish law, English common law, and local tribal customary law
Structure of government	
Executive branch	*Chief of state:* President (elected by popular vote, 1990/1999)
	Head of government: Prime minister (appointed by president, most recent appointment 2001)
	Cabinet: Appointed by president
	Elections: Universal suffrage, minimum voting age 18
Legislative branch	*Upper chamber:* Shura Council (111 seats; appointed by the president)
	Lower chamber: House of Representatives (301 seats; members elected by popular vote, most recent 2003)
Judicial branch	Supreme Court
Administrative divisions	17 governorates
Most recent local elections held	2001
Political parties (seats in parliament)	General People's Congress (238), Yemeni Congregation for Reform (46)
Year women received right to vote	1967
Women in parliament (%)	0.7
Women at ministerial level (%)	..
Independence	May 22, 1990, merger of South and North Yemen
Constitution	May 16, 1991, amended 1994 and 2001
Ethnic groups	Predominantly Arab
Religious groups	Sunni Muslim (99%), other (1%)
Circulation of daily newspapers, 1996 (copies printed per 1,000 people)	14.6
Internet users (%)	0.1

Measures of public sector performance (2000 or most recent)

	Yemen	MENA13	LIC
Number of procedures to start business	..	..	11
Judicial efficiency (contract enforcement)			
Number of procedures	27	23	25
Number of days	240	284	263
Government expenditure (% GDP, 1999)	27	31	18
Public spending on education (% GDP, 1998)	..	6.7	2.7
Public spending on health (% GDP, 1998)	2.1	2.9	1.3
Infant mortality (per 1,000 live births)	85	31	81
Maternal mortality (per 100,000 live births, 1995)	850	180	..
Illiteracy (% population age 15+)	53	28	38
Female illiteracy (% female population age 15+)	75	38	47
Ratio of girls to boys in primary and secondary education	50	93	..
Access to improved water (% population)	69	83	76
Access to improved sanitation (% population)	38	85	44
Roads, paved (% total roads, 1999)	11.5	65	16
Telephone mainlines (per 1,000 people)	19	123	27

Measures of governance quality

(0–100, higher is better)	Yemen	MENA15	LIC
Index of public accountability (IPA)	19	32	38
Index of quality of administration (IQA)	33.5	47	30
Index of governance quality (IGQ)	22.5	37	28

Governance quality

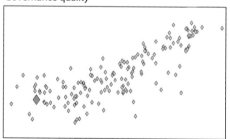

Per capita income

Quality of administration

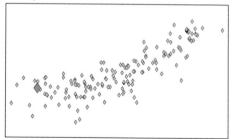

Per capita income

Public accountability

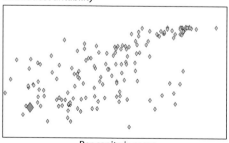

Per capita income

References

The word "processed" describes informally produced works that may not be commonly available through libraries.

Background Papers

Produced for This Book

al-Azmeh, Aziz. 2003. "Governance from a Socio-Historical Perspective: The Mashreq." World Bank, Washington, D.C. Processed.

Charfi, Mohammed. 2003. "Gouvernance et Développement en Tunisie." World Bank, Washington, D.C. Processed.

Farhi, Farideh. 2003. "Governance and Development in Iran." World Bank, Washington, D.C. Processed.

Filali-Ansari, Abdou. 2003. "Le Maroc à l'Aube du XXIe Siècle: Amorce de Modernisation Politique." World Bank, Washington, D.C. Processed.

Ghalioun, Burhan. 2003. "Etat, Société Civile, et Développement en Syrie." World Bank, Washington, D.C. Processed.

Hejailan, Salah. 2003. "Governance in Saudi Arabia." World Bank, Washington, D.C. Processed.

Khafaji, Isam. 2003. "Rentierism, Atomization and Governance: The Case of Iraq." World Bank, Washington, D.C. Processed.

Khouri, Rami. 2003. "Jordan: A Tribal-Constitutional Monarchy in Transition." World Bank, Washington, D.C. Processed.

Mahiou, Ahmed. 2003. "Analyse et Bilan de la Gouvernance en Algérie." World Bank, Washington, D.C. Processed.

Saeed Ali, Abdel Monem. 2003. "Governance in Egypt." World Bank, Washington, D.C. Processed.

Salem, Paul. 2003. "Lebanon: Governance Reform and Development." World Bank, Washington, D.C. Processed.

Tozy, Mohamed. 2003. "Eléments pour une Lecture de Sociologie Historique de la Gouvernance au Maghreb." World Bank, Washington, D.C. Processed.

References

Abed, George T. 2003. "Unfulfilled Promise: Why the Middle East and North Africa Region Has Lagged in Growth and Globalization." In "The Middle East: On the Threshold of Change," *Finance and Development* 40(1).

Acemoglu, Daron, Simon Johnson, and James A. Robinson. 2001. "The Colonial Origins of Comparative Development: An Empirical Investigation." *American Economic Review* 91(5): 1369–401.

———. 2003. "An African Success Story: Botswana." In Dani Rodrik, ed., *In Search of Prosperity: Analytical Narratives on Economic Growth*. Princeton, N.J., and Oxford, U.K.: Princeton University Press.

Ades, Alberto, and Rafael Di Tella. 1999. "Rents, Competition, and Corruption." *American Economic Review* 89: 982–93.

Adwan, Charles D., and Mina Zapatero. 2002. "Cutting through Red Tape in Lebanon." In *Global Corruption Report, 2003*. Berlin: Transparency International.

Alesina, Alberto, and Roberto Perotti. 1996. "Income Distribution, Political Instability, and Investment." *European Economic Review* 40: 1203–28.

Alesina, Alberto, Sule Ozler, Nouriel Roubini, and Phillip Swagel. 1996. "Political Instability and Economic Growth." *Journal of Economic Growth* 1(2): 189–211.

Alston, Lee, Gary Libecap, and Bernardo Mueller. 1999. *Titles, Conflict and Land Use: The Development of Property Rights and Land Reform on the Brazilian Amazon Frontier*. Ann Arbor: University of Michigan Press.

Anderson, Lisa. 1986. *The State and Social Transformation in Tunisia and Libya, 1830–1980*. Princeton, N.J.: Princeton University Press.

———. 1991a. "Absolutism and the Persistence of Monarchy in the Middle East." *Political Science Quarterly* 106(1): 1–15.

———. 1991b. "The State in the Middle East and North Africa." *Comparative Politics* 20(3): 1–18.

———. 1991c. "Obligation and Accountability, Islamic Politics in North Africa." *Daedalus, Journal of the American Academy of Arts and Sciences, Religion and Politics* 120(3).

Anderson, Robert E., and Albert Martinez. 1996. "Supporting Private Sector Development in the Middle East and North Africa." In Nemat Shafik, ed., *Prospects for Middle Eastern and North African Economies: From Boom to Bust and Back?* New York: St. Martin's Press.

Ansari, Muhammad Jabir. 1996. *Al-Fikr al-Arabi wa-sira al-addad* [On the Conflict of Fundamentalism and Secularism as Opposites in Contemporary Arab Thought]. Beirut: al-Muassasah al-Arabiyah lil-Dirasat wa-al-Nashr.

———. 1998. *Intihar al-Muthaqqafin al-'Arab wa-qadaya rahinah fi al-thaqafah al-'Arabiyah* [The Suicide of the Arab Intellectuals and Current Ussues in Arab Culture]. Beirut: al-Muassasah al-Arabiyah lil-Dirasat wa-al-Nashr.

Arab Decision Project. 2003. Available online at http://www.arabdecision.org. Accessed 2003.

Auty, Richard M., ed. 2001. *Resource Abundance and Economic Development*. New York: Oxford University Press.

Ayubi, Nazih N. 1995. *Over-Stating the State: Politics and Society in the Middle East*. London: I. B. Tauris.

al-Azmeh, Azíz. 1995. "Nationalism and the Arabs." *Arab Studies Quarterly* 17: 1–2.

Banerji, Arup, and Caralee McLiesh. 2002. "Governance and the Investment Climate in Yemen." Middle East and North Africa Working Paper Series 28. World Bank, Washington, D.C.

Banerji, Arup, and Hafez Ghanem. 1997. "Does the Type of Political Regime Matter for Trade and Labor Market Policies?" *World Bank Economic Review* 11(1): 171–94.

Barro, Robert J. 1991. "Economic Growth in a Cross Section of Countries." *Quarterly Journal of Economics* 106: 407–44.

———. 1999. "Determinants of Democracy." *Journal of Political Economy* 107(S6): S158–29.

Barro, Robert J., and Jong-Wha Lee. 1994. "Panel Data Set Cross Countries." Data Diskette.

———. 2000a. "International Data on Educational Attainment: Updates and Implications." CID Working Paper 42. Harvard University, Cambridge, Mass.

———. 2000b. "International Measures of Schooling Years and Schooling Quality." *American Economic Review* 86: 218–23.

Bayat, Asef. 2002. "Activism and Social Development in the Middle East." *International Journal of Middle East Studies* 34(1): 1–28.

Beblawi, Hazem. 1987. "The Rentier State in the Arab World." In Hazem Beblawi and Giacomo Luciani, eds., *The Rentier State*. New York: Cromm Helm.

Bellin, Eva. 1994. "The Politics of Profit in Tunisia: Utility of the Rentier Paradigm?" *World Development* 22(3): 427–36.

———. 2001. "The Robustness of Authoritarianism in the Middle East: A Comparative Perspective." Harvard University, Cambridge, Mass. Processed.

Ben Nefissa, Sarah, ed. 2002. *Pouvoir et Associations dans le Monde Arabe*. Paris: CNRS Editions.

Bennani-Chraibi, Mounia, and Olivier Fillieule, eds. 2003. *Résistances et Protestations dans les Sociétés Musulmanes*. Paris: Presse de Sciences Politiques.

Bill, James A., and Robert Springborg. 1990. *Politics in the Middle East.* Glenview, Ill.: HarperCollins.

Brand, Laurie A. 1992. "Economic and Political Liberalization in a Rentier Economy: The Case of the Hashemite Kingdom of Jordan." In I. Harik and D. Sullivan, eds., *Privatization and Liberalization in the Middle East.* Bloomington: Indiana University Press.

Broadman, Harry, and Francesca Recanatini. 2002. "Corruption and Policy: Back to the Roots." *Journal of Policy Reform* 5(1): 37–49.

Brown, Nathan. 2001a. "Arab Judicial Structures." Program on Governance in the Arab Region (POGAR), United Nations Development Programme, New York. Processed.

———. 2001b. "Mechanisms of Accountability in Arab Governance: The Present and Future of Judiciaries and Parliaments in the Arab World." Program on Governance in the Arab Region (POGAR), United Nations Development Programme. Available online at http://www.undp-pogar.org/publications/governance/nbrown. Accessed 2003.

Bruno, Michael, Martin Ravallion, and Lyn Squire. 1998. "Equity and Growth in Developing Countries: Old and New Perspectives on the Policy Issues." In V. Tanzi and K. Chu, eds., *Income Distribution and High-Quality Growth.* Cambridge, Mass.: MIT Press.

Brynen, Rex, Bahgat Korany, and Paul Noble, eds. 1995. *Political Liberalization and Democratization in the Arab World,* Vol. 1: *Theoretical Perspectives.* Boulder, Colo.: Lynne Rienner Publishers.

Burns, Nancy, Key Lehman Schlozman, and Sidney Verba, eds. 2001. *The Private Roots of Public Action. Gender Equality and Political Participation.* Cambridge, Mass.: Harvard University Press.

Calderón, Cesar, and Alberto Chong. 2000. "On the Causality and Feedback between Institutional Measures and Economic Growth." *Economics and Politics* 12(1): 69–81.

Campos, J. Edgardo, and Sanjay Pradhan. 1997. "Evaluating Public Expenditure Outcomes: An Experimental Methodology with an Application to the Australia and New Zealand Reforms." *Journal of Policy Analysis and Management* 16: 423–45.

Carapico, Sheila, ed. 1998. *Civil Society in the Yemen: The Political Economy of Activism in Modern Arabia*. Cambridge Middle East Studies. Cambridge, U.K.: Cambridge University Press.

Center for Democracy and Technology. 2002. *The E-Government Handbook for Developing Countries*. Available online at http://www.dct.org/egov/handbook/2002-11-14egovhandbook.pdf. Accessed 2003.

Center for International Development and Conflict Management. 2000. *Polity IV Project, Political Regime Characteristics and Transitions, 1800–1999*. University of Maryland, College Park. Available online at http://www.cidcm.umd.edu/inscr/polity/index.htm. Accessed 2003.

Central Intelligence Agency. 2002. *The World Factbook 2002*. Available online at http://www.bartleby.com. Accessed 2003.

Chang, Ha-Joon, ed. 2002. *Kicking Away the Ladder: Development Strategy in a Historical Perspective*. London: Anthem Press.

Chaudhry, Kiren Aziz. 1997. *The Price of Wealth: Economies and Institutions in the Middle East*. Ithaca, N.Y.: Cornell University Press.

Cheng, Tun-Jen, Stephan Haggard, and David Kang. 1998. "Institutions and Growth in Korea and Taiwan: The Bureaucracy." *Journal of Development Studies* 34(6): 87–111.

Collier, Paul, and Anke Hoeffler. 1998. "On Economic Causes of Civil War." *Oxford Economic Papers* 50(4): 563–73.

———. 2000. "Greed and Grievance in Civil War." World Bank Policy Research Paper 2355. World Bank, Washington, D.C.

Commonwealth Secretariat. 2002. *Current Good Practices and New Developments in Public Sector Service Management*. Second Edition. London.

Crone, Patricia. 2002. *Roman, Provincial, and Islamic Law: The Origins of the Islamic Patronate*. Cambridge, U.K.: Cambridge University Press.

Crystal, Jill. 1994. "Authoritarianism and Its Adversaries in the Arab World." *World Politics* 46: 262–89.

———. 1995. *Oil and Politics in the Gulf: Rulers and Merchants in Kuwait and Qatar*. Cambridge, U.K.: Cambridge University Press.

De Dios, Emmanuel S., and Paul D. Hutchcroft. 2002. "Philippine Political Economy: Examining Current Challenges in Historical Perspective." In Arsenio Balisacan and Hal Hill, eds., *The Philippine Economy: On the Way to Sustained Growth?* New York: Oxford University Press; also Quezon City, Philippines: Ateneo de Manila University Press.

Deacon, Robert. T. 1999. "Deforestation and Ownership: Evidence from Historical Accounts and Contemporary Data." *Land Economics* 75(3): 341–59.

De Haan, Jakob, and Clemens L. J. Siermann. 1996. "New Evidence on the Relationship Between Democracy and Economic Growth." *Public Choice* 86: 175–98.

De Long, J. B., and L. Summers. 1991. "Equipment Investment and Economic Growth." *Quarterly Journal of Economics* 106(2): 455–502.

Denoeux, Guilain. 1993. *Urban Unrest in the Middle East: A Comparative Study of Informal Networks in Egypt, Iran and Lebanon.* New York: State University of New York Press.

deSoysa, Indra. 2000. "The Resource Curse: Are Civil Wars Driven by Rapacity or Paucity?" In Mats Berdal and David M. Malone, eds., *Greed and Grievance: Economic Agendas in Civil Wars.* Boulder, Colo.: Lynne Rienner Publishers.

Diaz-Cayeros, Alberto, and Beatriz Magaloni. 2000. "From Authoritarianism to Democracy: The Unfinished Transition in Mexico." Paper presented at the Democratization Seminar, Stanford University, Palo Alto, Calif. Available online at http://democracy.stanford.edu/Seminar/diaz_mag. Accessed 2003.

Djankov, Simeon, Rafael La Porta, Florencio Lopez de Silanes, and Andrei Shleifer. 2000. "The Regulation of Entry." NBER Working Paper 7892. National Bureau of Economic Research, Cambridge, Mass.

Dollar, David, and Aart Kraay. 2002. "Growth Is Good for the Poor." *Journal of Economic Growth* 7(3): 193–225.

Doornbos, Martin. 2001. "Good Governance: The Rise and Decline of a Policy Metaphor." *Journal of Development Studies* 37(6): 93–108.

Dresch, Paul. 1989. *Tribes, Government, and History in Yemen.* Oxford, U.K.: Clarendon Press.

Dreze, Jacques, and Amartya Sen. 1982. *Hunger and Public Action*. Oxford, U.K.: Oxford University Press.

Easterly, William, and Ross Levine. 2002. "Tropics, Germs, and Crops: How Endowments Affect Economic Development." NBER Working Paper 9106. National Bureau of Economic Research, Cambridge, Mass.

Economist, The. 2003. "Jordan's Election, Nail-Biting." *The Economist* 367(8329): 38–39 (June 21).

Eifert, Benn, Alan Gelb, and Nils Borje Tallroth. 2003. "Managing Wealth: The Political Economy of Oil-Exporting Countries." In "The Middle East: On the Threshold of Change," *Finance and Development* 40(1).

Eken, Sena, George Schieber, and David Robalino. 2003. "Living Better: MENA Countries Need to Improve Social Policies to Raise Living Standards." In "The Middle East: On the Threshold of Change," *Finance and Development* 40(1).

Elbadawi, Ibrahim A. 2002. "Reviving Growth in the Arab World." Working Paper Series 0206. Arab Planning Institute, Safat, Kuwait.

Elections Around the World. 2003. Available online at http://www.electionworld.org. Accessed 2003.

Encyclopaedia Britannica. 2003. *Encyclopaedia Britannica Book of the Year 2001*. Chicago.

Engelman, S., and K. Sokoloff. 2002. "Factor Endowments, Inequality, and Paths of Development among New World Economies." *Economia* 3(1): 41–109.

Entelis, John P. 1976. "Oil Wealth and the Prospects for Democratization in the Arabian Peninsula: The Case of Saudi Arabia." In Maiem A. Sherbiny and Mark A. Tessler, eds., *Arab Oil: Impact on the Arab Countries and Global Implications*. New York: Praeger.

Esfahani, Hadi Salehi. 2000. "What Can We Learn from Budget Institutions Details?" University of Illinois, Urbana-Champaign, Ill. Processed.

———. 2003. "Alternative Public Service Delivery Mechanisms in Iran." University of Illinois, Urbana-Champaign, Ill. Processed.

Esposito, John L., and John O. Voll. 1996. *Islam and Democracy*. New York: Oxford University Press.

Evans, Peter. 1995. *Embedded Autonomy: States and Industrial Transformation*. Princeton, N.J.: Princeton University Press.

Evans, Peter, and James Rauch. 2000. "Bureaucratic Structure and Bureaucratic Performance in Less Developed Countries." *Journal of Public Economics* 75(1): 49–71

Fawzi, Samiha, ed. 2002. *Global Firm Competitiveness in the Middle East and North Africa Region*. Washington, D.C.: World Bank.

Feder, Gershon. 1993. "The Economics of Land Titling in Thailand." In Karla Hoff, Avishay Braverman, and Joseph E. Stiglitz, eds., *The Economics of Rural Organization: Theory, Practice, and Policy*. New York: Oxford University Press.

Freedom House. 2002a. *Freedom in the World 2001–2002*. Available online at http://www.freedomhouse.org. Accessed 2003.

———. 2002b. *Press Freedom Survey 2003*. Available online at http://www.freedomhouse.org. Accessed 2003.

Galal, Ahmed. 1996. "Can Egypt Grow without Institutional Reforms? If Not, Which Institutions Matter Most?" In *Industrial Strategies and Policies, Management and Entrepreneurial Skills*. Beirut, Lebanon: United Nations Economic and Social Commission for Western Asia.

Gausse, Gregory F. 1996. "Regional Influences on Experiments in Political Liberalization in the Arab World." In Rex Brynen, Bahgat Korany, and Paul Noble, eds., *Political Liberalization and Democratization in the Arab World*, Vol. 1: *Theoretical Perspectives*. Boulder, Colo.: Lynne Rienner Publishers.

Ghalioun, Burhan. 1991. *Le Malaise Arabe. L'Etat Contre la Nation*. Paris: La Découverte.

———. 1997. *Islam et Politique, la Modernité Trahie*. Paris: La Découverte.

Girvan, Norman. 2002. "Problems with UNDP Governance Indicators." Association of Caribbean States. Available online at http://www.acs-aec.org/column/index45.htm. Accessed 2003.

Giugale, Marcelo, Olivier Lafourcade, and Vinh H. Nguyen, eds. 2001. *Mexico—A Comprehensive Development Agenda for the New Era*. Washington, D.C.: World Bank.

Global Attitudes Project. 2003. *Views of a Changing World, June 2003*. Washington, D.C.: Pew Research Center for the People and the Press.

Granados, Estanislao C., and Eulogio Martin Masilungan. 2001. "Philippines Pilot E-Procurement System." Available online at http://www1.worldbank.com/publicsector/egov/philippines_eproc.htm. Accessed 2003.

Gupta, Sanjeev, Hamid Davoodi, and Rosa Alonso-Terme. 2002. "Does Corruption Affect Income Inequality and Poverty?" *Economics of Governance* 3(1): 23–45.

Hall, Robert, E., and Charles I. Jones. 1999. "Why Do Some Countries Produce So Much More Output per Worker than Others?" *Quarterly Journal of Economics* 114(1): 83–116.

al-Hamad, Laila. 2002. "Women's Organizations in the Arab World." *Al Raida [The Pioneer]* 19(97–98): 22–27.

Hammoudi, Abdellah. 1997. *Master and Disciple, the Cultural Foundations of Moroccan Authoritarianism*. Chicago: University of Chicago Press.

Hellman, Joel, Geraint Jones, and Daniel Kaufmann. 2001. "Seize the State, Seize the Day: State Capture, Corruption, and Influence in Transition." World Bank Policy Research Working Paper 2444. World Bank, Washington. D.C.

Henry, Clement Moore, and Robert Springborg. 2001. *Globalization and the Politics of Development in the Middle East*. Cambridge, U.K.: Cambridge University Press.

Herb, Michael. 2002. "Do Rents Cause Authoritarianism?" Georgia State University, Atlanta, Ga. Processed.

———. 2003. "Taxation and Representation." Georgia State University, Atlanta, Ga. Processed.

Heritage Foundation/*The Wall Street Journal.* 2002. *2003 Index of Economic Freedom.* Available online at http://www.heritage.org/research/features/index. Accessed 2003.

Hibou, Béatrice, and Mohamed Tozy. 2002. "De la Friture sur la Ligne des Réformes: La Libéralisation des Télécommunications au Maroc." *Critique Internationale* 14: 93–94.

Hirschman, Albert. 1970. *Exit, Voice, and Loyalty: Responses to Decline in Firms, Organizations, and States.* Cambridge, Mass.: Harvard University Press.

Hofman, Bert. 1998. "The Australian Experience with a Medium Term Expenditure Framework." In *China: Managing Public Expenditures for Better Results.* Economic Report 20342. Washington, D.C., World Bank.

Hotelling, H. 1933. "Analysis of a Complex of Statistical Variables into Principal Components." *Journal of Educational Psychology* 24: 417–41, 498–520.

Hudson, Michael. 1995. "Arab Regimes and Democratization: Responses to the Challenge of Political Islam." In Laura Guazzone, ed., *The Islamist Dilemma. The Political Role of Islamist Movements in the Contemporary Arab World.* London: Ithaca Press.

Human Rights Watch. 2002. "Syria: Clampdown on Free Expression." *Human Rights News.* Available online at www.hrw.org/press/2002/02/syria0211.htm. Accessed 2003.

Huntington, Samuel. 1993. "The Clash of Civilizations?" *Foreign Affairs* 72(2): 22–49.

Ibn Khaldun, Abdul-Rahman. 1969. *The Muqaddimah: An Introduction to History.* Abridged ed. Princeton, N.J.: Rosenthal and Dawood.

Imam Abdul-Fattah Imam. 1994. *Al-Taghiyah, dirasah falsafiyah li-suwar min-al-istibdad al-siyasi* [The Despot: A Philosophical Study of Aspects of Political Authoritarianism]. Kuwait: National Council for Culture, the Arts, and the Humanities.

InfoDev and The Center for Democracy and Technology. 2002. *The E-Government Handbook for Developing Countries*. Available online at www.infodev.org. Accessed 2003.

Inglehart, Ronald. 1997. *Modernization and Post-Modernization: Cultural, Economic, and Political Change in Forty-Three Societies*. Princeton, N.J.: Princeton University Press.

Inglehart, Ronald, and Pipa Norris. 2002. "Islam and the West: Testing the Clash of Civilizations Thesis." Faculty Research Working Paper Series, John F. Kennedy School of Government, Harvard University, Cambridge, Mass. Processed.

International Finance Corporation. 2001. "Trends in Private Investment in Developing Countries, Statistics for 1970–2000, and the Impact on Private Investment of Corruption and the Quality of Public Investment." Washington, D.C.

International Monetary Fund. 2003. *World Economic Outlook, Growth, and Institutions*. World Economic and Financial Surveys. Washington, D.C.

Inter-Parliamentary Union. 2003. "Women in National Parliaments." Available online at http://www.ipu.org/english/home.htm. Accessed 2003.

Isham, Jonathan, Daniel Kaufmann, and Lant Pritchett. 1997. "Civil Liberties, Democracy, and the Performance of Government Projects." *World Bank Economic Review* 11(2): 219–42.

Jimenez, Emmanuel. 1984. "Tenure Security and Urban Squatting." *Review of Economics and Statistics* 66(4): 556–67.

Jimenez, Emmanuel, and Yasuyuki Sawada. 2000. "Do Community Managed Schools Work? An Evaluation of El Salvador's EDUCO Program." *World Bank Economic Review* 13(3): 415–41.

Kamrava, Mehran. 1998. "Non-Democratic States and Political Liberalization in the Middle East: A Structural Analysis." *Third World Quarterly Journal of Emerging Areas* 19(1): 63–85.

Karl, Terry Lynn. 1997. *The Paradox of Plenty: Oil Booms and Petro-States*. Berkeley, London, and Los Angeles: University of California Press.

Kaufmann, Dani. 2002. "Growth Without Governance." World Bank, Washington, D.C. Processed.

———. 2003. "Rethinking Governance: Empirical Lessons Challenge Orthodoxy." World Bank, Washington, D.C. Processed.

Kaufmann, Dani, Aart Kraay, and Maximo Mastruzzi. 2003. "Governance Matters III, Governance Indicators for 1996–2002." World Bank, Washington, D.C. Processed.

Kaufmann, Dani, Aart Kraay, and Pablo Zoido-Lobaton. 2002. "Governance Matters II." World Bank Policy Research Working Paper 2772. World Bank, Washington, D.C.

Kazemi, Farhad. 2002. "Perspectives on Islam and Civil Society." In Nancy Rosenblum and Robert Post, eds., *Civil Society and Government*. Princeton, N.J.: Princeton University Press.

Keefer, Philip. 2003. "A Review of the Political Economy of Governance: From Property Rights to Voice." In Herbert Kitschelt, ed., "The Consequences of Political Institutions in Democracy." Duke University, Durham, N.C. Processed.

Keefer, Philip, and Stuti Khemani. 2003. "The Political Economy of Providing Services to the Poor." World Bank, Washington, D.C. Processed.

Kennedy, Peter. 1994. *A Guide to Econometrics*. Third Edition. Cambridge, Mass.: MIT Press.

Khouri, Philip, and Joseph Kostiner, eds. 1990. *Tribes and State Formation in the Middle East*. Berkeley, Los Angeles, and Oxford: University of California Press.

King, R. G., and R. Levine. 1993. "Finance and Growth: Schumpeter Might Be Right." *Quarterly Journal of Economics* 108(3): 717–37.

Knack, Stephen, and Philip Keefer. 1995. "Institutions and Economic Performance: Cross-Country Tests Using Alternative Institutional Measures." *Economics and Politics* 7(3): 207–27.

Knack, Stephen, and Gary Anderson. 1999. "Is Good Governance Progressive? Property Rights, Contract Enforceability, and Changes in

Income Equality." Paper presented at the 1999 Annual Meeting of the American Political Science Association, Atlanta, Ga.

Koshi, Heli, and Tobias Kretschmer. 2002. "Entry Standards and Competition: Firms' Strategies and Diffusion of Mobile Telephony." Paper presented at the International Conference on Convergence in Communications Industries, Warwick Business School, Coventry, U.K.

Krueger, Anne. 1974. "The Political Economy of Rent-Seeking Society." *American Economic Review* 64(3): 291–303.

Kumar, Arvind, and Subhash Bhatnagar. 2001. "VOICE: Online Delivery of Municipal Services in Vijaywada, India." Available online at http://www1.worldbank.org/publicsector/egov/voice_cs.htm. Accessed 2003.

Landell-Mills, Pierre, and Ismail Serageldin. 1992. "Governance and the External Factor." In Lawrence Summers and Shekhar Shah, eds., *Proceedings of the World Bank Annual Conference on Development Economics 1991*. Washington, D.C.: World Bank.

Langseth, Peter, ed. 1997. *Post Colonial Conflict Uganda: Towards an Effective Civil Service*. Nairobi, Kenya: Claripress.

La Porta, Rafael, Florencio Lopez-de-Silanes, Andrei Shleifer, and Robert Vishny. 1999. "The Quality of Government." *Journal of Law, Economics, and Organization* 15(1): 222–79.

Layachi, Azzedine. 2001. "Algeria Flooding and Muddied State-Society Relations." *Middle East Report Online MERIP*. December. Available online at http://www.merip.org/mero/mero121101.html. Accessed 2003.

Leenders, Reinoud, and John Sfakianakis. 2002. "Middle East and North Africa." In *Global Corruption Report 2003*. Berlin: Transparency International.

Leite, Carlos, and Jens Weidmann. 1999. "Does Mother Nature Corrupt? Natural Resources, Corruption and Economic Growth." IMF Working Paper WP/99/85. International Monetary Fund, Washington, D.C.

Lewis, Bernard. 1964. *The Middle East and the West*. New York: Harper Torchbooks.

————. 1993. *The Islam and the West.* New York: Oxford University Press.

Li, Hongyi, Lixin Colin Xu, and Heng-Fu Xou. 2000. "Corruption, Income Distribution and Growth." *Economics and Politics* 12(2): 155–82.

Lipset, Seymour Martin. 1959. "Some Social Requisites of Democracy: Economic Development and Political Legitimacy." *American Political Science Review* 53: 69–105.

Luciani, Giacomo. 1984. "Allocation vs. Production States: A Theoretical Framework." In Hezam Beblawi and Giacomo Luciani, eds., *The Rentier State.* New York: Cromm Helm.

————. 1987. *The Rentier State.* New York: Croom Helm.

————. 1994. "The Oil Rent, the Fiscal Crisis of the State, and Democratization." In Ghassan Salame, ed., *Democracy Without Democrats? The Renewal of Politics in the Muslim World.* London: I. B. Tauris.

Lust-Okar, Ellen. 2003. "Why the Failure of Democratization? Explaining 'Middle East Exceptionalism.'" Yale University, New Haven, Conn. Processed.

Lust-Okar, Ellen, and Amaney Jamal. 2002. "Regimes and Rules: Reassessing the Influence of Regime Type on Electoral Law Formation." *Comparative Political Studies* 35(3).

Madani, Dorsati, and John Page. 2000. "Global Rules for Business: Challenges to Firm Competitiveness and Opportunities for Success." The Egyptian Center for Economic Studies, Cairo, Egypt. Processed.

Mahdavy, Hussein. 1970. "The Patterns and Problems of Economic Development in Rentier States: The Case of Iran." In M. A. Cook, ed., *Studies in Economic History of the Middle East.* London: Oxford University Press.

Mankiw, Gregory, David Romer, and David Weil. 1992. "A Contribution to the Empirics of Economic Growth." *Quarterly Journal of Economics* 106: 407–37.

Mansour, Antoine. 2002. "Support Services and the Competitiveness of Small and Medium Enterprises in the MENA Region." In *Global Firm Competitiveness Report in the Middle East and North Africa Region.*

Washington, D.C: World Bank and Mediterranean Development Forum.

Mauro, Paolo. 1995. "Corruption and Growth." *Quarterly Journal of Economics* 110: 681–712.

al-Mawardi, Abu Hasan Ali Ibn Mohamed (d. 1058). 1982. *Traite des Statuts Gouvernementaux.* Paris: al-Ahkam al-Sultaniyah.

McClosky, Herbert. 1968. "Political Participation." In David L. Sills, ed., *International Encyclopedia of the Social Sciences*, Vol. 12. New York: Macmillan and Free Press.

McNutt, Patrick. 1999. "Public Goods and Club Goods." Available online at http://encyclo.findlaw.com/0750book.pdf. Accessed 2003.

Mehlum, Halvor, Karl Moene, and Ragnar Torvik. 2002. "Institutions and the Resource Curse." University of Oslo, Oslo, Norway. Processed.

Mo, Pak Hung. 2001. "Corruption and Economic Growth." *Journal of Comparative Economics* 29(1): 66–79.

Moaddel, Mansoor. 2002. "The Worldviews of Islamic Publics: The Cases of Egypt, Iran, and Jordan." Eastern Michigan University, Ypsilanti, Mich. Processed.

Moreno Ocampo, Luis. 2001. "State Capture: Who Represents the Poor?" *Development Outreach.* (Winter).

Morocco (Kingdom of). Constitution of. 1996. Available online at http://www.mincom.gov.ma/english/generalities/state_st/constitution.htm. Accessed 2003.

———. 2000. "Plan de Développement Economique et Social 2000–2004." Département de la Prévision Economique et du Plan.

Mustafa, Mohammad A. 2002. "Benchmarking Regulators." *Public Policy for the Private Sector* 247. Washington, D.C.: World Bank.

Nabli, Mustapha, and Marie-Ange Veganzones-Varoudakis. 2002. "Reforms and Growth in MENA Countries: New Empirical Evidence." World Bank, Washington, D.C. Processed.

Narayan, Deepa. 1999. "Social Capital and the State: Complementarity and Substitution." World Bank Policy Research Working Paper 2167. World Bank, Washington, D.C.

Niblock, Tim. 1998. "Democratization: A Theoretical and Practical Debate." *British Journal of Middle Eastern Studies* 25(2): 221–33.

North, Douglas C. 1981. *Structure and Change in Economic History*. New York: W. W. Norton.

———. 1990. *Institutions, Institutional Change, and Economic Performance*. Cambridge, U.K.: Cambridge University Press.

Norton, Augustus Richard, ed. 1993. "The Future of Civil Society in the Middle East." *Middle East Journal* 47 (Spring).

———. 1996. *Civil Society in the Middle East* (Parts 1 and 2). Leiden, the Netherlands: E. J. Brill.

Norton, August Richard, and Farhad Kazemi. 1996. "Civil Society, Political Reform, and Authoritarianism in the Middle East: A Response." *Contention* 5: 111.

Norton, Seth W. 1998. "Poverty, Property Rights, and Human Well-Being: A Cross-National Study." *Cato Journal* 18(2): 233–45.

Nugent, Jeffrey B. 2002. "Dispute Resolution and Firms' Competitiveness in the MENA Region." In *Global Firm Competitiveness Report in the Middle East and North Africa Region*. Washington, D.C.: World Bank and Mediterranean Development Forum.

Nugent, Jeffrey B., and Nauro F. Campos. 2002. "Who Is Afraid of Political Instability?" *Journal of Development Economics* 67(1): 157–72.

Nugent, Jeffrey B., Nauro F. Campos, and James A. Robinson. 1999. "Can Political Instability Be Good for Growth? The Case of the Middle East and North Africa." University of Southern California, Los Angeles, Calif. Processed.

O'Donnell, Guillermo, and Philippe Schmitter. 1986. *Transitions from Authoritarian Rule*, Vol. 4: *Tentative Conclusions about Uncertain Democracies*. Baltimore: Johns Hopkins University Press.

Olson, Mancur. 1965. *The Logic of Collective Action.* Cambridge, Mass.: Harvard University Press.

O'Rourke, Kevin. 1999. "Culture, Politics, and Innovation: Creamery Diffusion in Late 19th Century Denmark and Ireland." Department of Economics, University College, Dublin, Ireland. Processed.

Orrego, Claudio, Carlos Osorio, and Rodrigo Mardones. 2000. "Chile's Government Procurement E-System." Available online at http://www1.worldbank.com/publicsector/ egov/eprocurement_chile.htm. Accessed 2003.

Page, John. 1998. "From Boom to Bust—and Back? The Crisis of Growth in the Middle East and North Africa." In Nemat Shafik, ed., *Prospects for Middle Eastern and North African Economies: From Boom to Bust and Back?* London: Macmillan.

Page, John, and Linda Van Gelder. 1998. "Missing Links: Institutional Capability, Policy Reform, and Growth in the Middle East and North Africa." World Bank, Washington, D.C. Processed.

Panizza, Ugo. 2001. "Electoral Systems, Political Rules and Institutional Quality." *Economics and Politics* 13(3): 311–41.

Patrinos, Harry Anthony. 2002. "A Review of Demand-Side Financing Initiatives in Education." World Bank, Washington, D.C. Processed.

Pearson, Karl. 1901. "On Lines and Planes of Closest Fit to Systems of Points in the Space." *Philosophical Magazine* 2: 559–72.

Pettersson, Thorleif. 2003. "Islam and Global Governance, Orientations towards the United Nations and Human Rights among Four Islamic Societies and Four Western." Paper presented at the conference on Explaining the World Views of the Islamic Publics. Cairo, Egypt, February 24–26, 2003.

Political Risk Services. 2001. *International Country Risk Guide.* New York: PRS Group. Available online at http://www.prsgroup.com. Accessed 2003.

Pomfret, John. 2003a. "SARS Reported in Rural China." Available online at http://stacks.msnbc.com/news/904928.asp?cp1=1. Accessed 2003.

———. 2003b. "China to Open Field in Local Elections." *Washington Post* (June 12). Available online at http://www.washingtonpost.com/wp-dyn/articles/A52277-2003Jun12.html. Accessed 2003.

Posusney, Marsha. 2002. "Multi-Party Elections in the Arab World: Institutional Engineering and Oppositional Strategies." *Studies in Comparative International Development* 36(4): 34–62.

Princeton Survey Research Associates. 2003. *The Global Poll, Multinational Survey of Opinion Leaders 2002.* Washington, D.C.: Princeton Survey Research Associates.

Przeworski, Adam, and Fernando Limongi. 1993. "Political Regimes and Economic Growth." *Journal of Economic Perspectives* 7: 51–69.

Przeworski, Adam, Michael Alvarez, Jose Antonio Cheibub, and Fernando Limongi. 2000. *Democracy and Development: Political Institutions and Well-Being in the World, 1950–1990.* New York: Cambridge University Press.

Putnam, Robert. 1993. *Making Democracy Work: Civic Traditions in Modern Italy.* Princeton, N.J.: Princeton University Press.

Rasappan, Arunaselam. 1999. "Budget Reform—Malaysia (with Singapore Comparisons where Applicable)." World Bank, Washington, D.C. Processed.

Reporters Without Borders. 2003. "Jordan—2003 Annual Report." Available online at http://www.rsf.org/article.php3?id_article= 5387. Accessed 2003.

Richards, Alan, and John Waterbury. 1996. *A Political Economy of the Middle East: State, Class, and Economic Development.* Boulder, Colo.: Westview Press.

Rodrik, Dani. 1998. "Where Did All the Growth Go? External Shocks, Social Conflict, and Growth Collapses." NBER Working Paper 6350. National Bureau of Economic Research, Cambridge, Mass.

———. 1999. "Institutions for High-Quality Growth: What They Are and How to Acquire Them." Paper presented at the International Monetary Fund Conference on Second-Generation Reforms, Washington, D.C. November 8–9.

Rodrik, Dani, Arvind Subramanian, and Francesco Trebbi. 2002. "Institutions Rule: The Primacy of Institutions over Geography and Integration in Economic Development." NBER Working Paper 9305. National Bureau of Economic Research, Cambridge, Mass.

Ross, Michael. 1999. "The Political Economy of the Resource Curse." *World Politics* 51: 297–322.

———. 2001. "Does Oil Hinder Democracy?" *World Politics* 53: 325–61.

———. 2003. "Does Taxation Lead to Representation?" Processed. Available online at http://www.polisci.ucla.edu/faculty/ross/taxrep.pdf. Accessed 2003.

Sachs, Jeffrey D., and Andrew M. Warner. 1995a. "Economic Reform and the Process of Global Integration." *Brookings Papers on Economic Activity* 1995(1): 1–118.

———. 1995b. "Natural Resource Abundance and Economic Growth." Harvard Institute for International Development Discussion Paper 517a. Cambridge, Mass.

———. 1997. "Natural Resource Abundance and Economic Growth." Center for International Development. Harvard University, Cambridge, Mass. Available online at http://www.cid.harvard.edu//ciddata/ciddata.html. Accessed 2003.

Sala-i-Martin, Xavier, and Elsa V. Artadi. 2002. "Economic Growth and Investment in the Arab World." In *World Economic Forum 2002*. New York and Oxford: Oxford University Press.

Salamé, Ghassan, ed. 1994. *Democracy Without Democrats? The Renewal of Politics in the Muslim World*. London: I. B. Tauris.

Salem, Paul. 2003. "Designing Democracy in Iraq: Reflections from Lebanon." *The Daily Star* (Lebanon). June 17.

Sato, Tsugitaka. 1997. *Islamic Urbanism in Human History*. London and New York: Kegan Paul International.

Schedler, Andreas. 1999. "Conceptualizing Accountability." In A. Schedler and others, eds., *The Self-Restraining State: Power and Accountability in New Democracies*. Boulder, Colo.: Lynne Rienner.

Schiavo-Campo, Salvatore, and Pachampet Sundaram. 2000. *To Serve and to Preserve: Improving Public Administration in a Competitive World.* Manila: Asian Development Bank.

Scully, Gerald. W. 1988. "The Institutional Framework and Economic Development." *Journal of Political Economy* 96(31): 652–62.

Sen, Amartya. 1995. "Economic Development and Social Change: India and China in Comparative Perspectives." Development Economic Research Paper 27. Development Economic Research Programme, London.

———. 1999. *Development as Freedom.* New York: Alfred Knopf.

Sewell, David. 2001. "Governance and the Business Environment in West Bank/Gaza." Middle East and North Africa Working Paper Series 23. World Bank, Washington, D.C.

Shafik, Nemat, ed. 1998. *Prospects for Middle Eastern and North African Economies: From Boom to Bust and Back?* London: Macmillan.

Sharabi, Hisam. 1988. *Neo-Patriarchy: A Theory of Distorted Change in Arab Society.* New York: Oxford University Press.

Shils, Edward. 1991. "The Virtue of Civil Society." *Government and Opposition* 26(1): 3–20.

Singerman, Diane. 1995. *Avenues of Participation.* Princeton, N.J.: Princeton University Press.

Skocpol, Theda. 1985. "Bringing the State Back In: Strategies for Analysis in Current Research." In Peter Evans, Dietrich Rueschemeyer, and Theda Skocpol, eds., *Bringing the State Back In.* New York: Cambridge University Press.

Stiglitz, Joseph, E. 1998. *Economics of the Public Sector.* Second Edition. New York and London: W. W. Norton.

Stone, Andrew H. W. 2000. "The Regional Business Environment in the Global Context." In *Global Firm Competitiveness in the Middle East and North Africa Region.* Washington, D.C.: World Bank.

Syrian Arab Republic. 1973 Constitution. Available online at http://www.oefre.unibe.ch/law/icl/sy00000_.html. Accessed 2003.

Tanzi, Vito, and Hamid Davoodi. 1997. "Corruption, Public Investment, and Growth." International Monetary Fund, Washington, D.C. Processed.

Tendler, Judith. 1999. *Good Government in the Tropics*. Baltimore, Md.: Johns Hopkins University Press.

Tessler, Mark. 2002. "Do Islamic Orientations Influence Attitudes Toward Democracy in the Arab World? Evidence from Egypt, Jordan, Morocco, and Algeria." Processed.

Transparency International. 2002. *Global Corruption Report 2003*. Berlin.

Tzannatos, Zafiris. 2000. "Social Protection in the Middle East and North Africa: A Review." Paper presented at the Third Mediterranean Development Forum. Available online at http://www.world bank.org/wbi/mdf/mdf3/papers.html. Accessed 2003.

United Nations Division for Public Economics and Public Administration, and American Society for Public Administration. 2002. *Benchmarking E-Government: A Global Perspective—Assessing the Progress of UN Member States*. New York: UN Publications.

UNDP (United Nations Development Programme). 2002a. *Arab Human Development Report 2002*. New York.

_____. 2002b. *Human Development Indicators in Human Development Report 2002*. New York.

Vandewalle, Dirk. 1998. *Libya Since Independence: Oil and State-Building*. Ithaca, N.Y.: Cornell University Press.

van Eeghen, Willem, and Kouassi Soman. 1998. "Government Programs for Poverty Reduction and Their Effectiveness: An Overview." Paper presented at the 1998 Mediterranean Development Forum, Marrakech, Morocco.

Wallack, Jessica Seddon, Alejandro Gaviria, Ugo Panizza, and Ernesto Stein. 2002. "Political Particularism Around the World." Stanford University, Stanford, Calif. Processed.

Waterbury, John. 1994. "Democracy Without Democrats." In Ghassen Salamé, ed., *Democracy Without Democrats? The Renewal of Politics in the Muslim World*. London: I. B. Taurus.

Weiner, Myron, and Samuel P. Huntington, eds. 1987. *Understanding Political Development*. Boston and Toronto: Little, Brown, and Company.

WHO (World Health Organization). 2000. *World Health Report. Reducing Risks, Promoting Healthy Life*. Geneva, Switzerland.

World Bank. 1997. *World Development Report: The State in a Changing World*. New York: Oxford University Press.

———. 1999a. "Consumer Food Subsidy Programs in the MENA Region." Report 19561-MNA. Washington, D.C.

———. 1999b. "Education in the Middle East and North Africa: A Strategy Towards Learning for Development." World Bank, Human Development, Middle East and North Africa. Washington, D.C.

———. 1999c. "West Bank and Gaza: Strengthening Public Sector Management." Washington, D.C. Available online at http://wbln0018.worldbank.org/mna/mena. Accessed 2003.

———. 2000a. "Pilot Investment Climate Assessment: Moroccan Manufacturing Sector at the Turn of the Century: Results of the Firm Analysis and Competitiveness Survey, FACS-Morocco." Washington, D.C. Available online at http://www.worldbank.org/privatesector/ic/docs. Accessed 2003.

———. 2000b. *Reforming Public Institutions and Strengthening Governance: A World Bank Strategy*. Washington, D.C.

———. 2000c. *The Quality of Growth*. New York: Oxford University Press.

———. 2000d. "Tunisia: Social and Structural Review." World Bank Country Study. Washington, D.C.

———. 2000e. *Voices of the Poor: Crying Out for Change*. New York: Oxford University Press.

———. 2001a. "Country Policy and Institutional Assessment." Available online at http://www.worldbank.org/ida/cpiaq2001.pdf. Accessed 2003.

———. 2001b. "Introduction to Public Expenditure Management." Available online at http://www.worldbank.org/publicsector/pe/pemanagement.htm. Accessed 2003.

———. 2002a. "Algeria: Second Rural Employment Project: Project Appraisal Document." Report 24715. Washington, D.C.

———. 2002b. "Jordan Development Policy Review: A Reforming State in a Volatile Region." Report 24425. Washington, D.C.

———. 2002c. "Morocco Civil Society Note." Washington, D.C. Processed.

———. 2002d. "Poverty Reduction in Egypt: Diagnosis and Strategy." Report 24234-EG. Washington, D.C.

———. 2002e. "Public Health in the Middle East and North Africa, a Situation Analysis." Washington D.C. Processed.

———. 2002f. "Reducing Vulnerability and Increasing Opportunity: Social Protection in Middle East and North Africa." Washington, D.C.

———. 2002g. "The BEEPS II Interactive Dataset: Enterprise Survey in Transition." Available online at http://info.worldbank.org/governance/beeps2002. Accessed 2003.

———. 2002h. *Transition—The First Ten Years: Analysis and Lessons for Eastern Europe and the Former Soviet Union.* Washington, D.C.

———. 2002i. *World Development Report 2002: Building Institutions for Markets.* New York: Oxford University Press.

———. 2003a. "Access to Basic Services through Registration: Progress Reports." Processed. Available online at http://www.development-marketplace.org/report944.html. Accessed 2003.

———. 2003b. "Algeria Investment Climate Assessment." Washington, D.C. Processed.

———. 2003c. "Doing Business." Available online at http://rru.worldbank.org/DoingBusiness. Accessed 2003.

———. 2003d. "Iran Medium-Term Framework for Transition, Converting Oil Wealth to Development, A Country Economic Memorandum." Report 25848-IRN. Washington, D.C.

———. 2003e. *MENA's Employment Challenge in the 21st Century: From Labor Force Growth to Job Creation.* MENA Development Report. Washington, D.C.

———. 2003f. "Public Expenditure." Available online at http://www1.worldbank.org/publicsector/pe/index.cfm. Accessed 2003.

———. 2003g. *Trade, Investment, and Development in the Middle East and North Africa: Engaging with the World.* MENA Development Report. Washington, D.C.

———. 2003h. *World Development Report 2004: Making Services Work for Poor People.* New York: Oxford University Press.

World Economic Forum. 2002. *The Arab World Competitiveness Report, 2002–2003.* New York: Oxford University Press.

Yao, Yang. 2001. "Building Support for Policy Change by Improving Governance in China: The Case of Shunde." *Transition Newsletter: The Newsletter about Reforming Economies.*

Zaalouk, Malak. 2001. "Community Schools: Egypt's Celebrity Model." *The UNESCO Courier.* Available online at http://www.unesco.org/courier/2001_05/uk/education2.htm. Accessed 2003.

Zogby, James. 2002. *What Arabs Think: Values, Beliefs and Concerns.* Washington, D.C.: Zogby International; also Beirut, Lebanon: Arab Thought Foundation.

Index

Abu Bakr, 27[quoted]
accountability, 2–20*passim*, 27–31,
    38, 42–55, 135, 140, 141,
    144, 183
    channels of, 29–30, 38, 121, 155
    defined, 26, 73*n*.1
    democratic, 183
    inclusiveness and, 30, 31
    mechanisms, 31, 108
    performance and, 121
    procurement, 131
    stronger, 157–158
accountability, external, 2, 5, 19,
    20, 21, 28, 29, 38, 43, 122,
    133, 142, 148–149, 157,
    169, 178
    elections, 52–53
    local actions, 162–166
    mechanisms, 52–55
    national actions, 158–162
    oversight by the media and
      civil-society intermediaries,
      53–55
    see also public accountability
accountability, internal, 2, 5, 11,
    19, 21–22, 28, 29, 32, 38,
    43, 86, 94, 123–124, 128,
    148, 157, 178
    administrative measures,
      168–172
    checks and balances, 44–48,

    166–168
    institutional arrangements,
      48–52
    mechanisms, 44–52
administration (in public sector),
    6, 7, 56–57, 58–62, 72, 77
    East Asia vs. MENA, 86
    growth and, 103*n*.12
    income and, 58, 61
    oil-dependent countries, 9
    quality of, index (IQA), 58–62,
      73*n*.7, 83, 86, 102*n*.10,
      102–103*n*.11, 126–127, 179,
      183–188
administrative actions, 22, 49–50
    judiciary review, 47
administrative environment, 76
administrative measures, 18, 19,
    178
    internal accountability and,
      168–172
administrative regulations, 64
advocacy, 144, 161–162
Algeria
    accountability, 50
    elections, 53, 161
    electricity, 100
    governance quality measures,
      215
    inclusiveness, 39
    language, 39

media, 54, 55
National Ombudsman, 169
public sector performance
measures, 215
socioeconomic indicators, 214
sociopolitical indicators, 214
transparency, 42, 43
Arab Decision Project, 43
Argentina, public procurement,
90–91
association laws, 55
authoritarianism, 202, 205n.5
authority, 25–26, 31–32
abuse of, 32
autonomy, 140

Bahrain
governance quality measures,
217
parliament, 46, 154, 175
public sector performance
measures, 217
regulatory and institutional
framework, 89
socioeconomic indicators, 216
sociopolitical indicators, 216
women, 40
Bangalore, citizen surveys, 136
black market, 184
Botswana, good governance, 72
Brazil, participatory budgeting,
144
budgeting system, 61, 127
effectiveness, 124, 125,
126–127
management, 13, 185
performance-oriented, 14,
128–131
bureaucratic environment, 76
bureaucratic performance and
predictability, 77–78
bureaucratic quality, 184
corruption and, 208–210

bureaucrats, discretionary power,
170
business environment, 10, 11,
76–77
business registration, 63, 95–96
business registration procedures,
185

checks and balances, 44–48
children, 102n.7
China, SARS and external
accountability, 142
citizens
accountability, 29, 42
advocacy and oversight, 55
agencies and, 13
leverage, 122
parliament and, 47
politicians and, 141–148
civic responsibility, 157
civil liberties, 180–181
civil service, 22, 48, 61
recruitment, 50
reform, 131, 132–133, 170–171
civil society
cooperation, 166
informed, 163
institutions, 72
intermediaries, oversight, 53–55
organizations (also groups, associations), 26, 30, 55,
145–148, 161–162, 164, 166
class structure, fluidity, 204
clientelism, 50
clients (as citizens), 120–123
accountability, 29, 42
empowering, 133–134
public services, 141
surveys, 135–136
coalitions, 123
collective action, 123
Colombia, voucher system, 139
commercial environment, 76, 78

commitment, 23, 175–176
community
    for action, 141
    groups, 21
    school management, 143
    see also civil society and clients
competition, 21, 42, 138–141,
        149*n*.1
    public service agencies, 163
competitiveness
    executive recruitment, 182
    participation, 182
conflict, 39, 68, 72, 172
consensus, 18
constitutions, 44–45, 167
contestability, 2, 3, 4–5, 20, 27,
        38, 42, 43–44, 88, 158,
        167
contract enforcement, 63
corruption, 2, 32, 60–61, 72, 89,
        92, 97–98, 99, 103*n*.14,
        183–184, 208–210
    high-level (or grand), 97, 99
    low-level (or administrative),
        97, 99
    prevention, 138
    variation, 98
costs of doing business, 92–98
Country Policy and Institutional
        Assessment (CPIA), 180,
        183, 184–185
court system, 93
cultural explanation, 203–204
customs, 94–95
cynicism, 154

dawra, 56
decentralization, 22, 134, 155,
        165, 166
deconcentration, 134, 171
democracy, 32
    democracies, competitive, 173
democratic accountability, 183

democratic processes, 154
development, 9, 14–15
    governance gap and, 151–152
disenfranchisement, 27
dispute resolution, 93–94
distributive justice, 39
Dutch Disease, 199, 205*n*.2

economy
    development, 75–103
    environment, 87–88
    explanation, 202
    opportunities, 151–152
    performance, 80
    policies, 10–11, 173
    security, elite, 72
    shocks, 85–86
    volatility, 11
education, 110–116*passim*, 127,
        138–139, 149*n*.2
    spending, 116, 118
    school enrollment, 105, 108,
        109
    schools, 114, 143
e-government, 135, 137, 159
Egypt, Arab Republic of
    administrative regulations,
        64
    business registration, 95–96
    civil service, 48
    civil-society associations, 55
    elections, 52–53
    executive, 45, 47
    governance quality measures,
        219
    inclusiveness, 36–37
    infant mortality, 4, 12, 42
    judiciary, 48
    laws, 93
    literacy, 105
    litigation, 93
    media, 53
    parliament, 46, 154

public sector performance measures, 219
regulatory and institutional framework, 89
road-building, 12, 105
sanitation, 109
school enrollment, 42, 114
socioeconomic indicators, 218
sociopolitical indicators, 218
telephones, 106
transparency, 4
unemployment, 75, 101*n*.2
El Salvador, community management of schools, 143
elections, 4, 13, 29, 39, 41–42, 52–53, 142–143, 145, 160–161
electricity, 100
enterprise surveys, 136–137
entry points, 155
equality, 1–2, 3, 27, 28, 38, 39, 40, 156
equitable treatment, 2, 3, 38, 40, 42
equity, equitable, 1–2, 3, 27, 28, 38, 39, 40, 42, 156
ethic (of public service), 22–23, 27, 73*n*.2, 133, 171–72
Europe and Central Asia (ECA), 173
executive branch, 44, 45, 167
  constraints, 182
  judiciary and, 47
  parliament and, 45–46
exogenous factors, 15, 172
exogenous rents, 200

financial management, 185
food subsidies, 112, 114
foreign direct investment (FDI), 81, 83

framework, analytical (for governance) 1–2, 13, 25–33, 38
Freedom House (FRH), 179, 180–181
freedom of information, 158–160
freedom of the press, 4, 181
  see also media
fundamentalists, 204

GDP growth, 83, 85
  East Asia vs. MENA, 79
  per capita, 75, 79
  rate, estimating, 193–198
  volatility, 80
gender, 42
  see also women
geopolitics, 15, 66–67 (*see also* 153)
girls' school, 114
goods and services, state role, 106, 107–108
governance
  challenge, 152–153
  debate, 16
  definition, 25–26, 38
  enhancing, 18–19
  example, 35, 36–37
  good, 31–33, 35, 72, 152
  macro, 157–158
  measuring, 56, 57, 102*n*.6
  micro, 158
  monitoring and data, 162
  moving forward, 172–178
  overall, 56, 58
  program formulation, 177–178
  quality of, index (IQG), 5–6, 20–21, 58, 59, 76–77, 102*n*.10, 179–187
governance gap, 35–73
  comparison, 60
  costs, 78
  development and, 76–78, 151–152

growth and, 83–87
index, 67
literature review, 199–243
overcoming, 152–172
persistence, 65–72
group formation, 201
growth, 14–15, 80–81, 88, 102*n*.8,
207–210
estimating, 193–198
governance gap and, 83–87
policies and, 88
rate, 72
slow, 78–87
sustaining, 85
volatility, 8–9
Gulf Cooperation Council (GCC)
countries, IQA,
102–103*n*.11

health services, 112–113, 115,
126, 138–139, 149*n*.3
spending, 115, 117
Heritage Foundation/*Wall Street
Journal* (HWJ), 184
human capital, 101
human development, 25, 76

identification card, 36–37
immunization, 105, 112, 126
inclusiveness, 2, 3–4, 10, 11, 17,
18–20, 27, 28, 39–42, 178
accountability and, 30, 31
defined, 26
enhancing, 156–157
gap, 60–61
perceived lack, 89
income, 5–6, 7–8, 37, 62–63, 81,
84
correlation with governance
indicators, 187–192
IQA, 58, 61
link to governance, 5–6, 7–8,
37, 62–63, 65

per capita, 189, 190
premium, 73*n*.6
service delivery and, 149*n*.5
indexes, 58–59
administration, quality of, 86,
183–186
governance, 102*n*.10, 179–186
political particularism, 191
public accountability, 7, 71,
179–183
India
citizen surveys, 136
Internet information system,
138
infant mortality, 4, 76,
105–116*passim*, 126
informal governance mechanisms,
30, 146–147
information
availability, 20, 21, 42, 48,
49–50, 88, 122, 158–160
flow, 11, 135–138, 170
freedom of, 158–160
infrastructure services, 83, 98,
99–100, 109–110, 127, 140
regulation and, 119
institutional arrangements, 48–52
institutional framework, 89
integrity, code of, 170
see also ethics
intermediation, 122–123
Internet, 106
e-government, 135, 137, 159
information system, 138
public procurement, 91
investment, 87
climate, 10, 87–101, 140,
151–152
public, 81, 82, 83, 102*n*.5
rates, 81, 82
Iran, Islamic Republic of
budget reform, 130
civil-society associations, 56

elections, 52, 53, 175
GDP per capita growth, 75
governance quality measures, 221
media, 54–55
military spending, 70
parliament, 46
public sector performance measures, 221
public services competition, 163
socioeconomic indicators, 220
sociopolitical indicators, 220
telephones, 110
transparency, 4, 42–43
Islam
quietism, 203–204
radicalism, 204

Jordan
business environment, 10
civil service reform, 131
civil-society associations, 55
education, 111
elections, 52
governance quality measures, 223
investment climate, 87
judiciary, 48
literacy, 76, 105
litigation, 93
media, 54
parliament, 44
public sector performance measures, 223
red tape, 94
regulatory and institutional framework, 89
socioeconomic indicators, 222
sociopolitical indicators, 222
telecommunications regulators, 140
transparency, 42

tribal governance, 147
women, 40
judges, 73n.4
judiciary, 22, 47–48, 92
independence, 48, 49, 168
just tyrant model, 31

Kuwait
governance quality measures, 225
judiciary, 48
oil revenue, 206n.10
parliament, 46, 47
public sector performance measures, 225
socioeconomic indicators, 224
sociopolitical indicators, 224

labor market issues, 103n.15
Latin America, decentralization, 155
law, 20, 178n.2
decentralization, 165
inclusiveness and, 156
leadership, 11, 32
Lebanon
administrative regulations, 64
civil-society associations, 55, 56
elections, 52, 53
governance quality measures, 227
immunization, 3, 12, 105
judiciary, 48
literacy, 105
litigation, 93
media, 54, 55
public sector performance measures, 227
red tape, 94
regulatory and institutional framework, 89
socioeconomic indicators, 226

sociopolitical indicators, 226
transparency, 43
life expectancy, 126
disability-adjusted, 149*n.*3
literacy, 4, 12, 76, 105, 110, 116,
118, 127
litigation, 93
local action, 18, 19, 178
external accountability, 162–166
Local Authorities Law, 165
local elections, 53
local government, 14, 21, 141,
164

Majliss, 40
maternal mortality, 126
measures, actionable, 156
media, 4, 21, 53–55, 146, 148, 162
broadcast, 53
print, 53
see also Internet; transparency
Mexico, political pluralism and
economic recovery, 174
migration, 101, 151
military spending, 68, 69–70
modernization theory, 202
monitoring, 162
of public agencies, 156–157
of services, 123-124
surveys, 137–137, 144
Morocco
business environment, 10
civil society, 166
civil-society associations, 55,
146
constitution, 44
customs, 94–95
electricity, 100
governance quality measures,
229
governance reforms, 176
investment climate, 87
judiciary, 48

literacy, 4, 12, 76, 105
media, 54
parliament, 46, 47, 154, 175
public administration, 131–132
public sector performance
measures, 229
socioeconomic indicators, 228
sociopolitical indicators, 228
telecommunications regulators,
140
unemployment, 75, 101*n.*2
women, 40

national actions, 178
external accountability,
158–162
checks and balances, 18,
166–168, 178
National Social and Economic
Council, 160–161
nation-building, 70, 73*n.*10
neoorientalism, 203–204
neopatrimonialism, 203–204
networks, exclusionary, 89–90
new businesses, 10–11, 77

Office of Citizen Relations, 51
oil and gas
cycle, 11
prices, 78
rents, 68
revenue, 37, 39, 81, 172,
206*n.*10
volatility, 78–79
wealth and governance, 68,
70–71
oil-reliant countries, 62
public accountability gap and,
68, 70, 71
Oman
governance quality measures,
231
military spending, 70

public sector performance
measures, 231
school enrollment, 12, 105
socioeconomic indicators,
230
sociopolitical indicators, 230
ombudsman, 50, 51, 157
Algeria, 50, 168–169
Tunisia, 50–51, 168
orientalism, 203
outcomes, governance and, 32
oversight, 13, 22

parliament, 37, 44–47, 167
authority, 22
executive and, 45–46
independence, 46
public and, 47
representation, 145, 154
stronger, 167–168
participation, 2, 3, 15, 16–17, 20,
21, 38, 40, 72, 143–145,
154–155, 160, 161–162,
163, 176, 182
informal, 56, 146
process, 17–18
participatory budgeting, 144
partners, external, 153
patriarchy, 203
patrimonialism, 202
performance budgeting,
128–131
performance orientation, 22, 52,
128
personal connection, 36
personal status code, 146
personalized transactions, 13
policymakers, 13, 77, 120,
121–122
accountability, 29, 42
service agencies and, 123–133
political climate, 53
political rights, 180

political particularism, index of,
191
political pluralism, economic
recovery and, 174
political regime, 103n.13
type, 204–205
Political Risk Services (PRS), 180,
183–184
politicians, 13, 120
citizens and, 141–148
service agencies and, 123–133
polity score, combined, 182
population growth, 14, 151
predictability, 92–93
principal component analysis
(PCA), 179, 186n.1,
198n.1
private activities, regulation, 119
private investment, 81–83
private sector activity, governance
and, 76–77
procurement, accountability, 131
productivity, 8, 81–83
growth, 98
investment, 83
property rights, 102n.7, 184, 208
public accountability, 12, 57–58,
62–65, 66, 72, 77, 86,
102n.9, 134, 151
index of, 7, 71, 179–183
growth and, 209–210
oil-dependent countries, 9
quality of index (IPA), 58, 59,
73n.8, n.9, 83, 179, 187
public administration, 131–132,
151, 185
reform, 132
service delivery and, 124–126
public agencies, monitoring,
156–157
public commitment, 17
public debate, 158–160
public disclosure, 158–160

public expenditure
    education, 166–118
    health, 115–117
    management, 22, 168–170
    tracking surveys, 137
public goods, 101–102*n*.4
    definition of nonexcludability,
        101–102*n*.4, 107
    definition of nonrivalry, 101*n*.4,
        107
    delivery of, 78
public institutions, 207–208
public investment, 81, 82, 83,
    102*n*.5
public organizations, citizens and,
    51
public procurement, state capture
    and, 90–91
public sector management, 61–62
public services, 151
    access, 3–4, 40–41
    accountability framework,
        120–123
    agencies, 12–13
    commitment, 110–114
    competition, 163
    delivery, 102*n*.7, 114–119,
        119–148
    ethic, 73*n*.2, 133, 171–172
    external accountability, 142
    governance and, 98–101
    parties involved, 120
    performance, 14, 21
    performance information, 163
    provision, 12–14, 21
    regulation, 139–140
    surveys, 164

Qatar
    governance quality measures,
        233
    internal accountability, 44
    oil revenue, 206*n*.10

public sector performance
    measures, 233
    socioeconomic indicators, 232
    sociopolitical indicators, 232
quality, bureaucratic, 86
quietism, Islam, 203–204

radicalism, Islam, 204
red tape, 60–61, 94
registration, business, 63, 95–96
regulations, 51, 60, 92, 94, 119,
    149*n*.7, 184
    administrative, 64
    agencies, regulatory, 22,
        119–120, 171
    customs, 94–95
    executive recruitment, 182
    framework, 89
    inclusiveness and, 156
    participation, 182
    public services, 139–140
    quality, 63
    telecommunications, 120
regulators, 140
    independence, 171
rentierism, 205*n*.4
rentier state, 200–202, 205*n*.6
    thesis, 200–201
rent-led patronage, 201
rents, locational, 205*n*.7
representation, 2, 40
repression thesis, 201–202
republics, 37
resource curse, 199–200
resource-rich countries, 199
revenue mobilization, efficiency
    of, 185
rights, 2, 28, 38
    protection, 27
    roads, 12, 105
rule-based governance, 184
rule of law, 92–94, 101*n*.3,
    208

sanitation. *See* water and sanitation
Saudi Arabia
GDP per capita growth, 75
governance quality measures,
235
infant mortality, 105–106
military spending, 70
oil wealth, 206*n*.11
public sector performance
measures, 235
representation, 40
socioeconomic indicators, 234
sociopolitical indicators, 234
school enrollment, 105, 108, 109
see also education
service agencies
client-citizens and, 133–141
motivating, 48
politicians and policymakers
and, 123–133
service delivery, 106
income and, 149*n*.5
outcomes, 108–119
service ethic, 22–23
service providers, 120, 121
accountability, 29, 42
services
implementation, 123
monitoring, 123, 124
standardized, 106
settler mortality index, 191
Shura councils, 40, 160–161
social development, 105–149
social explanation, 204
social safety net programs, 113,
118–119
spending effect, 201
state-building, 70, 73*n*.10
state capture, 89
public procurement and, 90–91
suffrage, 35, 37
development, 172

Supervising Citizen Team, 51
surveys, 137–138, 144
citizen, 135–136
enterprise, 136–137
public expenditure tracking, 137
public services, 163, 164
Syrian Arab Republic
civil service recruitment, 50
constitution, 44
elections, 52
governance quality measures,
237
media, 54
public sector performance
measures, 237
regulatory and institutional
framework, 89
socioeconomic indicators, 236
sociopolitical indicators, 236

taxation
assessments, 93
effect, 200–201
evasion, 103*n*.14
revenue, 206*n*.9, *n*.10
telecommunications, 83, 105, 106,
109–110, 127
regulation and, 119, 120
regulators, 140
tolerance, 153–154, 157
transparency, 2, 3, 4, 20, 27, 38,
42–43, 48–49, 88, 97, 158,
183
tribal governance, 147
Tunisia
accountability, 50
elections, 52
GDP per capita growth, 75
governance quality measures,
239
judiciary, 49
literacy, 76
military spending, 70

public organizations and citizens, 51
public sector performance measures, 239
socioeconomic indicators, 238
sociopolitical indicators, 238
telephones, 3, 12, 83, 105, 206

unemployment, 75, 101*n*.2
United Arab Emirates
   GDP per capita growth, 75
   governance quality measures, 241
   infant mortality, 4, 12
   military spending, 70
   public sector performance measures, 241
   socioeconomic indicators, 240
   sociopolitical indicators, 240

village work, 141
voting, 39–40
voucher system, 139

wasta, 36
water and sanitation, 3, 76, 105, 109
welfare services, 117–118
West Bank and Gaza, service delivery surveys, 164
women, 39–40, 41, 42, 102*n*.7

Yemen, Republic of
   civil service reform, 131
   decentralization, 165, 175
   electricity, 100
   governance quality measures, 243
   policy formulation, 89
   public sector performance measures, 243
   road-building, 12, 105
   socioeconomic indicators, 242
   sociopolitical indicators, 242